A HIST(
SCOTLAN⌐

Book One

Foundation

From Ice Age to Indyref –

a History in Three Books

Prehistory-1542

CRAIG WELDON

www.craigweldon.com

Forget the old battles, those days are over,
Hatred corrupts, and friendship refines.

Ian Richardson, *Scotland Will Flourish*

Contents

List of figures

Introduction

Scotland! Kilted clansmen running through the mist. Presbyterian engineers building steamships. But what else do you know of Scotland's past? If you are like me, you will know snatches of stories and of legends, but which were true? And where did they fit with the bigger picture? I wanted to know. So eleven years ago, I embarked on a voyage of discovery. I read all the history books I could get my hands on. As I got into deeper waters, it became clear that I needed to know some English history too, so I started reading that. (You could write a general history of England, and many people have, with scant regard to Scotland. The same is rarer in reverse.) But that wasn't enough. A discouraging truth materialised, like a barren anchorage out of the mist instead of a hoped-for harbour. England was just the start: to properly understand Scottish history, I also needed to know what was going on in France. And not just France and England, but Rome, Norway, Ireland, India, North America, Germany... Eventually, everything in the world became connected: popes and crusades, merchants and empires, American railroads and James Watt out for a walk on Glasgow Green. I thought I was just going to be discovering who the MacDonalds were fighting in fifteen-oatcake!

There were things I didn't expect. Ian Richardson wisely recommends we forget the old battles, but in early Scottish history, they are hard to avoid. The famous battles get fair coverage: but in this book you'll also discover how often Scottish armies made unprovoked attacks on England; the complicated loyalties of the nobility during the Wars of Independence; the grudging nature of Parliaments to grant tax; and the early nature of anti-Gaelic prejudice.

By this point I realised there was a book in what I'd learned, an accessible, yet complete and up-to-date Scottish history. So it was time to cut back the horizon-scanning and refocus on the original goal: Scotland's story.

This first book, *Foundation*, covers up to the year 1542, and the events that led, against the odds, to the enduring existence of a place called *Scotland*.

The second book, *Covenant*, covers the years from 1542 to 1815, and the pivotal moments of the Protestant Reformation, Union, Empire, and the titanic showdown with Napoleonic France.

The final book, *Citizen*, covers from 1815 to recent times, when the Scots made their mark abroad in increasing numbers, while ordinary people fought for dignity and representation at home.

I'm not a professional historian. But the resources to check the facts are all there, both online and at the National Library of Scotland in Edinburgh. I'm no George RR Martin either, but have you ever heard any Scottish history? It's hard to tell a dull story when the raw material is this good.

And like every story, it starts at the beginning...

Want to see more? Visit:

craigweldon.com/a-history-of-scotland

for a timeline of Scottish history,

and character vignettes of key players.

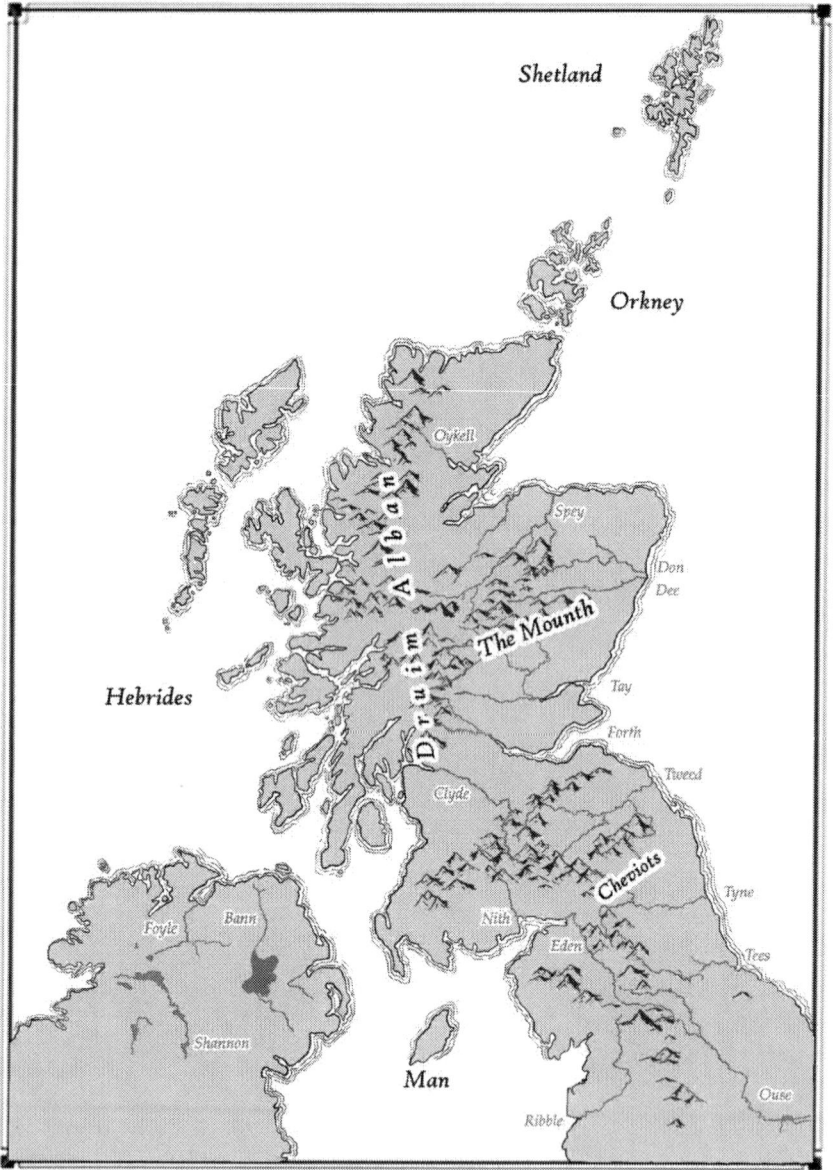

Figure 1: Scotland, Physical

CHAPTER ONE

The Matter of Scotland

Longships tethered above high tide, Lochlanners in oiled knitwear[1] sat around their campfires and told each other tales of the beginning. There was nothing but an endless void called Ginnungagap they said, letting their thoughts wander into the night, separating the elements: a region of fire, and a region of ice, that existed long before our own world.[2]

Others had a different story. In the beginning, said the King James Bible, God created the heavens and the earth. The earth was without form, and void; and darkness was upon the face of the deep. And the Spirit of God moved upon the face of the waters. And God said, Let there be light: and there was light.[3]

Then again, said geologists, tapping rock with their hammers, the earth was born a spinning planet of lava, which shifted around the earth's surface like the crust on cooling porridge to become our oldest rocks. There were vast mountains. There were tropical forests, which time and pressure transformed into coal. There was a desert, flooded by a shallow sea. There was the embrace of continents before the great rift that formed the Atlantic, land torn, volcanoes spurting, their litter making the Mournes, Hebrides, the Faroes, Iceland, and Eastern Greenland. American rocks were left behind on the European side, the Cheviot Hills marking the boundary between former continents, and the southern border of Scotland today. Finally, there was ice. Glaciers blanketing the land, gouging rock, excavating lochs and glens, depositing moraine and drumlins, and with a great geological sigh of relief as the crushing weight of ice melted, rebounding the shoreline.[4]

---

[1] Traditional sea-wear described in Severin, *The Brendan Voyage*, p.loc 2014.
[2] Guerber, *Norsemen*, p.2.
[3] Genesis 1:1-4.
[4] McKirdy, *Set in Stone*, pp.14-16.

This was before Scotland. This was before everybody.

And then people came, following the first animals of the tundra.

Travelling Folk

The human story starts with great sheets of ice. The land that would one day be called Scotland was buried a mile deep under icecaps. Polar bears roamed the ice edge, looking for food. But the earth warmed. The ice cracked and retreated north. Twelve thousand years ago, vast herds of reindeer and bison followed the edge of the ice, eating the lichens and grass that appeared.[5] Humans followed the herds. They were able to walk across from the Continent: icecaps had sucked all the water out the English Channel. For millennia, the tiny human population led a hunter-gatherer lifestyle, living off the land, moving on when necessary, returning time and again to the best spots.[6] The people knew how to make fire, and kept dogs to help them hunt and scare off bears. They lived in caves and tipis in a landscape whose every element was alive with its own spirit. There were water spirits, and tree spirits, sky and sea and animal spirits. At night they sat round shore-side fires or on the margins of the great forest, and told each other stories as wolves howled in the distance: stories of supernatural spirits and animals who could talk, stories of brave hunters and wise matriarchs, stories that helped the people co-operate and survive.[7]

We don't know their names and can only guess at their stories: but these were the Scots' ancestors, the first people to come to this land.

Metal

Six thousand years ago, the greatest change in human history began to arrive: farming. Farmers sailed over from Europe with cows, sheep, chickens, grain, and cats. With their tools of bone and stone, wood and fire, they built houses

---

[5] Moffat. *Before Scotland*, p.42..
[6] *Ibid*, p.65.
[7] It is not possible to know for sure what tales the earliest people of Scotland told each other, but these are the kind of folk tales told by the Agta people of the Philippines. See Smith, Schlaepfer, Major, et al., "Cooperation and the evolution of hunter-gatherer storytelling" *Nat Commun* 8, 1853 (2017)

and burned the forests to cultivate new land;[8] land that people would now claim to own. The ownership of land created complex new social hierarchies,[9] and people built monuments at places like Callanish and Brodgar to worship their Gods, forces of nature who were appeased through ritual and sacrifice:

Bloodthirsty Dee
each year takes three
but bonny Don
yearly needs none.[10]

What exactly took place in the great stone rings is lost to time. But there were rituals performed that echo down to this day. Rituals such as the festival of Samhain, taking place by torchlight at tribal focal points like the great hillfort of the Eildon Hills, on the night of the year when it was believed the veil between our own world and the spirit world thins to nothing. We know of this festival today as Halloween.[11]

Metals that could be made into tools were discovered around four thousand years ago. Bronze was an alloy of copper and tin, two metals that are rarely found together, and trade with the rest of Europe in copper, tin, bronze, gold and amber led to the earliest recorded languages.[12] The earliest place names like Clota (or Clyde), and Orkas (Orkney), were not recorded until around 300BC, but may date from this period.[13]

A more useful metal, iron, was discovered around 800BC. This metal is harder than bronze and makes better tools and weapons. Around the same

---

[8] Moffat, *Before Scotland*, pp.97-100.
[9] Suzman, How Neolithic Farming Sowed The Seeds Of Modern Inequality 10,000 Years Ago, [online] The Guardian.
[10] A rhyme of supposedly ancient origin, that hints at the hunger of water spirits for human sacrifice.
[11] Moffat, *Before Scotland*, pp.181-190.
[12].Armit, *Celtic Scotland*, pp.22-26. Ian Armit suggests that like the spread of Swahili and Malay, the pre-Roman Atlantic gained a common language based on trade.
[13] Cunliffe, *Facing the Ocean*, pp.91-93.

time the climate worsened. Marginal farmland was abandoned as swamps and bogs encroached on the land. The people divided into many constantly warring tribes. Brochs and crannogs were built, defensive structures for small, family-sized groups,[14] as the great hillforts of earlier times were burned and abandoned.[15]

Figure 2: The Ring of Brodgar

By the time of Jesus Christ, the people of all Britain and Ireland lived in several tribes, in small villages of round stone houses with turf or thatched roofs. They wore tattoos and gaudy jewellery, believed in reincarnation and strange taboos, raised children communally, fought each other constantly, were familiar, with the concept at least, of female leaders, and feared above all a tongue-lashing from their bards.[16]

---

[14] Armit, *Celtic Scotland*, pp.33-43.
[15] *Ibid*, pp.50-54.
[16] Encyclopædia Britannica, Fili | Ancient Gaelic Poets.

4

These bards were part of a brahmin-like middle class called druids, who believed in bravery, doing no evil, and reincarnation. To keep their knowledge sacred they wrote nothing down, memorising their learning by rhyming them out loud in triads.[17] Britain was the centre of excellence for these druids, and druids from Gaul crossed the Channel to complete their education.[18] The name first recorded for Britain by explorers from the Mediterranean was *Prettanike*, named for the inhabitants, the *Pritani*. It is widely accepted that this means 'painted', after the British habit of wearing tattoos. But *pritios* in the Atlantic languages had another meaning different to 'picture.' It meant 'creator, craftsman, enchanter or poet.' Perhaps the correct name for Britain is not the *painted isle* but the *loquacious isle*.[19] In the words of Shakespeare:

Be not afeard; the isle is full of noises,
Sounds and sweet airs, that give delight and hurt not.[20]

Though druids did not keep records, we can still taste their world as the ancient epics of Ireland survived long enough in oral tradition to be recorded by literate Christian monks. *Táin Bó Cúailnge* describes an Iron Age world of gaudy high-status wealth, powerful female leaders, endemic violence, cattle raids, sex, tattoos, and pointless taboos.[21] And Mediterranean adventurers who travelled north had their own perspective. They commented on the position of women in this society.[22] Women had higher status in Britain and Ireland than they did in the Mediterranean, where they were the property of men. According to Plutarch, it was standard practice north of the Alps for women to act as mediators in political and military disputes. In Britain, women could own property and sometimes had multiple sexual partners.[23] But if classical writers were correct in this observation, then it is unlikely to

---

[17] Berresford Ellis, *A Brief History of The Celts*, pp.47-53.
[18] According to Caesar, *Caesar's Commentaries*, Book 6, Chapter 13.
[19] This intriguing alternative to the orthodox view is presented by Robb, *The Ancient Paths*, p.216.
[20] Shakespeare, *The Tempest*, Act 3, Scene 2.
[21] The *Táin* is paraphrased in Rolleston, *Celtic Myths And Legends*, pp.178-252.
[22] Berresford Ellis, *A Brief History of The Celts*, pp.81-95.
[23] Caesar, *Gallic War*, Book 5, Chapter 14.

be an early example of female emancipation: it seems more likely a by-product of a society dedicated to violence. A communal attitude to sex and property is one way that warrior societies have dealt with the likelihood of a child's father not being around to raise them.[24]

It was into this world of eloquence and violence the Romans came.

Imperium

The Romans had the first great European Empire, the one to which all other empires hark back. But Scotland lay at the edge of the known world, and by the time the Romans arrived their expansion had reached its limits. They had conquered Gaul (or France), and Britannia (or England and Wales), but Caledonia (or Scotland) was a step too far. The Empire stretched from the River Clyde to the Sahara Desert, from the Pillars of Hercules at Gibraltar to the Persian Empire in Iran: and there was constant fighting along its frontiers. It was too big to manage.

"That which cannot be held must be given up," said the Emperor in 163.[25] So despite defeating the carnyx-blowing Caledonian confederacy in battle at Mons Graupius in AD83, and building a turf wall between Forth and Clyde in 142, the Romans retreated behind Hadrian's Wall between the Solway and the Tyne. Boys from the Mediterranean looked north over the barren moors of Tynedale, awaiting the appearance of tattooed warriors spoiling for a fight, men who arrived for battle secure in the knowledge that should they die, the tribe would care for their children. This was the age of the Fingalians, a mythical band of heroes who roamed the bens and glens of Gaeldom hunting deer and wild boar.

Meanwhile, the south of Britannia became accustomed to Roman rule. In the words of Tacitus:

---

[24] This is speculation, based on contemporary research into polyamorous societies. High male mortality is identified as one of the main drivers of polyandry by Starkweather and Hames, "A Survey of Non-Classical Polyandry." *Human Nature*, 23(2), pp.149-172.
[25] Moffat, *Before Scotland*, p.279.

Gradually they went astray into the allurements of evil ways, colonnades and warm baths and elegant banquets. The Britons, who had no experience of this, called it 'civilisation' although it was part of their enslavement.[26]

Britannia west of the Severn and north of the Humber remained a military occupancy for the entire Roman period, tying up three legions, but occasionally their governors took them to the Continent to get involved in Roman politics. The Caledonians and the tribes of the Pennines took advantage of their withdrawal, terrorising southern Britannia. Eventually, in 209, an Emperor called Severus arrived with the largest army yet seen in what is now Scotland. He met a tribal chief from Clackmannan called Argentocoxus, who accepted all Severus' demands and persuaded him to return to the great legionnaire base at Eboracum, or York, without a fight. As the men talked, their wives did too. Empress Julia was having an affair with a Roman senator, and made pointed remarks to Argentocoxus' wife about the fact she slept with the tribes' warriors. The Caledonian queen wasn't having Julia's hypocrisy, and said:

"I proudly have the best of men in full public knowledge, whilst you skulk in secret with the worst."[27]

Within a year, the Caledonians broke the terms of Argentocoxus' truce. Severus ordered the army north in a great slaughter. The Romans had already complained of losing fifty thousand men to disease and guerrilla warfare.[28] Caledonia was a cold Roman Vietnam, inflicting nightmares of ambush by the enemy, warriors hiding in swamps with only their eyes visible.[29] But the effect on Caledonia of the Roman genocide was far worse. The south-east of Scotland was emptied of human life.[30] When Severus died in 211, his son

---

[26] Moffat, *The Faded Map*, p.48. Quoting Tacitus, *Agricola*, XXI.
[27] Dio, *Epitome Of Book 77*, 16.4-5. It is regretful that the name of Argentocoxus' wife was not recorded.
[28] *Ibid*, 13.2.
[29] *Ibid*, 12.4.
[30] Moffat, *Before Scotland*, p.283.

made a hasty peace with the remaining Caledonians so he could return to Rome and secure his throne.

The Romans had come to Caledonia, made a desert, and called it peace. As a pacification, Severus' campaign was a success: for over eighty years, southern Britain was not bothered by attack from the north.[31] The people north of Hadrian's Wall didn't get the roads, trade, togas, central heating, written records, or taxes that the people to the south did. They didn't leave their own records, so we can't know how they felt about this. They might have resented their exclusion. Or they might have thought, like Tacitus, they'd kept something more important.

Their freedom.

These Britons north of Hadrian's Wall became known as the Picts, plaid-wearing warriors[32] whose leaders were occasionally chosen by descent from their mothers, and they terrorised the lands to the south of the Wall in ever greater numbers through the 4th century. The same story was true across all the Empire's frontiers: the Western Roman Emperors were unable to prevent barbarians crossing their limits. Eventually Huns, Vandals, and Visigoths crossed the Danube in massive numbers and in 410 attacked Rome itself. The legions were withdrawn permanently from Britannia to protect the Mediterranean core. Caledonia entered a new age: one of invasions. Four distinct cultures would jostle for space in the infant Scottish nation: the Picts in the north, the Britons to the south, the Angles from the east, and the Gaels to the west.

---

[31] Or at least, none were recorded: the next mention was in regard to a 297 invasion south of the Wall by a newly named people called 'The Picts', Lynch, *Scotland, A New History*, p.7.
[32] Uncredited, *Who Wore Scotland's Oldest Piece Of Tartan?* [online] The Scotsman.

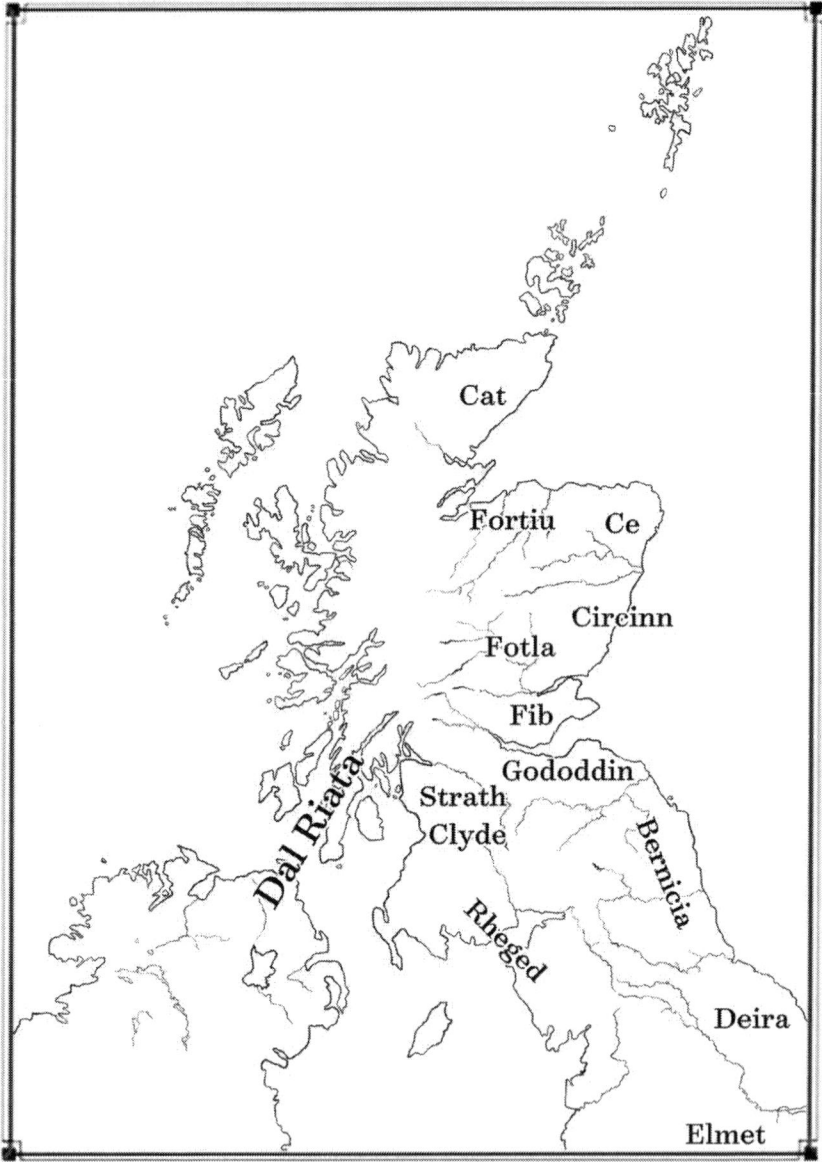

Figure 3: Kingdoms of Post-Roman Scotland

CHAPTER TWO

Hen Ogledd

In Scotland south of the Forth, the religion of Jesus Christ created a link in people's minds with the departed Empire. Rome gained a deathless glamour from its past glories, its Latin language, and its Pope in the Vatican. These Britons called themselves the Cymry,[1] they identified with their fellow Christians south of Hadrian's Wall, and they particularly disliked the pagan Picts, whose stronghold lay north of the Forth. To Gildas, a chronicler from Alt Clut (or Dumbarton), the Picts were:

> *Dark swarms of worms... [who] emerge from the narrow crevices of their holes when the sun is high and the heat increasing.*[2]

To help fight the Picts, the southern Britons around the Thames had invited mercenaries over from Germany called Saxons and Angles. But the cure became worse than the problem. After the Romans left, the Saxons and Angles landed in ever greater numbers, fighting for control of the land. For a season they were held back by the Arthurian figure of Emrys Wledig, but a plague spread along trade routes of the former Roman Empire and devastated Southern Britannia.[3] It was a wasteland such as that described in the ancient Welsh epic *the Mabinogion*: neither smoke nor fire, neither man nor dwelling-place, the court buildings empty, desolate, uninhabited, without people, without animals in them.[4]

The weakened Southern Britons were in no state to resist a renewed offensive of Saxons and Angles, and control of their land was eventually lost.

---

[1] Davies, *The Isles, A History*, p.207. Aneirin called the Christian Britons from outside Hen Ogledd the *Brythonaid*, the wider group of people of which the Cymry were part.

[2] Gildas, De Excidio Britanniae, p.45.

[3] Plague theory mentioned in Morris, *The Age of Arthur*, pp.222-224.

[4] Davies, *The Mabinogion*, p.37.

But between the Forth and Humber, the Cymry of *Hen Ogledd* (or the Old North), fought on. Led by the charismatic King Urien of Rheged, a kingdom centred on the Solway Firth, an alliance of kings from Ulster, Ystrad Clut (or Strathclyde), Elmet (in the Pennines), and Bryneich (or Northumberland) combined to sweep the Angles out of their northern territory once and for all. In the 580s and 90s, they nearly succeeded: the Angles were expelled from the mainland and put up a last-ditch defence on Ynys Metcaut (or Lindisfarne). But they were saved by King Morcant of Bryneich. Jealous of Urien's status, Morcant had him assassinated.[5] Without their leader, the Christian alliance collapsed. The Angles quickly took advantage: Morcant's fate was to be overthrown by Anglian warriors who took permanent control of his kingdom, renaming it Bernicia.

All that was left to the Britons of the east coast was their stories.

In the west lived a colourful Christian king: Rhydderch Hael of Strathclyde. He was known for his generosity, but was angry on discovering his wife Langoureth had cheated on him. When he came across a handsome youth sleeping by the Clyde near his castle of Alt Clut, or Dumbarton, and saw him wearing his wife's ring, he quietly took it, threw it in the river, then bid Langoureth wear her ring on their next feast day. In panic Langoureth rode to Glasgow to confess to St Kentigern, who instructed her to catch a salmon in the Clyde: she did, and found her ring in its guts.[6] Rhydderch had fought the Angles with Urien, knew a wise man called Merlin, was cuckolded by his wife, and possessed a magical sword that burst into flame whenever a righteous man wielded it: though none dared try.[7]

In the east lived a rich Christian king, Mynyddog Mwynfawr, known for his wealth. He hadn't joined Urien's alliance, but after its collapse decided to fight the Angles by himself. His base was Din Eidin in Lothian, where he entertained 300 warriors for a year in a great hall before riding out to attack Bernicia in 600, described in an ancient poem called *Y Gododdin*:

[5] Fraser, From Caledonia To Pictland, pp.128-129.
[6] Jocelyn of Furness, *The Life Of Kentigern*, Chapter XXXV.
[7] Bromwich, *Trioedd Ynys Prydein*, p.259.

Three hundred gold-torqued men attacked,
Guarding their land, bloody was the slaughter,
Although they were slain, they slew;
And until the end of the world they will be honoured.[8]

The Angles won. Din Eidin fell to these pagans, who renamed it Edinburgh. In the lands the Angles conquered, from the Forth to the Bristol Channel, the native Britons were treated as second-class citizens. They were named the Welsh, or 'foreigners' by their conquerors.[9] Gildas of Dumbarton knew exactly what was to blame for the Cymry's fall. Too many British kings had abandoned their reverence for Christian teaching, taking instead to adultery and murder. This fall from grace, Gildas said in *De Excidio Britanniae* (or *On the Ruin of Britain*),[10] had cost the native Britons their island. In the Cymric or Welsh language, England eventually came to be called *Lloegr*, the lost lands.[11]

In the south lived a madman, Myrddin Wyllt (or Merlin the Wild), known for his prophecy. He roamed the Forest of Caledon near Selkirk, musing over his life and the death of his master, who was killed at the Battle of Arfderydd by Rhydderch Hael. He felt responsible for the pointless battle, which had started over an argument about a lark's nest, and the stress of it had caused him to wander. When Myrddin died he was buried at Drumelzier on the Tweed. He had supposedly prophesied that the native inhabitants of Britain would one day throw the Angles and Saxons back into the sea.[12]

But this was wishful thinking. The Angles were here to stay.

The Angles

The early story of the Angles is one of constant battle; rogue Germanic mercenaries fighting first for the Britons and then against them. They had been invited across the sea as mercenaries to fight the Picts and Scots, but

---

8 Aneirin, *Y Gododdin*, XC.
9 Tichy and Rocek, *Wilisc*. [online] Bosworth-Toller Anglo-Saxon Dictionary.
10 Denunciation of the Five Princes in Gildas, *De Excidio Britanniae*, pp.69-252.
11 Moffat, *Before Scotland*, p.323.
12 Clarkson, *Scotland's Merlin*, p.23.

after the collapse of the Roman Empire, they had flooded into Britain and overwhelmed their former masters.

They had withstood Urien's alliance; they had defeated Mynyddog Mwynfawr of Lothian in 600; and in 603, they ambushed Áedán of Dal Riata as he marched on Bernicia to install a puppet king.[13] Having proved themselves equal to all comers, the Angles were in a position to start expanding into Hen Ogledd. King Aethelfrith of Bernicia became renowned as the man who:

> *More than all the chieftains of the Angles, ravaged the nation of the Britons... For no one among the kings, made more of their lands to be either tributary to, or to be inhabited by, the nation of the Angles, by exterminating or subjugating the natives.*[14]

But it was not only Britons he attacked. To the south of Bernicia lay Deira (or Yorkshire), another kingdom conquered by the Angles, and Aethelfrith wanted it too. His invasion ultimately led to him being killed by the exiled Deiran king. Aethelfrith's sons fled to their uncle Eochaid Buidhe's kingdom of Dal Riata (or Argyll). It was to prove a pivotal moment in the development of the pagan Angles. Because Dal Riata was different. It was a Christian kingdom.

The Gaels of Dal Riata

The nearest land to Britain is not France, but Ireland: only 19km separates Antrim from Kintyre. To the ancient Irish bards, Alba (or Scotland), was an exotic land of giants and amazons, where a young hero could be trained in the arts of war and love by the Queen of Skye, or a princess could find escape from a possessive king in the peace and tranquillity of Glen Etive and Glendaruel.[15] To the Romanized Britons, the Irish Gaels were no more welcome than the Picts, and yet another source of trouble: they attacked by sea, and though they called themselves the Gael, the Romans and their successors called them the Scots. In 367 they'd joined forces with the Picts

---

13 Moffat, *The Faded Map*, pp.167-172.
14 Gidley, *Bede's Ecclesiastical History of the English Nation*, p.96.
15 From the Ultonian Cycle. Rolleston, *Celtic Myths And Legends*, pp.178-252.

and Saxons in a co-ordinated, multinational attack on Britannia that had heralded the start of the end of Roman rule.

One of these possibly legendary Scots, Coirpre Riata, formed a dynasty: his legacy was a transoceanic kingdom called Dal Riata.[16] It was ruled by kings in Antrim in Ireland. But in 500 Fergus Mor Mac Erc moved his seat of power across the North Channel to Argyll, a coastal region separated from the rest of Scotland by the mountain barrier of Druim Alban. The Gaels had embraced Christianity through St Patrick, and in 563 the most famous Christian in Scottish history set sail from Ireland to Argyll. His name was Crimthann, a prince of the Cenel Conaill of Donegal. He had secretly copied a religious textbook, which led to a legal argument over copyright. Crimthann lost, decided to take the law into his own hands, and the dispute ended up on an Irish battlefield with three thousand men killed.

Crimthann was exiled from Ireland in disgrace. As penance he vowed to win for Christ as many souls as had died through his actions. His cousin King Conall of Dal Riata gave him a site that had been sacred to the druids called Iova, or *yew island*,[17] a small island off Mull. After his destructive start, Crimthann became known as Colm Cille, *the dove of peace*. We know him today as St Columba, and his island as Iona.

Colm Cille

Columba travelled to Inverness in 565 for an audience with King Bridei of the Picts. According to legend he performed various impossible feats, saving a follower swimming across the River Ness from a kelpie by making the sign of the cross, and throwing open the gates of Bridei's citadel through the power of prayer alone.[18] Bridei was impressed. He allowed Columba to set up Christian cells across Pictland. Meanwhile Iona became famed far and wide as a beacon of sanctity and learning, the most important early church in Scotland.

With Columba's influence and blessing, the new King Áedán of Dal Riata dominated the North Channel, his authority formalised at the Convention

---

[16] Clarkson, *The Picts: A History*, p.72.
[17] Watson, *The History Of The Celtic Place-Names Of Scotland*, p.88.
[18] Adomnán, *Life Of St. Columba*. Book 2, Chapters 28,36.

of Druim Cett in Ulster in 575. His coronation a year earlier at Iona was the first in Britain to be conducted by a bishop.[19] That ceremony bound Áedán to God: another ceremony at Dunadd would bind Dalriadan kings to the land. During this ceremony, kings placed their bare foot in a footprint carved out of a faultline in the rock at the top of his citadel of Dunadd and looked, not back to Ireland, but north-east to the rest of Scotland. *This too*, the alignment of the land itself seemed to say, *can be yours*. Áedán laid waste Rhydderch Hael's fortress of Alt Clut, defeated a force of the Maetae on the shores of the Forth, and sent an expedition north to raid Orkney. In 603 he marched on the Angles, taking with him Hering, a deposed prince of Bernicia, but was defeated by Aethelfrith at Degsastan.

And so it was not Áedán, but his descendants who would have the biggest influence on Bernicia, after Aethelfrith's sons Oswald and Oswiu fled for sanctuary in the Gaelic kingdom. Eochaid Buidhe took them in, and in 634, Domnall Brecc gave them a Scottish army to retake their father's kingdoms. At Heavenfield near Hexham, the Scots and Angles faced the army of Cadwallon of Gwynedd in Wales, who was threatening to re-conquer Bernicia and Deira for the Britons.

The Britons lost; Oswald was confirmed on his thrones. And he wanted his pagan people to have the same Christian benefits he had enjoyed in Dal Riata.

Bretwaldas

The Pope had sent a delegation to the Angles in 627, and they set up base in the former legionary capital of Ebrauc (or York). But Oswald had grown up at the Dalriadan court, could speak Gaelic, and preferred an Irish mission to the Roman one. At Oswald's request Iona sent Aidan, who was given Lindisfarne and made a great success of Christianising the Angles. As Aidan's influence spread, monasteries were founded across Bernicia, including at Old Melrose, Dryburgh, Kelso and Coldingham. But in the 660s Oswald's successor, his brother Oswiu, was embarrassed to have begun feasting in celebration of Easter while his wife Eanflæd was still fasting for Lent. Eanflæd had grown up in Kent and followed the Roman church, which

---

[19] Adomnán, *Life Of St. Columba.* Book 3, Chapter 5.

calculated the date of Easter differently to the Ionans. A synod at Whitby was convened to determine which system the Angles would follow. Leading the charge, Bishop Wilfred argued that the rest of Western Christendom followed Rome, and that:

> *"The only people stupid enough to disagree with the whole world are these Scots and their obstinate adherents the Picts and Britons, who inhabit only a portion of these two islands in the remote ocean."*[20]

Oswiu decided to go with his wife and with Rome. The church was consolidating; and the Anglian kings of Bernicia and Deira wanted to do the same. They conquered Elmet, reached the Solway, and claimed the Isle of Man. The poem *Dream of the Rood*, carved on the side of the early 8th century Ruthwell Cross on the Scottish side of the Solway Firth, is claimed to be the oldest existing piece of written English.[21] Oswald captured Din Eidin, and claimed tribute from the kingdoms of Mercia and the Lindisware to his south. His new kingdom between the Forth and Humber became called Northumbria. Oswiu continued the trend, defeating the Mercians and East Anglians in battle. His first wife had been Rienmelth, allowing him to legally inherit her kingdom of Rheged when she died. These men claimed the title of Bretwalda, or *Britain Ruler*.[22] It was a vanity title, but a revealing one. Even though they did not directly rule all Britain, or even the whole of the former Roman Province of Britannia, these Northumbrian kings were the most influential of their age. Through judicious marriage and ceaseless fighting, Northumbria had become the most powerful kingdom of Britain. And their long possession of Edinburgh before the Gaelic-speaking Scots took over meant that the Kingdom of Scotland would come with a powerful cultural force baked-in: the English language.

For the first time since the Romans, covetous eyes even looked north of the Forth. Oswiu stretched his influence over his nephew Talorcan, King of the Picts, taking direct control over Southern Pictland when Talorcan died. When Oswiu died in 670 and his successor Ecgfrith claimed Southern

---

[20] Lehane, *Early Celtic Christianity*, p.205.
[21] Moffat, *The Faded Map*, p.231.
[22] Davies, *The Isles: A History*, pp.203-204.

Pictland for his own, the Picts rose up and were slaughtered at the Battle of Two Rivers on the Plain of Manau near Falkirk. According to a Northumbrian chronicle:

> *He [Ecgfrith] slew an enormous number of the people, filling two rivers with corpses, so that, marvellous to relate, the slayers, passing over the rivers dry foot, pursued and slew a crowd of fugitives.*[23]

Ecgfrith installed an Anglian bishop at Abercorn on the Forth, right on the doorstep of Southern Pictland. He took tribute from Dal Riata and the Britons of Strathclyde. Some intrepid Angles even settled on the shores of Fife.[24]

But little did the Northumbrians know that the Bretwalda was about to meet his match.

[23] Clarkson, *The Picts: A History*, p.119.
[24] *Ibid*, p.130.

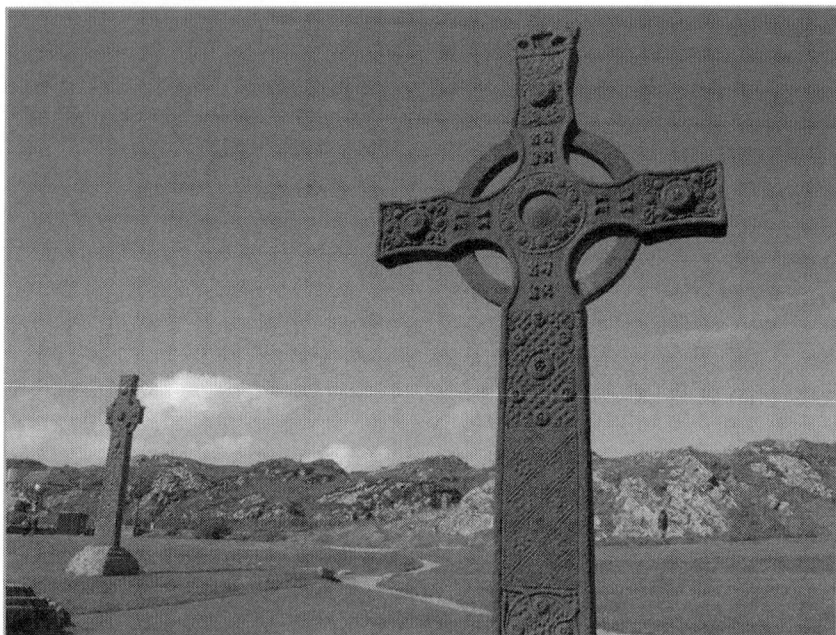

Figure 4: Celtic Crosses on Iona

CHAPTER THREE

The Picts

The least understood of all the peoples of early Britain are the Picts. The Gaels, Britons and Angles reveal themselves through their own writing; but as the Picts wrote little except ogham inscriptions on stones, other sources must be consulted to understand them. DNA evidence says the Picts were descended, like the Britons, from the earliest Celtic inhabitants of Northern Britain.[1] The Gaels claimed anyway that they were nomadic adventurers from Scythia on the Black Sea who had wanted to settle in Ireland, but were rebuffed, having to settle for Scotland instead. In 550, Pictish king Bridei mac Maelchon entered written history, thanks to an attack on Dal Riata. Like many Pictish kings, Bridei had inherited his throne not through his father but through his mother, a Pictish princess.[2] Another Irish legend says that this practice was a condition placed on the first Pictish settlers in return for taking Irish wives![3]

In 565 Bridei hosted St Columba, who performed a battle of wits with his chief druid Broichan before being given permission to evangelise Pictland.[4] By the end of the 7th century the church had important missions at Kinrymont (or St Andrews), Abernethy, and Portmahomack. [5]

The Picts followed the Gaels in religion. But in terms of warfare they remained unconquered, the blue-faced nightmare of Roman and Briton alike. Until 670, and the Battle of Two Rivers. Ecgfrith of Northumbria now lorded over the Picts south of the mountain barrier of the Mounth and their

---

[1] Moffat, *The Scots: A Genetic Journey*, pp.140-141.
[2] Woolf, *Pictish Matriliny Reconsidered*. [online] Academia. Woolf cautions that though Pictish kings had their mothers described, it doesn't necessarily mean that they inherited power exclusively down the female line.
[3] Mac Eoin, "On the Irish Legend of the Origin of the Picts" *Studia Hibernica*, no. 4, 1964, pp. 140-141.
[4] Adomnán, *Life Of St. Columba*, Book 2, Chapters 34,35.
[5] Fraser, *From Caledonia To Pictland*, pp.106-107,134,361.

three sub-kingdoms of Fib (or Fife), Fotla (Perthshire), and Circinn (or Angus).

But north of the Mounth, resistance was stirring.

For Ecgfrith was up against Bridei mac Bili. Bridei was the son of Bili, King of Strathclyde, and was grandson of a previous king of Picts. Bridei regrouped the Picts north of the Mounth, in the four sub-kingdoms of Ce (Aberdeenshire), Fortriu (presumed to be Moray & Ross), Fidich (possibly Speyside), and Cat (Sutherland and Caithness).[6] He reclaimed Orkney from the Gaels, who may have held the islands since the attack by Áedán of Dalriada a hundred years earlier. His army besieged and took the castles of Dunnottar and Dundurn, their garrisons loyal to Ecgfrith. Eventually Ecgfrith realised the seriousness of the threat Bridei posed to his hold over the Southern Picts. He gathered an army in the face of warnings from his spiritual advisor St Cuthbert, who had a vision of Ecgfrith's death.[7]

As Ecgfrith came on, Bridei refused at first to engage. Instead he retreated through a mountain pass, compelling Ecgfrith to follow him. On 20 May 685, Bridei sprung his trap, ambushing Ecgfrith at the battle of Linn Garan, or *Heron Lake*. It was a slaughter 'in angustias inaccessorum montium' (in defiles of unapproachable mountains),[8] and a great victory for the defending Picts. The Gaels called it the battle of Dun Nechtan, the Angles called it Nechtansmere.[9] It was long thought this was at Dunnichen in Angus where a symbol stone depicts a battle, though a new theory points towards the site being in Speyside, at Dunachton by Loch Insh.[10]

The result was a fatal blow to Northumbrian expansion. All their territory gained in the north since 650 was lost. Bridei ruled Pictland undisputed, and

---

[6] Cowan and McDonald, *Alba*, pp.24-42. These areas are speculative. The Picts have three separate kingdom lists, and they don't quite match up: Fib, Cat, Circinn and Ce are clear; but that leaves Fortriu, Fidich, and Fotla to be divided up between Strathearn & Menteith, Atholl, Moray & Ross in one list, and 'between the Forth and Tay', 'from Spey to Druimalban', and 'Moray and Ross' in another.
[7] Consitt, *Life of St Cuthbert*, p.96,106.
[8] Gidley, *Bede's Ecclesiastical History of the English Nation*, p.360.
[9] Clarkson, *The Picts: A History*, p.127.
[10] Fraser, *From Caledonia To Pictland*, pp.215-216.

Strathclyde and Dal Riata were freed from tribute to the Angles.[11] Bridei is barely known in Scotland's story, yet in repelling the Northumbrians his contribution is as crucial as that of Wallace or Bruce.

Bridei died in 693. He started the tradition of monarchs being interred in Iona: he had buried his enemy Ecgfrith there too. According to legend, not only had the burials begun earlier, but sixty kings from Scotland, Ireland, and Norway were buried at Iona, plus several medieval Lords of the Isles.[12] A legend grew that its sanctity was so great that at Armageddon all the earth would be inundated by a flood bar one small, holy island: Iona.

Floreat Picti

As the 8th century wore on, the Picts consolidated their dominance in the north. King Nechtan wrote to the Northumbrian abbey at Monkwearmouth-Jarrow for help setting up churches *'in the Roman style.'* Monks came to set up stone churches at Restenneth, which was dedicated to St Peter, and at the existing church of Kilrymont, dedicated to St Andrew. This latter church would become St Andrews Cathedral, the prime ecclesiastical site in Scotland. In 717 Nechtan went further: he expelled Ionan monks from practicing in Pictland.[13] These ascetics had become detached from mainstream Christian thought, and Nechtan decided, as the Northumbrians had done at Whitby, that only the doctrines endorsed by Rome would be allowed in his kingdom. As a result, a Pictish bishop attended a council in Rome in 721, which helped integrate Pictland further into the family of western Christian nations.[14] The bones of St Andrew himself ended up in St Andrews Cathedral. Legend speaks of a Roman Emperor, Constantine, deciding to move the saint's bones from their resting place in Greece to his new city of Constantinople, and a 4th century Greek monk called St Rule being told in a vision to move them instead to *'the farthest ends of the earth.'* Historians suggest instead that any relics were more likely transferred from

---

[11] Clarkson, *The Picts: A History*, p.130.
[12] Monro, Description Of The Western Isles Of Scotland, pp.19-21.
[13] Yorke, *The Conversion Of Britain*, p.132.
[14] *Ibid*, p.154.

St Andrews abbey in Hexham after 731, when Bishop Acca may have moved from Northumbria to Kilrymont.[15]

Nechtan retired to a monastery in 724, which triggered a bloodbath for his succession. The man who came out on top in 729 was Onuist map Uurguist, or Angus mac Fergus. He invaded Dal Riata to capture one of his escaped rivals, then ritually drowned him,[16] possibly – though this is speculation – in his sacred pool at Burghead. Dal Riata would bear the brunt of his attentions again. Two kindreds in Dal Riata, the Cenel Loarn and Cenel nGabhrain, struggled against each other for domination, fighting Britain's first recorded sea battle in 719.[17] But in 741 their struggle was rendered irrelevant, as the Gaelic kingdom came completely under Angus mac Fergus's rule. Dal Riata and Pictland became ever more intertwined. The Cenel Loarn and Cenel nGabhrain would eventually migrate into Pictland. The Cenel Loarn travelled from their homeland in Lorne up Strath Dearn to Moray;[18] the Cenel nGabhrain from their homeland in Kintyre up Strath Earn to Perthshire.[19]

Angus was also active to the south. As the power of the Britons of Strathclyde waned, the Northumbrians had taken over Rheged and appointed the bishops of Whithorn.[20] The Britons of Strathclyde were surrounded: Angles to the south and east, Picts to the north, and Pictish-ruled Dal Riata to the west. In 756 their worst fears were realized. Angus combined with Eadbert of Northumbria to launch an attack on Alt Clut, the capital of Strathclyde.[21] It was the last mention of the citadel for a century.[22]

But Eadbert had been played. In the aftermath of Linn Garan, Northumbria's star was fading, and the most powerful kingdom in Britain had become Mercia in the English Midlands. The true power alliance in Britain was not between Angus of the Picts and Eadbert of Northumbria. It

---

[15] Fraser, *From Caledonia To Pictland*, p.309.
[16] *Ibid,* p.298.
[17] Moffat, *Before Scotland*, p.311.
[18] Clarkson, *The Picts: A History*, pp.188-189.
[19] *Ibid,* p.184.
[20] Fraser, *From Caledonia To Pictland*, p.306,314.
[21] Clarkston, *The Picts: A History*, p.161; Fraser, *From Caledonia To Pictland*, p.316.
[22] Fraser, *From Caledonia To Pictland*, p.317.

was between Angus and the King of Mercia. They had already combined against the Northumbrians in 740.[23] And now, as Eadbert marched home, he was attacked and defeated. Who did it is not recorded: it could have been Angus, or even some Britons of Strathclyde looking for revenge.[24] This blow was the beginning of the end of Northumbria as a major political player. It may even have played a part in the legend of Scotland's flag.

The Legend of the Saltire

Legend has it that at Athelstaneford in East Lothian, King Angus of the Picts faced the invading army of Athelstan of Northumbria. Angus prayed to God for victory and saw a white cross of cloud in the blue sky: the symbol of St Andrew, patron Saint of the Picts. Encouraged by this sign from God, Angus routed Athelstan, and the Saltire was adopted as the national flag of Scotland. There was just one problem with the legend. East Lothian at the time was in Northumbria. If there was a battle at Athelstaneford, the Picts weren't defending their country: they were invading. It's not impossible, though admittedly it is also speculative, that the incident recalls Angus' attack on Eadbert, replacing his name with another Northumbrian leader.[25] Whatever the truth, the outcome is in no doubt. Thanks to the Picts' adoption of St Andrew, his white-on-blue saltire became the flag of the future country of Scotland.

---

[23] Fraser, *From Caledonia To Pictland*, p.310.
[24] Clarkson, *The Picts: A History*, pp.160-161.
[25] Fraser, *From Caledonia To Pictland*, pp.317-318.

Figure 5: The Saltire of St Andrew

A bad winter and famine came in 763-4,[26] and in 768 the last churches in Britain finally fell into line with Rome over Easter.[27] Famine, bad weather, and strange lights in the sky had combined to convince people that only adherence to the correct religious doctrine could appease divine wrath.[28] In 786, the Pope took advantage of this sentiment to send representatives to Northumbria to renew their faith. Northumbrians were ordered to stop copying the Pictish fashion for tattoos,[29] and other Pictish habits, like the docking of horses' tails and various styles of dress.

But a new force was about to arrive to test the status quo to destruction.

They were known as the Norse.

---

[26] Bambury and Beechinor, *The Annals Of Ulster*, U764.
[27] Yorke, *The Conversion Of Britain*, p.117.
[28] Swanton, *The Anglo-Saxon Chronicle*, pp.54-56.
[29] Moffat, *Before Scotland*, p.287. Bishop George of Ostia at a synod of Calcuth in Northumbria in 787, talked of the Picts' 'hideous scars' and the 'injury of staining'.

Vikings Attack

If the basic ingredients of early Scotland were the Picts, Gaels, Angles, and Britons, then the catalyst to bring these people together into one nation came through attacks by the Norse.

At the dawn of the 9th century they came over from Norway as pirates called Vikings, attacking undefended holy sites, killing, raping, looting, and taking slaves; terrors of the coast in versatile boats of shallow draft called longships. Iona was abandoned after the third devastating raid in 806,[30] its treasure sent inland well away from sudden Viking attack: the library went to Kells in Ireland and St Columba's bones ended up at Dunkeld in Perthshire. In 825 Blathmac mac Flann travelled to Iona with his suicidal acolytes who intended to endure a 'red martyrdom' of murder by the pagan Vikings. They got their wish.[31] In the space of a generation, Iona's light was destroyed, reduced from a radiant centre of influence to a killing field.

At the nunnery of Coldingham in 870 an even worse atrocity occurred. The abbess, fearing for her charges' virginity, sliced off her nose and upper lip with a knife to make herself unattractive to the marauding Vikings, and bade the other nuns follow her example. Their appearance so horrified the invaders that they burned the nunnery down with the women inside: burned alive, the chroniclers wrote approvingly, with their virginity and honour intact.[32]

Norwegians completely overran Orkney and Shetland, settled in great numbers in Caithness and the Western Isles, and set up pirate bases called longphorts in Ireland from which to terrorise the surrounding countryside and coasts. Via the long rivers of the Baltic and Russia, Scandinavians were in contact with Muslims in the Black Sea and Mediterranean who, like the Vikings themselves, had an insatiable appetite for Christian slaves.[33] North Atlantic farmers and fisherfolk were captured and sold by Vikings, to toil perhaps very far from home.

---

[30] Bambury and Beechinor, *The Annals Of Ulster*, U806.
[31] *Ibid,* U825.
[32] Goring, *Scotland: Her Story*, paras.10.17-24.
[33] Winroth, *The Age Of The Vikings*, p.116.

From Denmark came more Vikings, who sailed up the rivers of France[34] and settled in Northumbria in large enough numbers to change the language.[35] They were pagans who believed the greatest honour of all was to die in battle, at which point the warrior would be transported instantly to a giant feasting hall called Valhalla, perhaps the most boorish vision of heaven ever imagined.[36] For the Vikings, hell was not a hot torment but somewhere eternally cold and lonely. A flavour of this culture can be gained by a passage from *Haakon the Good's saga*:

> *The hero who knows well to ride*
> *The sea-horse o'er the foamingtide, -*
> *He who in boyhood wild rode o'er*
> *The seaman's horse to Skanea's shore.*
> *And showed the Danes his galley's bow,*
> *Right nobly scours the ocean now.*
> *On Scotland's coast he lights the brand*
> *Of flaming war; with conquering hand*
> *Drives many a Scottish warrior tall*
> *To the bright seats in Odin's hall.*
> *The fire-spark, by the fiend of war*
> *Fanned to a flame, soon spreads afar.*
> *Crowds trembling fly, – the southern foes*
> *Fall thick beneath the hero's blows:*
> *The hero's blade drips red with gore,*
> *Staining the green sward on the shore.*[37]

In 870, the Norse from their pirate base of Dublin made a devastating attack on Dumbarton, forcing it to be abandoned forever as the capital of Strathclyde.[38] They settled in Iceland, Greenland, and even North America, carrying in their exploratory longships the first Scots to land in America, a

---

[34] Winroth, *The Age Of The Vikings*, pp.22-24.
[35] The dales and fells of Yorkshire and the Lake District are the *dals* and *fjells* of Norse-speaking settlers.
[36] Guerber, *Norsemen*, pp.18-22.
[37] Sturlason, *Heimskringla: Haakon The Good's Saga*, Chapter 5.
[38] Bambury and Beechinor, *The Annals Of Ulster*, U870.

pair of fell-running slaves called Haki and Hekja who acted as their scouts.[39] In the north, from his base in Orkney, Sigurd the Mighty conquered Sutherland and Caithness for Norway, creating an international boundary along the River Oykell.[40] In the south, Danes overthrew the Angles of Northumbria and began ruling part of it for themselves as the Kingdom of York.[41] And in the islands of the west, two cultures mingled: the Viking settlers swapped their Norse language for Gaelic, accepted Christianity, and became known as the *Gall-gael*, or foreign Gaels; their ancestors from across the North Sea called the *Lochlanners*.

Alcuin of York had been in no doubt for the reason that Northumbria had been attacked: he blamed King Aethelred of Northumbria for the initial attack on Lindisfarne, saying it was a punishment by God for his sins, the catalogue of which included wearing his hair in a Viking style as he 'wished to resemble the pagans'.[42] We are so conditioned to the accounts from Christian martyrs of the brutality of Viking raids, that this domestic side can come as a surprise. But according to John of Wallingford:

> *Thanks to their habit of combing their hair every day, of bathing every Saturday and regularly changing their clothes, [they] were able to undermine the virtue of married women and even seduce the daughters of nobles to be their mistresses.*[43]

King Aethelred's motivation becomes clearer.

And if the Picts, Gaels, Britons and Angles didn't want to succumb entirely to the rule of these better-groomed Norwegians and Danes, they would have to band together and do something about it.

---

[39] Magnusson and Pálsson, *The Vinland Sagas*, p.95.
[40] Pálsson and Edwards, *Orkneyinga Saga*, pp.30-31. A bizarre story is told in the Orkneyinga Saga of the death of Sigurd. Victorious in battle against the Scots, he tied the head of his opponent Mael Tonn to his horse's saddle. But as he rode north, Mael's head bumped against Sigurd's thigh. The teeth opened a wound that became septic and Sigurd died.
[41] Davies, *The Isles, A History*, p.259..
[42] Browne, *Alcuin of York*, pp.130-131.
[43] Stevenson, *The Chronicles of John Wallingford*, pp.558-559.

29

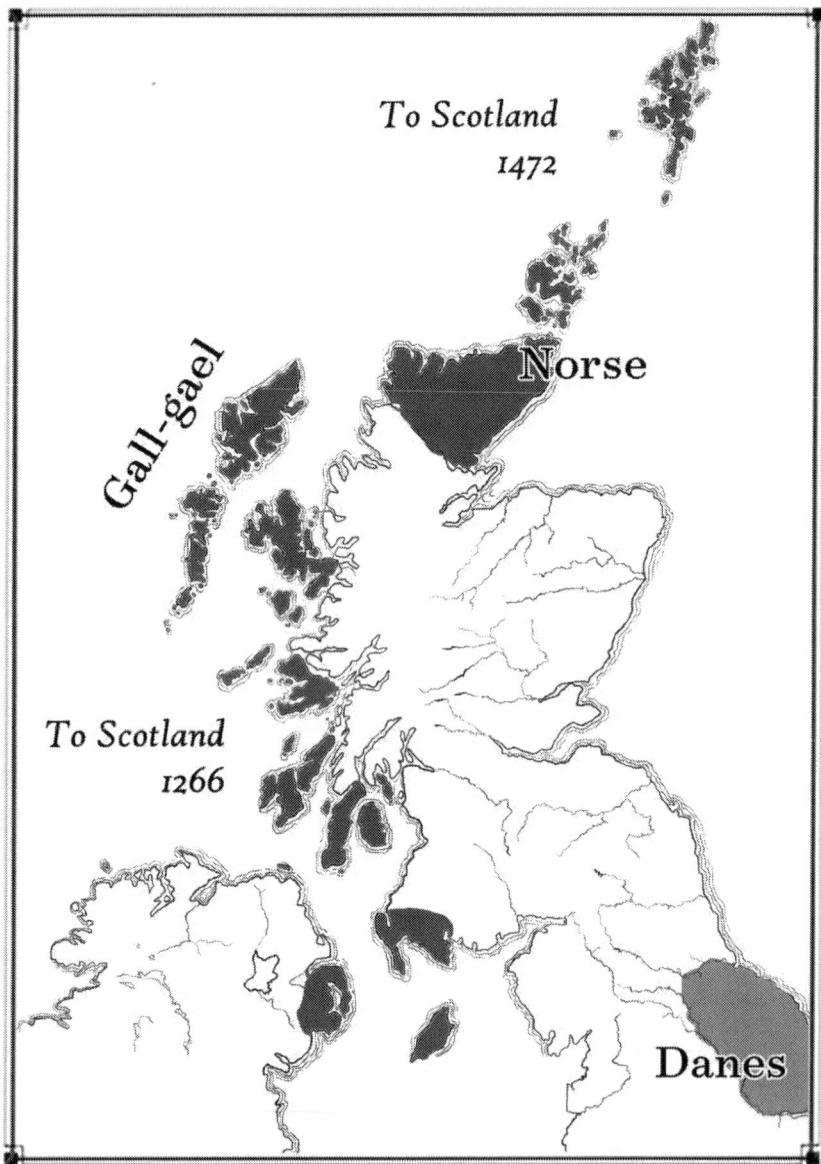

Figure 6: Viking Scotland

CHAPTER FOUR

Consolidation of a Nation

The bells tolled at St Andrews and in Northumbrian monasteries, and the monks prayed for the souls of the latest Christian kings to die. Their Pictish patron, King Uen, was dead.[1] He and his army had been scythed down like ripe corn in a disastrous battle against the Vikings. Lying alongside him on the battlefield was the body of King Aed of Dal Riata. It was 839. The Picts and the Scots needed new leadership, and they needed it fast.[2]

A new man inherited the Gaelic Kingdom of Dal Riata, and in 843, through his mother, he was proclaimed King of Picts. His name was Cináed mac Ailpin, or Kenneth MacAlpin, and by tradition he was the first King of Scots: though contemporary sources don't specifically refer to a *Rí Alban*, or Scottish king, until half a century later.[3] He moved the two great talismans of Dal Riata, the bones of St Columba and the Stone of Destiny, from Argyll to Perthshire. The saint's bones were placed in a jewelled box called the Brecbennach. The Stone was supposedly placed on the Moot Hill at Scone near Perth.[4] Tradition has it that this tiny hill was formed of soil from all parts of the land, brought by the nobility from their own lands when they came to acknowledge the creation of new kings.[5] It became the belly-button of a new country called Scotland. Although the Picts dominated in territory and population, the language, culture and laws of this new country would be of the Gaels of Dal Riata. A succession of kings with colourful names followed: Giric Mac Rath, Dòmhnall Dásachtach, Illdub an Ionsaighthigh,

---

[1] Taylor, *Kings, Clerics And Chronicles In Scotland*, p.25.
[2] Bambury and Beechinor, *The Annals Of Ulster*, U839.
[3] With the death of Dòmhnall Dásachtach in 900. Bambury and Beechinor, *The Annals Of Ulster*. U900.
[4] The Stone of Destiny is a talisman beswirled with legend. One tale has it that the stone never left Ireland in the first place, and that it is now the Blarney Stone at Blarney Castle. For the full story, see Gerber, *Stone Of Destiny*.
[5] Though Dr Oliver O'Grady suggests the mound was created entire around a thousand years ago. O'Grady, "Accumulating Kingship: The Archaeology Of Elite Assembly In Medieval Scotland." *World Archaeology*, 50:1, pp.137-149.

Dub Niger, Constantinus Calvus, Máel Coluim Forranach. Or: Lucky Giric, Donald the Mad, Illdub the Angry, Dub the Black, Constantine the Bald, Malcolm the Destroyer. They fought Norse and Danish warlords with equally colourful names: Olaf the White, Ivarr the Boneless, Sigurd the Mighty, Erik Bloodaxe, Thorstein the Red, and the legendary Ragnar Hairybreeks. The first Scottish king of note after MacAlpin is Constantine II, whose long rule from 900 to 943 saw the Norse finally held at bay, defeated by Scottish forces at a battle in Strathearn.[6] Constantine then combined with the Angles of Bernicia to fight the Danes at Corbridge.[7] But he also had a new threat to contend with.

England.

Just as, under the threat of attack by Scandinavians, the Picts and the Gaels combined to create a new country of Alba, or Scotland; so in southern Britain, the kingdoms of the Saxons and Angles had combined to form England. The rulers of both these new countries had managed to see off their Viking menace, but Athelstan, the ruler of England, decided that England alone was not the limit of his ambition. At the northern border of his lands at Eamont in Cumbria, he called all the rulers of Britain together to do homage to him. Constantine of Alba; Hywel Dda of Wales; Owain of Strathclyde; and Ealdred of Bernicia, the last independent Anglian kingdom, all acclaimed Athelstan as the greatest king in the islands.[8] After Ealdred died, in 934 Athelstan marched on Bernicia and annexed it to England.[9] He didn't stop there, and carried on in to Scotland, cornering Constantine in Dunnottar Castle.[10] This was too much, and Constantine gathered allies for a counter strike. In 937, Olaf of Dublin, Owain of Strathclyde, and Constantine of Alba landed on the Wirral at Dunbrunde,[11] or Brunanburh in Old English, where the Vikings already had a settlement. They were met by Athelstan with the men of Wessex and Mercia. The two sides fought each

---

[6] Woolf, *From Pictland To Alba*, pp.126-127.
[7] *Ibid,* p.142-144.
[8] Swanton, *The Anglo-Saxon Chronicle*, p.107.
[9] Woolf, *From Pictland To Alba*, pp.163-165.
[10] Stevenson, *The Historical Works Of Simeon Of Durham*, p.502.
[11] Wood, *Brunanburh: Where Did The Battle That Saved England Take Place?*, [online] HistoryExtra. The actual location of Dunbrunde is unknown.

other to a standstill in the bloodiest battle that had yet been recorded on British soil. After a day of slaughter, Constantine's forces retired from the field. Athelstan had won an immensely significant victory. Never again would England's dominance be seriously threatened by a combined army of her island neighbours. But Athelstan was too bruised to follow up his win with further attacks on Scotland. He died two years later, and his enemies lived long enough to see English advances reversed. Scandinavians retook the Kingdom of York and added half of Mercia to their domains. The new English king Edmund needed all the help he could get against the resurgent Scandinavians, so when Constantine II abdicated in 943, his successor Malcolm I made a pact to assist Edmund *'on sea and on land'* against Norwegians and Danes.[12]

The pact lasted only as long as Edmund did. When he died, Malcolm secured Cumbria for Scotland and invaded Bernicia.[13] But Malcolm had problems of his own.

The Kings of Scots were able to keep hold of their southern border, which was more lopsided than now,[14] but the north was another story. In Dal Riata the rival dynasties of Cenel Loarn and Cenel nGabhrain had fought over control. They had migrated into Moray and Perthshire respectively, intermarried with the local Pictish dynasties, and now their descendants north and south of the great mountain barrier of the Mounth came to blows. While Malcolm was away ravaging the North of England taking cattle and slaves, the Moravians of Northern Scotland took advantage of his absence and rose in revolt. When the king returned to face them in battle he was killed *'by deceit and guile'* on the plain outside the fortress of Dunnottar.[15]

An early death, whether at the hands of Norwegians or fellow Scots, was not that big a deal. It was easy to replace one vigorous leader with another. Kings were chosen from the derbfine, an eligible group that included every adult nephew, cousin, son or grandson of a past king, the most capable successor

[12] Swanton, *The Anglo-Saxon Chronicle*, p.110.
[13] Anderson, *Early Sources Of Scottish History, Volume One*, p.452.
[14] In the west the King of Scots controlled Cumbria down to at least the River Eamont, but in the east, no further south than the Firth of Forth.
[15] Anderson, *Early Sources Of Scottish History, Volume One*, p.453.

identified beforehand by his peer group and called the tanist.[16] This system had been imported from Ireland, but at the dawn of the 11th century, a new fashion caught the attention of the next king called Malcolm, Malcolm II. This fashion was primogeniture, or rule of the first-born son: it's the system of royal succession we are familiar with today. Malcolm was nicknamed *An Forranach* or 'the Destroyer' because he set about killing any potential rivals to his throne with the ruthlessness of an Ottoman Sultan. And having ensured nobody but his own son could inherit the throne, guess what?

He was blessed with daughters only.

---

[16] Encyclopædia Britannica, *Tanistry* | *Definition & Facts.*

Cináed mac Ailpín
(Kenneth I)
r. 834-859

Domnall mac Ailpín
(Donald I)
r. 859-863

Constantín mac Cináed
(Constantine I)
r. 863-877

Áed mac Cináeda
r. 877-878

Unnamed daughter

Eochaid
r. 878-889

Giric mac Rath
r. 878-889

Domnall Dásachtach
(Donald II)
r. 889-900

Causantín mac Áeda
(Constantine II)
r. 900-943

Máel Coluim
mac Domnaill
(Malcolm I)
r. 943-954

Ildulb an Ionsaighthigh
r. 954-962

Dub Niger
r. 962-967

Cináed an
Fionnghalach
(Kenneth II)
r. 971-995

Cuilén mac Illuilb
r. 967-971

Cináed an Donn
(Kenneth III)
r. 997-1005

Constantinus Calvus
(Constantine III)
r. 995-997

Máel Coluim
Forranach
(Malcolm II)
r. 1005-1034

Bethoc

Donada

Olith

Donnachd an
t-Ilgarch
(Duncan I)
r. 1034-1040

Macbeth
r. 1040-1057

Gruoch ── Gillecomain

Thorfinn the Mighty

Lulach
r. 1057-1058

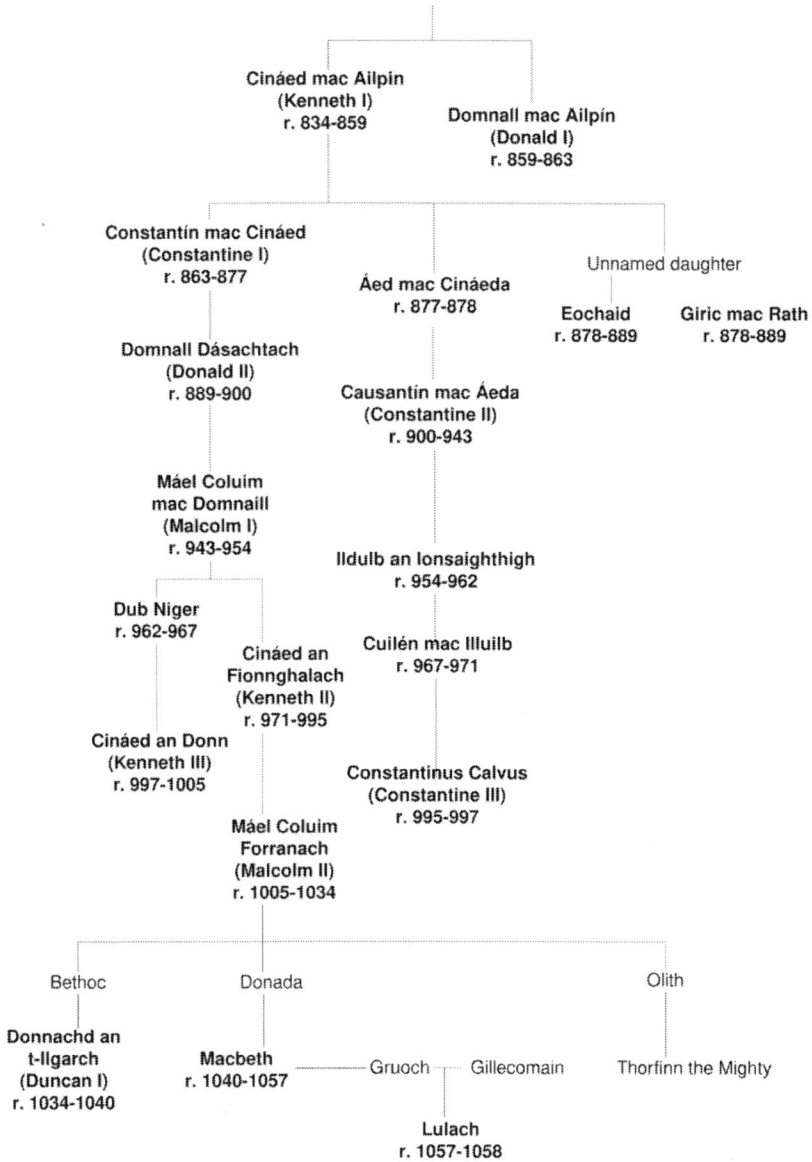

Figure 7: Kings of the Derbfine

35

They each had sons: Thorfinn became Jarl of Orkney, Macbeth became Mormaer of Moray, and Donnchad An t-Ilgarach, or Duncan the Unwell, the King of Scots. Had the derbfine got the vote, then Duncan may have been their last choice: but as son of his eldest daughter, Malcolm Forranach had nominated him king. It would prove fatal for the hapless Duncan. Like Malcolm Forranach, he attacked northern England: but unlike Malcolm, who annexed Lothian and the Merse to Scotland after winning the Battle of Carham in 1018 against English forces, Duncan was soundly defeated at Durham in 1039. Next Duncan turned his attention north, demanding tax and tribute from Thorfinn for Caithness. The Orcadian, who held Caithness in his own right, refused.[17] They clashed at the headland of Torfnes[18] where Duncan was defeated by Thorfinn,[19] before Macbeth arrived and delivered the final blow, killing the king with his own hand on 14 August 1040.[20]

You may have heard of Macbeth's treachery because of the famous play of that name. But forget your Shakespeare. The truth is Macbeth was the king Scotland needed. He came from the north – his father was descended from Cenel Loarn[21] – but he was also, through his grandfather Malcolm Forranach, descended from Kenneth MacAlpin and the Cenel nGabhrain line of kings. Scotland finally had a king able to unite all factions. He ruled wisely, and was secure enough in his kingdom to go on an extended pilgrimage to the Mediterranean in 1050 where he scattered silver coin like seed to the poor of Rome.[22] His Lady Macbeth was Gruoch, a woman whose first husband he had assassinated. Yet they married, and she persuaded Macbeth to nominate as his tanist her son Lulach from her first marriage, hinting at remarkable personal qualities in this lady. But trouble came from England when Duncan's sons grew up. His eldest, Malcolm, was supported in an invasion by the Earl of Northumberland. Malcolm had married Thorfinn's widow Ingibjorg, who may have provided Orcadian support from the north.[23] Macbeth was caught and killed at Lumphanan in

---

[17] Pálsson and Edwards, *Orkneyinga Saga*, p.50.
[18] Either Burghead or Tarbat Ness.
[19] Pálsson and Edwards, *Orkneyinga Saga*, pp.52-55.
[20] Anderson, *Early Sources Of Scottish History, Volume One*, p.579.
[21] Lynch, *Scotland: A New History*, pp.47-48; Chadwick, *Early Scotland*, p.96.
[22] Laing, *The Orygynale Cronykil Of Scotland, Vol II*, p.129.
[23] Woolf, *From Pictland To Alba*, p.265.

Aberdeenshire on 15 August 1057.[24] Lulach did not last much longer, being killed a year later. Scotland had a new king, Malcolm III, a.k.a. 'Canmore' or 'Big Chief', and, like Athelstan, he wasn't going to settle for his existing bounds. For Canmore had one great mission in life:

Annexe the rest of Bernicia, now called Northumberland, to Scotland.

The Normans
To the south, England was going through a great change. In 1066, their king died. The King of Norway made a failed attempt to seize the English throne, but from France came an even greater threat. This was Guillaume, (or William), Duke of Normandy, and at Hastings he defeated the English, who now suffered an executive takeover by French nobles and adventurers. When the North of England rose against the Duke of Normandy, William travelled across Yorkshire, burning, pillaging, slaughtering, and salting the land so it could not bear crops. 100,000 people starved to death,[25] the survivors reduced to cannibalism.[26] To his supporters, the new king was *Guillaume le Conquerant*, William the Conqueror. But the English had a less flattering name for him: *William the Bastard*.[27]

And there was no relief for the English people from the direction of Scotland. As Yorkshire was laid waste, Malcolm was busy himself in Northumberland, burning, pillaging, and taking slaves. According to the chroniclers:

> *Scotland was, therefore, filled with slaves and handmaids of the English race; so that even to this day, I do not say no little village, but even no cottage, can be found without one of them.*[28]

The legitimate heir to the English throne, a teenage boy called Edgar, fled with his mother and sisters to their childhood home of Hungary. But after

---

[24] Anderson, *Early Sources Of Scottish History, Volume One*, p.579.
[25] Forester, *The Ecclesiastical History of England and Normandy by Ordericus Vitalis, Vol. II*, p.28.
[26] Forester, *The Chronicle of Florence of Worcester*, pp.173-4.
[27] Laing, *The Orygynale Cronykil Of Scotland, Vol II*, p.157, where he is called 'Willeyham Bastarde'.
[28] Stevenson, *The Historical Works Of Simeon Of Durham*, p.553.

setting sail for the Continent, a great wind blew them off course. In despair they realised they were landing on the shores of Fife, right into the clutches of Malcolm Canmore. They charged themselves with courage and stepped onto land and an audience with the King of Scots.[29]

Mother of Scotland

There are moments in history around which the destiny of entire countries pivot, and this audience was one. Meeting Edgar's older sister Margaret was a thunderbolt moment for Canmore. He had married Ingibjorg, widow of Thorfinn the Mighty, a union which produced a son called Duncan.[30] But Ingibjorg was no more, and Canmore found he 'began to desire' Margaret, a woman who would eventually be canonised as a saint.[31] She was as different from her husband as could be.

Cultured, caring, and pious, Margaret carried with her a piece of the 'true cross' on which she believed Jesus had been crucified.[32] On holy days she took money from her husband's offerings of gold coins and gave it to beggars. She would bring 300 destitute people into her royal hall and except for the attendance of chaplains and some attendants, would personally serve meals to 'Christ in the person of His poor.'[33] She restored Iona Abbey, founded the abbey of Dunfermline, and instigated the Queens Ferry between Edinburgh and Fife. She encouraged manufacturers, the arts, and trade.[34] She was particularly keen to reform the Scots kirk. As a fervent believer in Roman forms of worship, she was appalled at Scottish practices.[35] (Her biographer doesn't describe them all, but it may have included worshipping outdoors.)

The illiterate Malcolm delighted to hear her argue points of doctrine with his most learned clerics and even though he couldn't read them, or perhaps

---

[29] Laing, *The Orygynale Cronykil Of Scotland, Vol II*, p.148; Simeon of Durham also has them first meeting at Wearmouth during Malcolm's raid on Northumberland. See Stevenson, *The Historical Works Of Simeon Of Durham*, p.552-4.
[30] Pálsson and Edwards, *Orkneyinga Saga*, p.72.
[31] Swanton, *The Anglo-Saxon Chronicle*, p.201.
[32] Forbes-Leith, *Life Of St. Margaret*, pp.76-7.
[33] *Ibid*, p.63.
[34] Forbes-Leith, *Life Of St. Margaret*, p.40.
[35] *Ibid*, pp.43-51.

because he couldn't, he kissed her books and bound them with covers of gold.[36] He gave her brother Edgar his support, and English aristocrats fleeing the Norman invasion flocked to Scotland where they knew that, thanks to Margaret's influence, they would be welcome at Malcolm's court. Her inability to speak the native language of Scotland[37] was the first of many steps that would lead the court and country away from Gaelic. More than any one person, St Margaret changed the nature of early Scotland.

But one thing she couldn't influence was Canmore's continuing desire to attack Northumberland. After yet another Scottish raid of Northern England in 1072, William the Conqueror marched north to have it out with the Scots King. He cornered Malcolm at Abernethy, who promised not to attack England again. William took Malcolm's eldest son by Ingibjorg, Duncan, hostage as a guarantee.[38] But this was no sacrifice for Canmore, who intended his sons by St Margaret to inherit the throne. Malcolm was back attacking Northern England in 1079 and 1091, gaining temporary control of Northumberland and forcing the English king to build a defensive fortress at Newcastle. But the Normans went a step further and moved knights and men into Malcolm's lands of Cumbria, laying claim to them by building a castle at Carlisle. Malcolm insisted on a diplomatic conference, but William's successor refused to attend in person. This snub meant war, and the Scottish attack on Northumberland in 1093 was unusually severe. But on his way home, Malcolm was ambushed and killed.[39]

Malcolm had suffered from what Dante would call:

The thirsting pride, that maketh fool alike
The English and Scot, impatient of their bound.[40]

He was buried at Tynemouth at the edge of the land he had spent his reign either despoiling or trying to conquer. When St Margaret heard of the death

---

[36] Forbes-Leith, *Life Of St. Margaret,* pp.38-40.
[37] Inferred by the fact her husband had to act as her interpreter into English. Forbes-Leith, *Life Of St. Margaret*, pp.44-5.
[38] Lynch, *Scotland: A New History*, p.75.
[39] *Ibid,* pp.75-76.
[40] Kuhns, *The Divine Comedy of Dante Alighieri*, p.402.

of her husband and eldest son, she fell into despair and died herself nine days later. But she had left a strong legacy in her family.

Four of St Margaret's sons had a go at ruling Scotland. First up was Edmund. In exchange for being nominated tanist, he supported as king his uncle Domnall, or Donald III, who:

Drove out all the English who were with King Malcolm before.[41]

Ingibjorg's son Duncan made a bid for the throne, and was killed by Donald. But Donald, who had fled from Macbeth as a child to Ireland, was soon deposed by Margaret's next son Edgar, whose claim to the throne was backed up by the King of England's army. Edgar was followed by his brother Alexander, and finally, the youngest, David.[42]

And it was this youngest son of Malcolm Canmore who would do what his father could not: peacefully rule Northumberland.

---

[41] Lynch, *Scotland: A New History*, p.77.
[42] *Ibid*, pp.77-78.

Donnchad an t-Ilgarach
(Duncan I)
1001-1040
r. 1034-1040

Máel Coluim ceann mòr (Malcolm III)
1031-1093
r. 1058-1093

Saint Margaret
c.1045-1093

Domnall Bán (Donald III)
1033-1099
r. 1093-1097

Ingibiorg Finnsdottir

Donnchad mac Máel Coluim (Duncan II)
1060-1094
r. 1094

Edmund

Edgar
1072-1107
r. 1097-1107

Alexander I
1077-1124
r. 1107-1124

Matilda
1080-1118

Henry I of England
1068-1135
r.1100-1135

Matilda, Queen of England
1102-1167
r.1141-1148

The MacWilliams

David I
1080-1153
r. 1124-1153

Maud, Countess of Huntingdon
c.1072-1130

Henry, Earl of Huntingdon
1114-1152

Ada de Warenne
c.1120-1178

The MacHeths

Malcolm IV
1141-1165
r. 1153-1165

Ermengarde de Beaumont
c.1170-1234

William I
1142-1214
r. 1165-1214

Marie de Coucy
c.1218-1285

Alexander II
1198-1249
r. 1214-1249

Joan of England
1210-1238

Yolande de Dreux
1263-1330

Alexander III
1241-1286
r. 1249-1286

Margaret of England
1240-1275

Margaret of Scotland
1261-1283

Eirik II of Norway
1268-1299
r.1280-1299

Margaret, Queen of Scots
1283-1290
r. 1286-1290

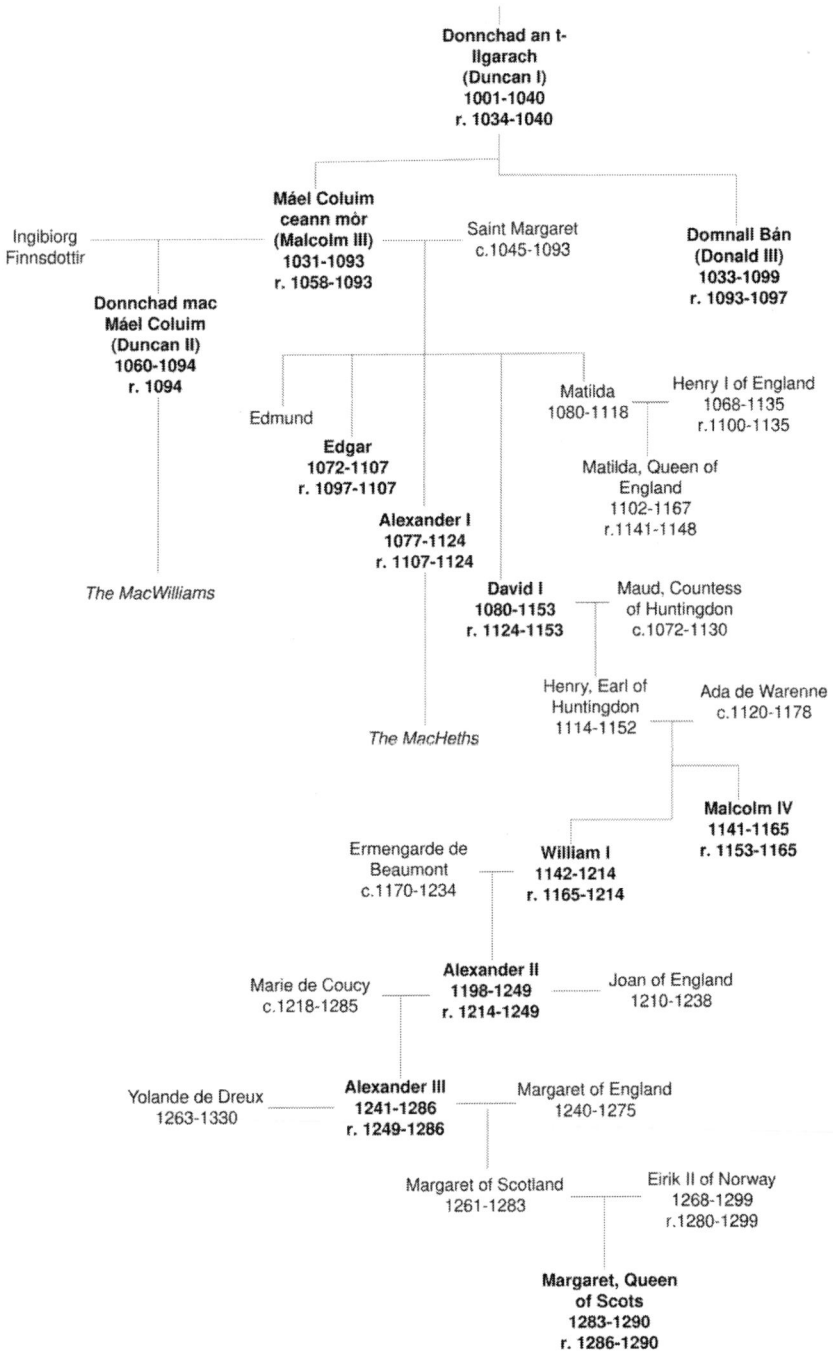

Figure 8: Early Scottish Kings

42

CHAPTER FIVE

David the Great

David picked up where his mother had left off. He founded Scotland's first royal burghs: towns with a monopoly on foreign trade.[1] He populated the towns not just with native Scots but with foreigners accustomed to town life: merchants from England, France, Germany, and Flanders, who were given rights over trade in exchange for paying tax to the king.[2] Royal charters were given initially to the burghers of Berwick, Roxburgh, Dunfermline, Edinburgh, Perth, Stirling, Aberdeen, Forres, Haddington, Peebles, Renfrew, Rutherglen, Elgin, Linlithgow, Montrose, Crail, Jedburgh, and Lanark.[3] David standardised coinage, and Berwick in particular grew rich and prosperous. Great abbeys were built to glorify God at Melrose, Jedburgh, Holyrood, Dundrennan, Kelso and Dryburgh, and were gifted large tracts of land. And David did something else: he invited Normans to settle in Scotland. These French knights had been in Scotland since the time of Macbeth, fighting for the king as mercenaries,[4] but David was first to systematically settle them. In England they had come as invaders and conquerors, but in Scotland they were invited by the king and given land.[5] David enthusiastically welcomed their prowess in battle on the open field, their heavy horse and armour the battlefield tanks of their day. From his base in Moray, Lulach's grandson rose against David, but was defeated in 1130. A Fleming called Freskin was given control of Moray and built Duffus Castle. In the train of men like Freskin came further Flemish, English, and French retainers, adding to and altering the culture in which they settled. Scotland under David had become a melting pot of different peoples and cultures. If the country was united, it was by the Christian religion and loyalty to the king. Yet while the mass of the people from Galloway to

---

[1] Though Tain claims to have been founded during the rule of Malcolm Canmore.
[2] Lynch, *Scotland: A New History*, pp.62-63.
[3] Pryde, The Burghs Of Scotland, pp.3-10.
[4] Barrell, *Medieval Scotland*, p.15.
[5] Lynch, *Scotland: A New History*, p.80.

Aberdeenshire spoke Gaelic, God spoke Latin, power talked French, the south-east English, with Norse in the far north, and shepherds in isolated pockets of Strathclyde possibly still clinging on to the Cymric language of Rhydderch Hael and Mynyddog Mwynfawr.[6]

Scotland under David had entered an age of trade and development. By contrast, England suffered further woes. David's sister Matilda had married Henry I of England and had no surviving sons. Their daughter, also Matilda, was nominated Henry's heir. But another person claimed the throne, a Frenchman called Étienne (or Stephen). He, crucially, had a penis, and so won the support of many of England's nobles. When Henry died in 1135, Stephen seized the throne and civil war broke out in England. The Anglo-Saxon chronicle described it as a period which was 'all strife and evil and robbery'.[7] To a King of Scots intent on grabbing English territory though, it was a golden opportunity. David invaded England to 'safeguard' Carlisle, Newcastle and Durham for his niece Matilda. When Stephen arrived with an army, the two sides agreed terms: David would retain Cumbria, Carlisle, and Doncaster, and English garrisons would be placed in the key fortresses of Newcastle, Alnwick, and Norham.[8] The war in England between Matilda and Stephen lasted eighteen years. The South of England suffered, but for once, thanks to David's stewardship after 1136, Northumberland remained largely untouched: bar one incident.

In 1138 David decided to reassert Matilda's claim by invading England with an army. It was a multi-cultural force that reflected the country he led, described by chronicles as consisting of Scots and Moravians, Cumbrians and Islanders, French and English, men of Teviotdale and Lothian, and the proud Galwegians.[9] As it had in 1135 and 1136,[10] the army plundered and slaughtered its way across Northern England, and in high spirits they marched in sight of Thurstan, Archbishop of York who had rallied the men of Yorkshire. The Yorkshiremen were led to face the superior Scottish force by a ship's mast on a cart flying the banner of their most venerated saint, St

[6] Koch, *Celtic Culture*, pp.515-516.
[7] Swanton, *The Anglo-Saxon Chronicle*, p.263.
[8] Oram, *David I*, paras.15.1-5.
[9] Anderson and Anderson, *Scottish Annals From English Chroniclers*, pp.198-200.
[10] Oram, *David I*, para.15.10.

Cuthbert. At Northallerton on 22 August the two armies clashed. The unarmoured Galwegians rushed impetuously onto the Yorkshire spears and arrows and were slain. The rest of David's army were unable to turn the tide of the battle, and Thurstan won a famous victory at this Battle of the Standard. Yet despite losing the battle, a second treaty with Stephen left David even more solidly in control north of the Rivers Tees and Ribble.[11] So while Southern England descended into a period of anarchy, Scotland and the North of England entered the 1140s at peace,[12] David effectively ruling between Ardnamurchan and the Tees, the Pentland Firth and the River Ribble. The southern expansion of Scottish kings, started by the capture of Edinburgh in 954, had reached full expression. David died in Carlisle Castle in his southern domains. But his claim on English territory would not long outlast him. David's sons were unlucky, both dying before him. It fell upon his eldest grandson, the pious and determined Malcolm IV, to rule an unruly kingdom.

In an age when the ideals of knightly chivalry and Christian piety were first introduced into Continental courts by the troubadours of the Languedoc, the teenage Malcolm IV was already ahead of fashion. His deliberately celibate approach worried his mother, who eventually took matters in hand by introducing a 'beautiful and noble virgin' into his bed chamber; but Malcolm rose and lay on the floor instead, and was discovered there next morning covered by his cloak with the girl left in his bed.[13] This level of self-discipline was much needed by the young king, as he fought to extend control over a decentralised kingdom: in a short but eventful reign he faced opposition to his rule in Moray, Galloway, and the Isles.[14] The MacHeths of Moray sought the throne, theirs, they believed, by right, through descent of an illegitimate son of Alexander I. They raised trouble for Malcolm for three years until Donald MacHeth was captured in 1156 and his followers in Moray were:

---

[11] Oram, *David I,* paras.15.42-43. David looked to expand further still, but was chased out of London when supporting Matilda and had to be content with what he had. *Ibid,* paras16.3-11.

[12] *Ibid,* paras.16.3-11.

[13] Stevenson, *The History of William of Newburgh*, p.433.

[14] For details, see Cowan and McDonald, *Alba*, pp.166-186.

Scattered throughout the other districts of Scotland so that not even one native of the land abode there.[15]

In Galloway, the Lord Fergus ruled as if in his own kingdom: he founded abbeys, took as wife a daughter of the King of England, saw his own daughter Affrica marry Olaf the Red, King of Man, and had tribute paid to him by a troubadour with the *Roman de Fergus*. Malcolm led three expeditions into Galloway, finally capturing Fergus in 1160. He was forced to retire to Holyrood Abbey where he became nicknamed 'sit by the king'.[16] French knights loyal to the king were granted land encircling Galloway.[17]

Malcolm's final and most formidable enemy was Somerled, *rí Innse Gall*, or Lord of the Isles. This half-Norse progenitor of the MacDonalds was related by blood and marriage to both the MacHeths and the King of Man. Through battle he himself became king of all the islands between Man and Lewis. Like his Gall-gael predecessors, he had no interest in submitting to any other king. Yet in 1164 at Renfrew, even Somerled fell when facing an army loyal to Malcolm.[18]

But there was one ruler who Malcolm would not oppose. This was Henry II, the new king of England. King David had held the lands north of the Rivers Tees and Ribble, but the chaotic circumstances that enabled that no longer applied. When Malcolm met Henry at Chester in 1157, he meekly accepted Henry's right to retain the lands south of the Tweed. Henry would not have the King of Scots controlling Northumberland and Cumbria. In compensation, Malcolm was confirmed in his father's Earldom of Huntingdon, a prime swathe of land just north of London, where the English king could keep a closer eye on him.[19]

William the Rough

When Malcolm died young and childless in 1165, his brother William inherited the throne. As a young man he had ruled Northumberland on

---

[15] Skene and Skene, *John of Fordun's Chronicle of the Scottish Nation*, p.252.
[16] *Ibid,* p.251.
[17] Cowan and McDonald, *Alba*, pp.181-182.
[18] For the life of this fascinating figure, see McPhee, *Somerled: Hammer Of The Norse.*
[19] Skene and Skene, *John of Fordun's Chronicle of the Scottish Nation*, p.250.

behalf of his grandfather King David, and was particularly peeved when Malcolm handed the North of England back to Henry II without even a fight. As King of Scots, William, nicknamed 'the rough',[20] was not about to be accused of the same lack of vim in regard to his southern neighbours. When Henry II became distracted by a rebellious wife and sons, William saw his chance. He invaded Northumberland, but dispersed his forces in various actions across the north of England, keeping only sixty men around him as a bodyguard. English ambassadors discovered this weakness, and at Alnwick William was surprised by a body of four hundred knights in Henry's service.[21] William acted courageously and immediately charged the enemy, supposedly shouting "now it will appear who knows how to be a knight!"[22] William was unhorsed, captured, and taken as a prisoner to Henry's impregnable fortress of Falaise in Normandy.

Had this been the days of tanistry, the end would have come quickly for William, and his successor quickly chosen from the derbfine. But politics had evolved to become more like a game of chess. Capture a king, and you captured his entire country. So Henry gave William a choice. He could remain in prison in Normandy, or he could be released in exchange for his country and 15 high-born hostages.[23] William reluctantly agreed. Since the very start, English kings had sought to control all of Britain. Now, there would be no doubt. The Plantagenet king Henry II, with his Kingdom of England, Dukedom of Normandy, marriage to the Countess of Aquitaine, and the submission of the King of Scots, now controlled a vast swathe of territory from the Pentland Firth to the Pyrenees.

But many Scots were unhappy with the situation, and William had to deal with rebellion at home. The aristocracy resisted the invited French knights who seemed to be taking over. In the words of Walter of Coventry:

---

[20] Bambury and Beechinor, *The Annals Of Ulster*, U1214.6.
[21] Sutton, *Rerum Scoticarum Historia,* Book VII, Chapter 35.
[22] Anderson and Anderson, *Scottish Annals From English Chroniclers*, p.253.
[23] Lynch, *Scotland: A New History*, p.80.

The modern kings of Scotland count themselves Frenchmen in race, manner, language and culture; they keep Frenchmen in their household and following and have reduced the Scots to utter servitude.[24]

William's brother Malcolm had already faced rebellions from Moray, Galloway, and Argyll; and while the king was held prisoner in Falaise, the new Lords of Galloway, Gille Bride and his brother Uchtred, rose and:

At once expelled from Galloway all the bailiffs and guards whom the king of Scotland had set over them; and all the English and French whom they could seize they slew.[25]

William had to deal with this rebellion on his release. Galloway only came under Scottish control again when Gille Bride died in 1185.

In Moray, the situation was even more serious; William was faced with a full-out insurrection by the MacWilliams, who held Moray and Ross against him between 1181-87. The MacWilliams were legitimate descendants of the deposed King Duncan II, Malcolm Canmore's son by Ingibjorg, and their ambition was for the throne of Scotland itself. The king led an expedition against them which fell out with itself, quarrelling because 'some loved the king not at all.' [26] But William was not entirely friendless. Roland, the new Lord of Galloway, allied himself to the King of Scots, and had more success than the king in leading an army north, killing the MacWilliam chief at Mam Garvia near Dingwall in 1187.[27] More good news for the King of Scots was to follow. England became ruled by Richard the Lionheart, a man who spent almost all his life abroad. His life's passion was war in the Holy Land. He was constantly looking for ways to pay for it, and he had an asset he could sell to a willing buyer: Scotland. For 10,000 merks in 1189, William bought back his rights to Scotland, answerable to God alone.[28] William and Richard became friends, and when Richard was captured on crusade, the Scottish

---

[24] Barrow, *Scotland And Its Neighbours In The Middle Ages*, p.72.
[25] Anderson and Anderson, *Scottish Annals From English Chroniclers*, p.256.
[26] Oram, *Domination And Lordship*, p.143.
[27] McDonald, *Outlaws of Medieval Scotland*, p.38.
[28] Skene and Skene, *John of Fordun's Chronicle of the Scottish Nation*, p.267. A merk was 2/3 of a pound.

king chipped in to pay for his ransom.[29] Their friendship culminated in Richard accepting a bid by William to buy Northumberland as well. But he added a catch: the castles had to keep their English garrisons. William refused, and the last realistic chance for a King of Scots to possess Northumberland slipped out of William's hands.[30]

Peace with England allowed further development of Scotland. According to *The Kings and Queens of Britain*, William governed with vigour, founding new burghs, increasing Anglo-Norman settlement, extending feudalisation, clarifying criminal law, widening the responsibilities of justices and sheriffs, and growing trade.[31] His royal standard, the red-on-yellow Lion Rampant, became the alternative flag for Scotland, leading to his other nickname: William the Lion.

Figure 9: The Royal Standard of William the Rough

William died of old age in 1214 after a long reign. He had never quite mastered the northern boundaries of his country: this was something

[29] Skene and Skene, *John of Fordun's Chronicle of the Scottish Nation,* p.269.
[30] Oram, *Domination And Lordship,* p.153.
[31] Cannon and Hargreaves, *The Kings And Queens Of Britain,* p.135.

William's son Alexander II was going to address. But first, he had a battle in England to fight.

Scotland's Herod

At the age of sixteen, the flame-haired son of the old king took the throne. He did so at a pivotal time for the neighbours to the south. English kings had refused to bend the knee to the kings of France for their French possessions like Normandy, and in 1214 at the Battle of Bouvines, Phillippe II kicked King John of England out of France for good.

John had burdened his English nobles by raising tax for wars in France, and alarmed them by imprisoning and killing the wife of one of his favourite barons, who was forced to flee.[32] The nobility cornered him at Runnymede on the Thames in 1215 and forced him to agree to Magna Carta, a charter of rights that said the king couldn't imprison 'free men', (which in the 13th century, meant aristocrats), without trial.[33] But John had no intention of honouring the agreement. With the Pope's help, he raised an army against his nobility. The King of Scots stood by the rebels, on one condition: Northumberland and Carlisle were to be his. The barons agreed, then offered the crown of England to Prince Louis of France.[34] Alexander marched his army down to Dover to join Louis in besieging the castle.[35] But its defender would not give up what he called 'the key of England' to a foreigner[36] and, while all this was going on, King John died. His son Henry III was only nine and easily persuaded to agree to Magna Carta. The barons no longer needed French prince Louis, and kicked him out. Alexander tried to take Northumberland by force in 1217, and failed.[37] He contemplated the lessons learned. The English barons, when it came to it, knew who their rightful king was. But did the Scots, with their history of tanistry and looser allegiance to the centre, have the same sense of loyalty to their own king?

---

[32] Connolly, *Heroines Of The Medieval World*, pp.144-146.
[33] Summerson et al, *The Magna Carta Project*, Clause 39.
[34] Oram, *Alexander II*, pp.34-35.
[35] *Ibid*, pp.40-43.
[36] Giles, *Roger Of Wendover's Flowers Of History*, p.401.
[37] Oram, *Alexander II*, pp.48-50.

It didn't seem so. On Alexander's accession to the throne, the loyal Ferchar MacTaggart had put down a rebellion of MacWilliams and MacHeths against the king in Northern Scotland.[38] But the MacWilliams in Moray rose yet again against Alexander. He decided to deal with them once and for all in the most brutal fashion possible. Channelling his ancestor Malcolm Forranach, Alexander put to death every MacWilliam he could find, including innocent children. In 1230 there was only one left. By royal proclamation, the last of the MacWilliams was held up in her swaddling cloths in front of the crowd at Forfar, taken by her legs, and her brains dashed out against the market cross.[39]

If you had never heard of the once influential MacWilliam family until now, you now know why.

And Galloway too finally fell: the last Lord of Galloway divided his patrimony in three for his daughters, but his illegitimate son Thomas, 'despising their age and sex',[40] set himself up independently as Lord of Galloway. Thomas was defeated by the trusty Earl of Ross, Ferchar MacTaggart, and the daughters of Galloway and their husbands remained loyal subjects of the Scottish king.

The diplomatic temperature between England and Scotland rose and fell: Henry III claimed ownership of Scotland, Alexander occupied Newcastle, and the Pope got involved to calm everyone down. In 1237 the line of the border was agreed, following the ancient faultline of the Cheviot Hills.[41] With the exception of the town of Berwick, the line of the border has remained the same to this day.[42] Peace with England allowed Alexander to complete his life's work: to bring Argyll and the Isles under his control, whose lords had proved far too independent-minded for either the Scottish or Norwegian kings to accept. The half-Gaelic, half-Norse warrior called Somerled had united all the isles from the Butt of Lewis to the Calf of Man,

---

[38] Anderson, *Early Sources Of Scottish History, Volume One*, p.404.
[39] Oram, *Alexander II*, p.96.
[40] Sutton, *Rerum Scoticarum Historia*, Book VII, Chapter 43.
[41] Wyckoff, *Feudal Relations Between the Kings of England and Scotland Under the Early Plantagenets*, p.120.
[42] With various medieval exceptions such as the Liberty of Tynedale, the Debateable Lands, and the English Pale.

and in 1164 brought 15,000 men in 164 galleys up the Clyde to have a pop at Scotland: but he was betrayed and killed by a nephew in the King of Scots' pay. That invasion had fizzled out, but Somerled's descendants became the MacDougalls and the MacDonalds, independent lords of Argyll and the Isles.

Both kings Alexander II of Scotland and Haakon IV of Norway claimed ownership of these Isles, whose inhabitants had a foot in both camps, but preferred to be ruled by neither. The spark came when Haakon appointed Ewan MacDougall as his Lord of the Isles. Ewan had travelled to Haakon's court in Bergen to present himself as a loyal subject, and Alexander accused him of treachery, because Ewan already held mainland Argyll on behalf of the Scots king.[43] "No man can serve two masters," said Alexander to Ewan. According to Clan MacDougall tradition, Ewan replied to the contrary:

"He can if they are not enemies."[44]

In response to this Alexander cried that his standard would fly on the cliffs of Thurso, and he would rule the Western Isles.[45] But as he prepared an army in July 1249 to attack MacDougall at his fortress of Dunstaffnage the king caught a fever, dying of it on Kerrera, the island that protects Oban harbour. It would be up to his son Alexander to complete his work.

---

[43] Wærdahl, *The Incorporation And Integration Of The King's Tributary Lands Into The Norwegian Realm*, p.49.
[44] Macdougall, *Clan MacDougall Handout*, [online] Clan Macdougall Society.
[45] Johnstone, *The Norwegian account of Haco's expedition against Scotland*, pp.3-4.

CHAPTER SIX

A Roch Wind Blawing

Alexander III was crowned King of Scots at an ancient ceremony on Moot Hill at Scone, sitting on the Stone of Destiny with a bard reciting his genealogy back to Fergus Mor Mac Erc, the king of Dal Riata who moved the seat of his kingdom from Ireland to Argyll, then further back into mythology, every ancestor, real or not, all the way to Scota, daughter of the Pharaoh of Egypt during the time of Moses. As the crown was placed on his head, the shout went up in Gaelic – *"Benach De Re Albanne!"* – God bless the King of Scots![1] Alexander may have been the son of a Frenchwoman and a three-quarters Anglo-Norman father, but his coronation ceremony had a taproot deep in the culture of the Gaels.

In a country that had entertained rival MacWilliam claims to the throne only nineteen years earlier, this was a powerful affirmation of right engineered by the mother of an eight-year-old boy.[2] But while the widowed queen Marie de Coucy knew how to leverage the power of tradition, she also operated in a world of men. The coronation secured, the regency of the boy king was placed in male hands, and Marie was encouraged to visit her ancestral lands in France. Alexander II had made provision for his son with a diplomatic marriage to Henry III's daughter Margaret, and so in 1251, the ten-year-old king and eleven-year-old queen were wed in York. After the wedding, Henry III had Alexander perform a homage ceremony for his father's English Earldom of Huntingdon, and asked amiably why he should not do the same for his Kingdom of Scotland. But Alexander had been well schooled for this eventuality by his advisors.

"I came in peace," he replied, *"not to answer arduous questions."*[3]

---

[1] Skene and Skene, *John of Fordun's Chronicle of the Scottish Nation*, pp.289-290.
[2] Marshall, *Scottish Queens*, p.21.
[3] Tytler, *Lives Of Scottish Worthies, Vol. I*, pp.10-11.

Alexander and Margaret were kept apart, the queen a virtual prisoner in Edinburgh Castle, until it was decided, at the age of fourteen, they were old enough to consummate their marriage. But the pair remained pawns in a power struggle between rival factions at court, and Marie de Coucy returned to Scotland to act as a regent until Alexander's majority at the age of twenty-one.[4]

And his first act as an adult was to pick up where his father left off.

The Dragon and the Thistle

In 1261 Alexander sent a delegation to Haakon making a formal claim to the islands off Scotland's west coast,[5] and a year later sent an ultimatum to Ewan MacDougall: choose your master. MacDougall prevaricated, and would only do so once the matter was settled.[6] In the meantime, Alexander provoked Haakon by sending the Earl of Ross to pillage the Norwegian-owned Isle of Skye. In the summer of 1263 Haakon gave his response. The elderly Norwegian king gathered 20,000 men in 160 ships.[7] His flagship was built entirely from oak with a dragon's head at the prow made from gold, a square sail on a swinging arm, and either fifty-four or seventy-four oars[8] with four men per oar.[9] This immense force was irresistible in the isles, fealty being reaffirmed by all he came in contact with. By the time the great fleet anchored in the Clyde off Lamlash it was nearly autumn. Alexander brought an army to Ayrshire and sought to buy time by negotiating. The two forces were formidable in their respective elements: none could resist Haakon in the islands, yet on the mainland Alexander's mounted, armoured knights would have the upper hand. But Alexander had an even more irresistible weapon: time. The Norse were summer warriors. No medieval navy could stay at sea all winter. Seeking to force Alexander into making a move before the season turned, Haakon moved his fleet to Fairlie roads off Cumbrae within striking distance of the Ayrshire shore, and sent sixty ships up Loch

---

[4] Marshall, *Scottish Queens*, p.21.

[5] Johnstone, *The Norwegian account of Haco's expedition against Scotland*, pp.7-8.

[6] McDonald, *Outlaws of Medieval Scotland*, p.57.

[7] Skene and Skene, *John of Fordun's Chronicle of the Scottish Nation*, p.295.

[8] Anderson, *Early Sources Of Scottish History, Volume Two*, p.610.

[9] Johnstone, *The Norwegian account of Haco's expedition against Scotland*, pp.14,21.

Long and down Loch Lomond to rape, pillage and burn.[10] Alexander sat tight despite the fires that could be seen burning over his right flank. Finally, on 1 October, a south-westerly gale drove five of Haakon's ships ashore at Largs.[11]

The Last Viking

It was not the landfall Haakon intended. A cagey, on-off, three-day encounter ensued on the Ayrshire beach. History records this as the Battle of Largs, though neither side committed their forces and casualties were light. But five days later Haakon was joined by his Loch Lomond force, moved his fleet back out to sea, and then in the face of autumn weather, headed home.[12] 'It was not by the power of man that Haakon was driven away,' said the Chronicle of Melrose, 'but by that of God.'[13]

At Kirkwall in Orkney, Haakon grew sick. He called for his priest to shrive his sins. As he grew weaker, he dismissed the priest and called for his skald to recite stories from the sagas. Haakon died in his hall in Kirkwall, his ears echoing to the stirring deeds of his pagan ancestors.[14]

Haakon's successor Magnus proved more amenable to Alexander's claims. In 1266 the two kings agreed the Treaty of Perth, which ceded the Hebrides and the Isle of Man to Scotland in return for 4,000 merks in silver plus an annual payment of another 100 merks, and the formal recognition by Alexander that Orkney and Shetland were Norwegian territory.[15]

The Hebrides finally came under Scottish control, and a period of peace and plenty ensued on the mainland. Scots built ships for Continental clients[16] and exported fish and wool to Europe. The farmers and monks who raised sheep on the slopes of the Southern Uplands transported them downstream on the Tweed to Berwick, where at the Hanseatic merchants' White Hall or the Flemish merchants' Red Hall they exchanged their goods for French wines

---

[10] Johnstone, *The Norwegian account of Haco's expedition against Scotland,* pp.42-45.

[11] *Ibid*, pp.45-47.

[12] *Ibid,* pp.58-64.

[13] Stevenson, *The Chronicle of Melrose,* p.214.

[14] Johnstone, *The Norwegian account of Haco's expedition against Scotland,* pp.67-68.

[15] Lynch, *Scotland: A New History*, p.90.

[16] Barrow, *Robert Bruce And The Community Of The Realm Of Scotland*, p.14.

and Flemish cloth.[17] Through trade with Europe, Berwick became Scotland's richest and most populous town. Later historians described this period of peace as Scotland's Golden Age.[18] It probably didn't feel particularly special at the time; but stormclouds were gathering.

Disaster for Scotland

Alexander's Queen Margaret died in 1275, survived by two sons and a daughter. The daughter married King Eirik II of Norway in 1281, taught the teenage king European fashion and manners,[19] and bore him a daughter before dying of complications from childbirth in 1283. Her younger brother had already died aged nine, and when Alexander's last remaining son died in 1284 at the age of twenty, the king, who had enjoyed his widowerhood in the company of 'nuns or matrons, virgins or widows,'[20] realised he needed to do something about his succession. His infant Norwegian granddaughter Margaret, the Maid of Norway, was designated his heir. But Alexander had a more direct plan for ensuring his succession. He was still only in his early 40s. He'd marry a young French noblewoman, Yolande de Dreux, and start again. Their marriage was celebrated at Jedburgh on 14 October 1285.[21] Later legends would grow up around their ill-fated match: as the king and his new wife celebrated by leading all the guests in the first dance, a skeleton, according to Hector Boece, was seen bringing up the rear of the procession: a macabre vision which brought a swift end to the celebrations.[22]

In spite of the alarming omens that would be recorded later, Alexander and Yolande spent the winter in the delights of each other's company. In the spring of 1286 the pair separated for a few days. Alexander left his queen at Kinghorn in Fife to conduct state business in Edinburgh, and on 19 March, having concluded discussions with his nobles, was impatient to return to Kinghorn to continue the business of begetting an heir. It was a filthy night,

---

[17] Herbert, *Berwick-Upon-Tweed And The Torching Of The Red Hall*, [online] University of St Andrews, describes the halls.
[18] Encyclopædia Britannica, *Alexander III*.
[19] Anderson, *Early Sources Of Scottish History, Volume Two*, p.680.
[20] Maxwell, *The Chronicle Of Lanercost*, p.40.
[21] Skene and Skene, *John of Fordun's Chronicle of the Scottish Nation*, p.304.
[22] This grisly legend is reported in Sutton, *Historia Gentis Scotorum*, Book XIII, Chapter 84.

with a storm howling round the castle rock, and Alexander's advisors implored him to wait it out. But nothing would detain the king.

At the Queens Ferry between Edinburgh and Fife, with waves crashing onto the shore, the ferryman questioned the wisdom of setting out on the Forth on such a rough night. The king teased him – "are ye feart?" and got the reply he wanted:

"I could not die better than in the company of your father's son." [23]

On arriving safely in Fife, Alexander was met by the concerned Baillie of Inverkeithing who issued a third warning, begging the king to stay the night with him. In response, the rampant Alexander spurred his horse on, outstripping his bodyguard, Yolande on his mind. The king never arrived.

His body was found on the beach the next morning. In the darkness he had ridden his horse over a sea cliff just a mile from his destination.

Scotland had lost its 44-year old king. It was about to lose much more. The people would lament:

> *Quhen [When] Alexander our kynge was dede,*
> *That Scotland lede in lauche and le, [love and law]*
> *Away was sons [plenty] of alle and brede,*
> *Of wyne and wax, of gamyn and gle.*
> *Our gold was changit into lede.*
> *Christ, born in virgynyte,*
> *Succoure Scotland, and ramede,*
> *That stade is in perplexite.*[24]

A Union of Crowns

A king dying without a male heir was a problem. But Alexander III had made plans. Before his marriage to Yolande and his hope of more children, his nobles had agreed to recognise Margaret, the infant princess in Norway, as the future Queen of Scots. In fact, Alexander had gone further. He had

---

[23] Barrow, *Robert Bruce And The Community Of The Realm Of Scotland*, p.4.
[24] Laing, *The Orygynale Cronykil Of Scotland, Vol II*, p.266.

proposed to his brother-in-law Edward I of England that Margaret be married at some future date to Edward's baby son, also Edward.[25] When they grew up, they and their descendants would rule both England and Scotland. And why not? Relations between the two royal families were cordial. There was no objection to a royal merger from the Scottish nobility, many of whom held land in England as well.[26]

The Guardians of Scotland

The nobles appointed six Guardians to act as regents for Margaret: two barons, two earls, and two bishops. They concluded arrangements for her diplomatic marriage to young Edward of England, and her journey to the kingdom that she had never yet seen. And so in 1290 Margaret, aged seven, started the voyage from her father's court in Norway to the mysterious land of Scotland of which she was queen. It was her last journey. In September, getting no further than Orkney, the poor child grew sick and died. The Guardians were in a quandary. With tanistry long dead, the Scots now had to choose a king despite there being no obvious direct heir. The most eligible nobles immediately started to jostle for advantage, and the Guardians found it impossible to maintain order.

Two of Scotland's leading families had already been fighting. In 1286 the Bruces, supported by the Stewarts, seized Balliol's tower of Buittle and the royal castles of Dumfries and Wigtown, and other nobles were forced to raise men 'to uphold the peace and tranquillity of the realm of Scotland.'[27] Now, with Margaret dead, Balliol styled himself 'heir of Scotland' and the Bruces were rumoured to be gathering an army.[28] With civil war looming between the Balliols and the Bruces, the Guardians turned to the only man

---

[25] Lynch, *Scotland: A New History*, p.114.
[26] Most notably, Rodger de Quincy had been both Earl of Winchester and Constable of Scotland; John de Balliol had been Lord of Galloway, of Barnard Castle in Durham, and Sheriff of Nottinghamshire; Robert de Brus was Lord of Annandale and of Writtle and Hatfield Broadoak in Essex; William de Vescy was Lord of Sprouston in Roxburghshire and Constable of Scarborough; and Henry de Beaumont held land in England and would claim the Earldom of Buchan.
[27] Barrow, *Robert Bruce And The Community Of The Realm Of Scotland*, p.24.
[28] *Ibid,* p.39.

they knew who had the clout to keep the warring factions in check. Alexander III's brother-in-law, Edward I of England.[29]

Edward: the man who had recently, and at incredible expense, completed the conquest of Wales.

The man who would become so obsessed with conquering Scotland that on his deathbed, he would give instructions that his bones have the flesh boiled from them, be placed in a casket, and carried at the head of every English army attacking Scotland until the conquest was complete.[30]

That was the man the Guardians trusted.

Oh dear.

[29] Lynch, *Scotland: A New History*, p.115.
[30] Linklater, *Robert The Bruce*, p.73.

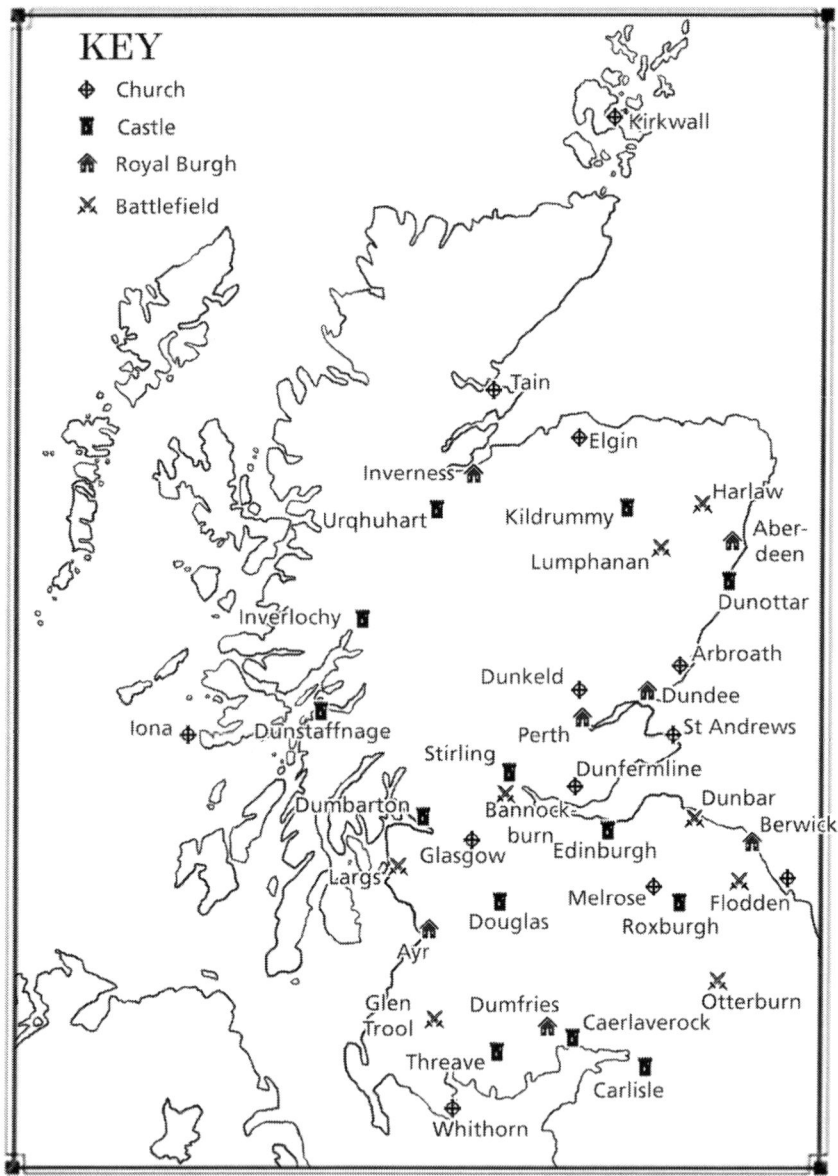

KEY
⊕ Church
▮ Castle
🏠 Royal Burgh
✖ Battlefield

Kirkwall

Tain

Elgin

Inverness

Urquhart

Kildrummy

Harlaw

Aber-
deen

Lumphanan

Dunottar

Inverlochy

Arbroath

Dunkeld

Dundee

Iona

Dunstaffnage

Perth

St Andrews

Stirling

Dunfermline

Dumbarton

Bannock-
burn

Dunbar

Berwick

Largs

Glasgow

Edinburgh

Melrose

Flodden

Douglas

Roxburgh

Ayr

Glen
Trool

Dumfries

Otterburn

Caerlaverock

Threave

Carlisle

Whithorn

Figure 10: Medieval Scotland

60

CHAPTER SEVEN

Survival

In May 1291, Edward called the nobility of Scotland to his castle of Norham on the Tweed. At this assembly he let it be known he would carefully consider every claim to the throne that was submitted. But there was a catch: only the claims of nobles who first swore fealty to him as 'Lord Paramount of Scotland' would be considered. Bishop Wishart of Glasgow was indignant. He had already smelt trouble when they were called to an English castle to decide the matter. The Scottish church had already fought, and won, a diplomatic battle against the Archbishops of York: in 1192 the Pope had decreed in that Scottish bishops reported not to an archbishop, but uniquely, directly to the Pope himself.[1] The church was as independent as its people, and they had no interest in giving that up.

Wishart boldly told Edward that his treatment of the leaderless Scots, dependant on disinterested advice, was deplorable. After all, asking Edward to arbitrate was no admission of suzerainty: in 1263, for example, the English had invited French king Louis IX to settle differences between Henry III and his barons.[2] Scotland was free, Wishart said, and:

"owed no one any homage whatever, save only God."[3]

The *bonny gents* hadn't been invited to Norham, those freeholders and small landowners who formed the backbone of Scottish society, and they also protested, saying such a promise was impossible to agree until after Scotland had a king of her own.[4] But legal disputes like this were meat and drink to Edward. He calculated that the leading nobles, blinded by the opportunity of gaining a throne, would trip over each other in their haste to swear fealty to him. In fact in an attempt to improve his own chances, Robert Bruce the

---

[1] Broun, *Scottish Independence And The Idea Of Britain*, p.124.
[2] Mackie, *A History Of Scotland*, p.66.
[3] Skene, *The Book Of Pluscarden, Vol II*, p.99.
[4] Mackie, *A History Of Scotland*, p.66.

Elder had confirmed his loyalty even before Norham.[5] Eventually twelve other Competitors joined him. Alexander III had refused to swear fealty to Henry III when he was ten, just as Edward himself had refused to swear fealty to the King of France for his French possessions: but both had done so from a position of strength. The Competitors were in a position of weakness: they knew that if they refused to bend a knee to Edward, their rivals would not.

Edward took his time. A stickler for playing by the rules, especially as in this case he had written them, he followed due process. All of the Competitors' claims were remote, and there was some doubt about the outcome between Bruce and Balliol. But by the winning interpretation of the laws of primogeniture, John Balliol's claim was slightly stronger than Bruce's. The Competitors were called to the Great Hall of Berwick Castle for 17 November 1292. In front of the great and good of Scotland, Edward decreed John Balliol to be John I, King of Scots. He was crowned at Scone on 30 November. On 26 December he travelled to Newcastle to do homage to his overlord, Edward I.[6]

It was not a position that could last.

Toom Tabard

King John gets a bad name. It was hardly his fault. He was legitimately King of Scots; and if he hadn't sworn fealty to Edward, someone else would have done so, and been chosen in his place. He did his best to implement good laws and govern well.[7] Yet he was a lamb amongst wolves. Robert Bruce the Elder refused to acknowledge John as king, going as far as resigning control over his estate of Carrick to his family to avoid forfeiture.[8] The nobles of Scotland learned that if they had a legal dispute in which the king ruled against them, they could petition Edward who could overturn the decision; encouraged by the English king, some could not resist. John was summoned to London for all kinds of reasons by Edward, who treated him as a subject

---

[5] Sadler, *Border Fury*, p.57.
[6] Sutton, *Historia Gentis Scotorum,* Book XIV, Chapter 5.
[7] For example, three new sheriffdoms were created in the west: in Skye, Lorn, and Kintyre. RPS, *1293/2/16-18.*
[8] Barrow, *Robert Bruce And The Community Of The Realm Of Scotland*, p.86.

of court amusement rather than a king in his own right.[9] King John would earn the unwanted nickname of 'toom tabard': empty vest.

The Auld Alliance

When Edward demanded a Scottish army fight for England against the French, the Scots could take no more. The leading nobles formed a council of twelve, the new Guardians, who in October 1295 concluded a treaty with France of mutual assistance against England.[10] This suited Edward: it was an excuse to invade Scotland. Edward marched his army north in March 1296 and ordered the massacre of the population of Berwick. The massacre took two days, mill wheels turning through the weight of blood spilling into the drains.[11] Berwick had been Scotland's richest town, a cosmopolitan centre of trade with Europe. It never fully recovered. A hastily convened Scottish army was easily defeated at Dunbar, the supporters of Bruce refusing to fight for Balliol and instead flying 'scathless from the field'.[12] After riding round the country burning and pillaging, Edward put John de Warenne in charge. John Balliol was humiliated by having his insignia of kingship physically torn off him. The deposed king was imprisoned in the Tower of London, placed under papal protection, and finally exiled to his ancestral estates in France.[13] In order to hamper the Scots in any legal disputes, Edward seized Scotland's official records, which were subsequently lost. He took other sacred objects: the Stone of Destiny and Queen Margaret's Black Rood.[14] He rode home thinking his work done, joking on handing over to de Warenne the great seal of Scotland:

> *"Bon besoigne fait qy de merde se delivrer."*

> *It's a good job to be delivered of a shit.*[15]

---

[9] Skene and Skene, *John of Fordun's Chronicle of the Scottish Nation*, p.315, has MacDuff, for example, successfully defending himself against King John by appealing to Edward.
[10] Mackie, *A History Of Scotland*, p.68.
[11] Sutton, *Historia Gentis Scotorum*, Book XIV, Chapter 6.
[12] Skene and Skene, John of Fordun's Chronicle of the Scottish Nation, p.319.
[13] Barrow, *Robert Bruce And The Community Of The Realm Of Scotland*, p.155.
[14] Mackie, *A History Of Scotland*, p.69.
[15] Stevenson, *The Scalacronica of Sir Thomas Gray*, p.123.

His lightning campaign had put him in control of Scotland. How satisfying! Scotland was bigger than Wales, and more advanced feudally. Yet victory had been easy compared to the eye-wateringly expensive, time-consuming conquest of Wales. As a man steeped in feudal law, perhaps Edward thought of this as a game of chess: topple the king, and the whole country must follow. A document now known as the Ragman Roll indicated Edward's complete legal domination of Scotland. It was a document swearing fealty to Edward as overlord, and it was his legal justification for the most terrible measures against any signatory who crossed him. In September 1296, every Scotsman of substance was forced to travel to Berwick to sign the roll. But study the document as closely as you can; and you will search in vain for the name of one particular man.[16]

William Wallace.

William Wallace

With the nobility and gentry all forced to submit to Edward, the prospects for Scotland as a self-governing country looked grim. But in their work of state-building, previous kings had created something bigger than themselves. Unlike earlier states that barely outlived the charismatic leader who created them, like Urien's Rheged for example, *Scotland* had become a concept in people's minds and practices. The king may be deposed, but 'the Lion' bound the people together. And if the nobility would not fight for Scotland? Others would.

William Wallace was already a wanted man. According to tradition, the constable of Dundee had demanded his dirk: Wallace plunged it in his heart, then fled. A year later, armed only with his fishing rod, he'd beaten five English soldiers who had come down to the River Irvine and demanded his day's catch.[17] This was in 1292: by 1296, Wallace was stirring up trouble for the English and secretly meeting his lover Marion Braidfute in Lanark. Incensed by his inability to bring Wallace to justice, Heselrig, the Sheriff of Lanark, seized and killed Braidfute instead.[18] The grieving Wallace gathered

[16] You can peruse the ragman rolls at: Thomson, *Instrumenta Publica Sive Processus Super Fidelitatibus Et Homagiis Scotorum Domino Regi Angliae Factis*, [online] Internet Archive.
[17] Mackay, *William Wallace*, pp.61-65.
[18] *Ibid*, pp.111-113.

his friends. They forced their way into Heselrig's chambers and stabbed him to death.[19]

It was spark to tinder.

Hearing of Heselrig's death, a handful of patriotic nobles rose in sympathy. Andrew de Moray, who had been made prisoner at the Battle of Dunbar[20] and escaped captivity,[21] rose the north, and Sir William Douglas the south. They harried and burned English garrisons across Moray and Central Scotland.

The Battle of Stirling Brig

This could not be tolerated by Edward, who ordered de Warenne to raise an army to defeat the Scots. De Warenne's army counted around 10,000, including cavalry, plus some Scottish nobles and their followers. Wallace travelled to Aberdeen to combine with Andrew de Moray, and their army of around half the size of de Warenne's, almost entirely infantry, marched down from the north. The two armies met on 11 September 1297 across the narrow bridge of Stirling. De Warenne had brought to the field of battle the vast majority of armour and mounted knights and was complacently aware of his superiority. Believing the rebel army to be no match for his cavalry, de Warenne deployed his force across the narrow bridge, two at a time. It was a fatal mistake. De Moray and Wallace waited for enough to cross before striking, and once de Warenne realised his vanguard were all to be slaughtered, he retreated, leaving them to their fate. Seeing how the day went, de Warenne's Scottish contingent switched sides to Wallace, and the victory was complete.[22] De Warenne escaped, but his chancellor Hugh de Cressingham was killed and had the skin flayed from his back. Wallace would use the skin as his sword belt.[23]

---

[19] Mackay, *William Wallace,* pp.113-114.
[20] Bain, *Calendar Of Documents Relating To Scotland Preserved In Her Majesty's Public Record Office, London. Vol II.,* pp.176-177.
[21] Barrow, *Robert Bruce And The Community Of The Realm Of Scotland,* p.112.
[22] *Ibid,* p.115.
[23] Maxwell, *The Chronicle Of Lanercost,* p.164.

Figure 11: New Stirling Brig

Scotland was once again open for business, and de Moray and Wallace wrote to the Pope and to merchants across the North Sea to inform them of the fact.[24] But Scotland was not free yet. Stung by this unexpected defeat, Edward made a temporary truce with France and returned to deal with the issue in person. To deal with the Scots he moved to York, the seat of English government for the next six years.[25] He brought a full-sized army drawn from his feudal levies of England, Wales, Ireland, Gascony, his Anglo-Scottish nobles, mercenaries from Flanders, and the Knights Templar from their base in Midlothian.[26] De Moray was dead through wounds inflicted at Stirling Bridge, and Wallace was left to prepare his forces alone. He was hastily knighted and made sole Guardian of Scotland. In the face of the English army he retreated, burning the Lothians so there was nothing for the invaders to live on. Edward was experiencing difficulties with supplies, his army getting drunk at Kirkliston and fights breaking out between the Welsh and English contingents.[27] But just as he was on the verge of humiliating retreat, spies in the pay of the Earl of Dunbar brought vital information from

---

[24] Uncredited, *Special Delivery: The William Wallace Letters*, [online] The Scottish Parliament.
[25] Barrow, *Robert Bruce And The Community Of The Realm Of Scotland*, p,128.
[26] Ferguson, *The Knights Templar And Scotland*, pp.54-55.
[27] Barrow, *Robert Bruce And The Community Of The Realm Of Scotland*, pp131-132.

the Scottish camp. They told him of Wallace's plans and that his army was nearby. Reinvigorated by this intelligence, Edward pushed on, and on 22 July 1298 the armies met at Falkirk.

"I hae brocht ye to the ring,"

said Wallace to his troops as the English approached,

"now see gif ye can dance."[28]

The Battle of Falkirk
Wallace had a tactic, the schiltron: a mobile forest of infantry pikes designed to stop the superior English cavalry. But Edward had a tactic too: the longbows of the recently conquered Welsh. If medieval politics was a game of chess, then medieval battle tactics were much simpler: a game of paper, scissors, stone. Well-drilled infantry in a schiltron could thwart a cavalry charge; fast, mobile cavalry could mow down archers; and well-placed archers could cause havoc upon infantry. The correct combination of these forces was the secret to success. Edward's knights rushed on the Scottish bowmen, and the Scottish cavalry, led by John Comyn the Red, rode off the field at this point. In the popular imagination Wallace was deliberately betrayed by the nobility, jealous of a commoner who dared command,[29] though others argue a simpler point. They may have taken fright at the overwhelming odds and made the pragmatic decision to live, and fight, another day.[30] Either way, the effect on the defenceless infantry was the same.

And so, without cavalry to ride down the longbowmen, Wallace's army stood defenceless under the arrowstorm. After the schiltrons were decimated by the archers, Edward's infantry and cavalry charged back in, destroying the Scottish army. Wallace escaped and became a fugitive. The Guardianship of

---

[28] Cowan, *'For Freedom Alone'*, p.23.
[29] Skene and Skene, John of Fordun's Chronicle of the Scottish Nation, p.323.
[30] Barrow, Robert Bruce And The Community Of The Realm Of Scotland, p.134-136.

Scotland passed from him to a secret three-way bond between Bishop Lamberton of St Andrews, Robert the Bruce, and John Comyn the Red.

Attrition

Edward had won a battle, but the war continued. Inspired by the church and the shadowy figure of Wallace, the community of Scotland remained in open revolt. English forces raided and burned Southern Scotland, and opposition to Edward's rule hardened. Although Edward kept garrisons in Southern Scotland, nobles such as the Red Comyn and his father, the Earl of Buchan, remained in control north of the Forth,[31] and conducted trade and diplomatic relations with Europe in the name of the exiled King John.[32] The fight was taken beyond Scotland to European courts. Wallace went abroad in 1299 to gather support, certainly to France and possibly to Rome and Norway,[33] but the French dropped the Auld Alliance in 1302 after the Flemish won a famous battle against them at Cortrai.[34] France tapping out gave English envoys the chance to put diplomatic pressure on the Pope. Edward's propagandists promoted a story that the British were descended from Brutus, a fictional character present at the Siege of Troy, and that the King of England was descended from his eldest son: and therefore superior over the whole of Britain.[35]

These stories were nonsense, said Baldred Bisset, Scottish representative to the Pope, calling for ink and vellum and scribing his own legal myth. The Scots, said Bisset, were in fact descended from the equally fictional Scota, daughter of an Egyptian Pharaoh, descendant of the lost tribe of Israel, whose people had travelled from Egypt to Scotland via Spain and Ireland: and whose lineage was considerably older than any character in Greek

---

[31] Barrow, Robert Bruce And The Community Of The Realm Of Scotland, p.136,138,149.
[32] Reid, "The Kingless Kingdom: The Scottish Guardianships of 1286-1306." *The Scottish Historical Review*, vol. 61, no. 172, 1982, pp. 105–129.
[33] Mackay, *William Wallace*, pp.214-221.
[34] Mackie, *A History Of Scotland*, p.71.
[35] Prestwich, *Edward I*, p.492.

mythology. Scottish royalty, therefore, had a far more senior lineage than the English.[36]

But the Scottish representation was in vain. In August 1302 the Pope retreated[37] from previous rulings that the Scots church was responsible not to York but to him alone.[38] And through steady attrition, Edward brought more and more of Scotland under his heel. The Earl of Buchan died in 1302. Robert the Bruce formally submitted to Edward in February of that year; the Red Comyn, along with most of the rest of the Scottish nobility, held out another two years, but surrendered in February 1304. The French had made peace with England and, without French support, many had come to believe the cause was hopeless. As part of the deal with Edward, Comyn insisted that the legal system remain as it was under Alexander III, and under the control of the Scots.[39] With consent to his rule finally in sight, Edward agreed to this compromise. In March 1304 Edward held a Parliament at St Andrews where he recognised the laws and customs of Scotland. Only one thing was left to do. The terms of the new agreement would not take effect until the remaining patriots were captured.

One of the men who had submitted to Edward in 1304 was Sir John de Menteith. For his acquiescence he was rewarded with the Sheriffdom of Dumbarton. In return he captured William Wallace at Robroyston in August 1305, and handed him over to English forces. Wallace was taken to London and tried for treason in the Great Hall of Westminster. In response to the charges Wallace replied:

> *'I cannot be a traitor to Edward, for I owe him no allegiance. He is not my Sovereign; he never received my homage; and whilst life is in this persecuted body, he never shall receive it.'*[40]

---

[36] Watt, MacQueen, MacQueen, *Walter Bower's Scotichronicon, Volume 3*, p.173..
[37] Mackie, *A History Of Scotland*, p.71.
[38] Papal bulls *Cum universi* and *Scimus, Fili.*
[39] Sadler, *Bannockburn: Battle For Liberty*, p.57.
[40] Tytler, *Lives Of Scottish Worthies, Vol. I*, p.279.

Wallace was dragged behind a horse to Spitalfields where a monument to his memory now stands. In front of a jeering mob he was tortured, half-hung, emasculated, disembowelled, and finally beheaded.

William Wallace had appeared out of nowhere and streaked across the pages of history like a shooting star, living a life of defiance and martyrdom. In a world dominated by the international elite of Anglo-French nobility, where a family like the Balliols held land in Scotland, Picardy, and seventeen English counties,[41] he led a genuine popular movement; a deep eruption of Scottish consciousness. Wallace's reward was the life of a fugitive and a horrific death. His head was displayed on a pike on London Bridge. His limbs were sent to hang above the four town gates of Newcastle, Berwick, Stirling, and Perth, as a warning against anyone who dared defy the will of Edward I. With the nobility now in his pocket, Scotland's castles captured, Wallace dealt with, and a lighter touch in allowing the Scots to remain in charge of their own laws and hold their own offices of state, it seemed that finally, fifteen years after the death of Margaret of Norway, Edward had completed the conquest of Scotland that he so craved.

The sensible thing had been to acquiesce to Edward's superior force. Faced with such a choice, it is what any reasonable person would do. It was what the Scottish nobility did. But unlike those who eventually betrayed him, Wallace never, ever, accepted English domination. The Scots found the example of Sir William Wallace, in the words of Robert Burns:

Poured a Scottish prejudice into my veins that would boil along until the floodgates of life shut in eternal rest.[42]

Edward was about to discover it had been easier to fight a living fugitive than a dead legend.

Bishops and Bruce

Autumn of 1302, Paris. Bishop Lamberton of St Andrews, returning from an audience with the Pope was deep in thought. Despite all his efforts in negotiating the Scottish cause, despite John Balliol's release from captivity,

---

[41] Lynch, *Scotland: A New History*, p.91.
[42] Burns, *Letter to Dr John Moore*, [online] National Library of Scotland.

the king had returned to his ancestral lands in France, indicating he had no further interest in pursuing the Scottish crown. But Lamberton was a former pupil of one Europe's foremost intellects, John Duns Scotus. Either from his earlier teaching, or from an encounter now in Paris, Duns Scotus had persuaded the bishop that a king was made not by God, but by the consent of those he ruled. This meant that the king could be replaced if he lost the consent of his people. It was a revolutionary concept, but it could get Scotland out of its hole. Lamberton returned home, convinced that replacing Balliol was the answer. And he had an obvious candidate: Robert the Bruce.[43]

The Bruce's relationship with Scotland's affairs was complicated. Unlike the single-minded Exocet of Anglophobia that was Wallace, Bruce played the conditions before him. In the aftermath of the Battle of Dunbar he had begged Edward to give him Scotland; Edward had replied with contempt "have I naught to do but win kingdoms for you?"[44] Yet when Edward ordered Bruce to fight against his fellow Scots he could not bear to do so, raised his banner in 1297 for Balliol, then surrendered without a fight to an English force at Irvine.[45] After the Battle of Falkirk he was appointed Guardian of Scotland in a secret ceremony along with the Red Comyn, but the two men fell out, coming to blows at a meeting in 1299 at Peebles and having to be separated by the Stewart.[46] When the French threatened to send an army to reinstate Balliol, Bruce made a public peace with Edward in 1302.[47] Any opposition to the English after this was very much the work of the Comyns and other nobles. But Lamberton felt convinced he had the right man. The enmity between Bruce and the Comyns was not hard to understand: they supported King John, and Comyn's father, the Earl of Buchan, had himself been one of the Competitors. The family were a direct threat to Bruce's own desires for the throne. Once the Comyns too, finally submitted to Edward, Bruce stole away to meet Lamberton at Cambuskenneth Abbey on 11 June 1304. Within sight and sound of Edward's siege of Stirling Castle, they made a secret bond; secret because publicly, Bruce had declared for Edward; secret, because the time to act was

[43] Penman, *Robert The Bruce: King Of Scots*, p.80.
[44] Davies, *The Isles: A History*, p.376.
[45] Wright, *The History Of Scotland From The Earliest Period*, pp.65-66.
[46]. Barrow, *Robert Bruce And The Community Of The Realm Of Scotland*, pp.140-141.
[47] *Ibid*, pp.159-161.

not yet ripe; secret, because Lamberton had something revolutionary to say to Bruce. It was Duns Scotus' advice. The country needed a king. If Balliol would not fight for Scotland, it was Bruce's destiny to do so. But not yet. Edward was formidable, but was old and would die soon. Let the trigger for Bruce to act be Edward's death. So they agreed to keep their council, and parted ways.

The Secret Outed

Lamberton was not the only man with whom Bruce made a secret bond. A picturesque story is told in later chronicles that Bruce also made contact with Red Comyn, the man with whom he had previously come to blows. Comyn agreed that when the time was ripe, he would support the Bruce in his bid for kingship in return for being granted Bruce's Scottish estates.[48] According to the medieval chroniclers, Comyn confessed the scheme to Edward, who had the Bruce travel to London to answer for it. Robert talked himself out of arrest, but after he had left, Edward informed his council that the Bruce would be executed in the morning.[49] Ralph de Monthermer, Edward's son-in-law and a friend of the Bruce, was alarmed. It would be treason to send a direct message so instead, Monthermer sent Bruce a messenger carrying a shilling and a pair of spurs. Bruce took the hint. He gave the servant the shilling as a tip, and took off into the night for Scotland. Arriving at his stronghold of Lochmaben Castle, he arranged to meet Comyn in Greyfriars Kirk in Dumfries as a matter of urgency.

This legend of Comyn's double-dealing and Bruce's close escape from London is a colourful embellishment to an already incredible story: for the Bruce was in Scotland all the time.[50] It, and stories like it, are an attempt to explain the reason the two men met privately at Greyfriars on the night of 10 February 1306. Exactly why they met, or what passed between them that night is unknown. But the result is in no doubt.

Because suddenly Bruce burst out of the church, covered in blood, having stabbed Comyn.

---

[48] Skene and Skene, *John of Fordun's Chronicle of the Scottish Nation*, pp.330-331.
[49] *Ibid,* p.331.
[50] Linklater, *Robert The Bruce*, p.45.

"Is he dead?" asked his followers.

"I know not."

"I mak siccar,"[51] replied Sir Roger de Kilpatrick, going inside the church to finish Comyn off.

Bruce was in serious trouble.

He had now been outed as plotting against Edward I. This was bad enough. But he had also committed the worst crime of all: murder in a church. The two rivals had met there because the sanctuary of holy ground was well understood by everyone. Bruce would be excommunicated. Every Christian in Europe would be duty-bound to bring him to justice. He was a fugitive from both the law and from God.

Only one man could save him now.

Bishop Wishart of Glasgow would have been informed of events soon afterwards. Bruce murdered Comyn! That had rearranged the chessboard. The church's patient plans of waiting for Edward to die were undone. And Bruce had murdered his rival in a church. Excommunication and civil war, in an occupied country, were now inevitable. Wishart did not hesitate. He absolved Bruce of the sin of the murder, and in March they rode for Scone, raising Lamberton, the Bishop of Moray, and the loyal nobility. Edward had removed the Stone of Destiny and Scottish regalia, but Wishart had hidden the royal vestments and banner which he now produced from a chest.[52] Traditionally the King of Scots had been crowned by MacDuff, the Earl of Fife. But the holder of that position was in Edward's thrall,[53] and his sister Isabella was married to a Comyn, the new Earl of Buchan. Knowing it would put her outside the protection of her family and the law, Isabella rode to Scone to do her duty. On 27 March 1306, Robert the Bruce was the first King of Scots, and perhaps the first king in Europe, to be crowned by a

---

[51] Way and Squire, *Collins Scottish Clan & Family Encyclopedia*, pp.411-412.
[52] Linklater, *Robert The Bruce*, p.47.
[53] Mackie, *A History Of Scotland*, p.72.

woman.[54] Bruce's ambition to be king had been achieved. Glowing, he asked his wife how she felt to be a queen.

"I fear we have been made King and Queen, as children play in summer games," she replied.[55]

But this was no game.

The Dragon Banner

The Comyns and their allies were numerous, angry, and out for Bruce's blood. The various branches of the Balliols and Comyns in southern and north-east Scotland ranged themselves against the Bruce; as did their ally in the west, MacDougall of Lorne; as did their allies in the east, the Earls of March, Dunbar, and Strathearn.

But Bruce was not friendless. Standing by him were James Stewart and, thanks partly to an existing feud with MacDougall, MacDonald of the Isles. Attending the coronation were the Earls of Atholl, Menteith, Lennox, and Mar.[56] And crucially, the church stood square behind him. Bishop Wishart swapped his surplice for armour to lead a siege of Cupar Castle, using timber granted for the repair of his cathedral to build instead a siege engine.[57] Bruce aside, the man who would prove Scotland's most effective commander now declared himself: James Douglas.[58] Douglas was desperate for revenge against the English who had taken possession of his lands and castle.

But by the end of March 1306, Scotland's English governors had consolidated their position in Dumfries, with reinforcements speedily called up. On 5 April Aymer de Valence was appointed commander of Eastern Scotland and Edward, the Prince of Wales the west. They rode out flying the Dragon Banner, which meant no quarter could be expected towards any who stood against them.[59] With the English and the Comyns and their allies against him, the Bruce's position was desperate. On 19 June, a force led by

---

[54] Connolly, *Heroines Of The Medieval World*, pp.159-160.
[55] Murison, *King Robert The Bruce*, p.47.
[56] Barrow, *Robert Bruce And The Community Of The Realm Of Scotland*, p.196.
[57] *Ibid*, p.197.
[58] *Ibid*, p.203.
[59] Barbour and Duncan, *The Bruce*, p.90.

de Valence surprised Bruce at Methven near Perth, utterly defeating him and taking his supporters captive, including Thomas Randolph who was forced to fight for the English. Bruce and the remnants of his force fled west, only to be set upon by MacDougall at Dalrigh near Tyndrum where the closest escape possible was made: in the desperate fighting, a brooch was ripped from the Bruce's cloak by MacDougall; traditionally it has been retained as a family memento to this day.[60] Bruce and the remains of his army reached the eastern shore of Loch Lomond where they found one boat. It took the whole day to ferry the company across. The Bruce sat under a yew tree near Firkin Point on the western side as his men gradually crossed, telling them stories to keep their spirits up.[61]

By the end of August, Wishart and Lamberton were prisoners in English dungeons, and Bruce's own castle of Lochmaben had fallen. His wife, daughter, sisters, and the woman who crowned him, Isabella MacDuff, were sent north to Kildrummy Castle and the care of Bruce's brother, Nigel. The Prince of Wales followed and laid siege. Nigel smuggled the ladies out to safety but was then betrayed by a traitor who set a fire, and in the chaos the castle was taken.[62] In September Nigel Bruce was executed at Berwick. On their way to safety in Orkney and Norway, Bruce's ladies were captured at the sanctuary of St Duthac of Tain by the Earl of Ross and handed over to the English.[63]

The Comyns and the English continued the hunt for Robert, or 'King Hob' as his enemies mocked him. They called him the 'king of the summer': a euphemism for a tramp. But he had disappeared. He had fled for sanctuary to the islands, beyond the reach of his enemies in the protection of Angus Og MacDonald of Islay.[64] No-one knows for sure exactly where he overwintered. He may have stayed at the unfortified house of Finlaggan where nobody could get past MacDonald's fleet. He may have stayed with his supporter Christina MacRuari, in one of her castles in the West

---

[60] It's known as the Brooch of Lorn.
[61] Barbour and Duncan, *The Bruce*, pp.132-133.
[62] *Ibid*, pp.154-159.
[63] Connolly, *Heroines Of The Medieval World*, p.160.
[64] Barrow, *Robert Bruce And The Community Of The Realm Of Scotland*, p.211-212.

Highlands. Traditionally, he went into hiding on Rathlin.[65] His sister Mary Bruce was imprisoned in a cage, hung over the wall of Roxburgh Castle for all to see and mock. She would spend four years in this torturous position.

The woman who crowned him, Isabella, Countess of Buchan, endured a similar fate. Legend has it that Edward ruled:

> *Let her be closely confined in an abode of stone and iron made in the shape of a cross, and let her be hung up out of doors in the open air at Berwick, that both in life and after her death, she may be a spectacle and eternal reproach to travellers.*[66]

Robert himself spent the winter of 1306-7 alone, utterly despondent. His fate, the fate of Scotland as an independent country, hung by a thread as thin as a spider's web.

---

[65] *Ibid*, p.212,215-220.
[66] Connolly, *Heroines Of The Medieval World*, pp.160-162, suggests the reality is likely to have been slightly more comfortable, a cage inside a tower.

CHAPTER EIGHT

King's Return

Whilst lying in his cave on Rathlin wondering whether or not to quit, Robert the Bruce saw a spider attempt to spin a web. Six times it attempted to swing across to a distant beam to start the web, and six times it failed. It occurred to Bruce that he had fought six battles and lost them all. The spider's next action, he decided, would determine whether or not he would abandon hope. The spider swung across a seventh time and this time, it was successful.

It's a great story, if probably untrue, a Bruce family tradition repeated by Sir Walter Scott in 1828's *Tales of a Grandfather*.[1] But its essence resonates: it illustrates Bruce's persistence in the face of discouraging odds. He made plans to return to mainland Scotland. Robert's brothers Thomas and Alexander were sent ahead to Galloway in eighteen galleys, and in February 1307, with a small force of MacDonalds, the king landed on Arran. From here he could see his estates of Carrick on the mainland. He was keen to know if the people would still rise for him, and so another man was sent to Carrick to discover the people's loyalty. If Carrick proved friendly, he was to light a fire on the shore as a beacon.

Robert waited. And then he saw it. The beacon! Sailing over with his men he landed, expecting to be reunited with his brothers and a band of loyal locals. Instead he was met with horrifying news: his brothers were dead. They had been captured by a kinsman of MacDougall, and sent to Carlisle to be executed.[2] It was sheer coincidence that someone else, innocent of Bruce's plans, had lit a bonfire on the shore.[3]

A lesser man may have given up at this point. John Balliol had abdicated under lesser travails. The Bruce pressed on.

---

[1] Scott, *Tales Of A Grandfather, Vol. I*, pp.115-118.
[2] Barbour and Duncan, *The Bruce*, p.152.
[3] *Ibid*, pp.176-193.

The Battle of Glen Trool

Robert's force attacked and killed the garrison of Turnberry, then disappeared into the wildest part of the Galloway Forest. Bruce's conqueror at Methven, Aymer de Valence, sent a bloodhound that had formerly belonged to the Bruce to track him down.[4] The dog narrowly failed, but de Valence subsequently discovered his quarry at large in Glen Trool. He set out in pursuit, only to find the Bruce in command of a defile impassable by horseback, and his fifteen hundred men were seen off by Bruce's three hundred. This battle of Glen Trool was a minor skirmish, but a significant morale boost for the Bruce: his first ever victory.[5]

The Battle of Loudoun Hill

Robert's second battle was more ambitious, again using childhood knowledge of the local terrain to his advantage. He ambushed troops chasing him under de Mowbray,[6] and Aymer de Valence laid down a challenge to meet in pitched battle. Bruce accepted, and they clashed at Loudoun Hill on 10 May. But Robert had prepared his ground well. According to John Barbour's *The Bruce*:

> *The king upon the other side,*
> *Whose prudence was his valour's guide,*
> *Rode out to see and chose his ground.*
> *The highway took its course, he found,*
> *Upon a meadow, smooth and dry.*
> *But close on either side thereby*
> *A bog extended, deep and broad,*
> *That from the highway, where men rode,*
> *Was full a bowshot either side.*[7]

The superior attacking force of de Valence was forced into a narrow front that could not outflank Bruce on either side. De Valence escaped the carnage, but Bruce's knowledge of terrain had again won him victory over

---

[4] Barbour and Duncan, *The Bruce*, pp.246-261.
[5] *Ibid*, pp.282-289.
[6] *Ibid*, pp.290-295.
[7] Barbour, *The Bruce*, p.197.

superior forces. Victory was becoming a habit. The Bishop of Moray unleashed a rumour that priests spread like wildfire from their pulpits. The English castellan of Forfar wrote in May to his superiors that:

> *Preachers have told the people they have found a prophecy of Merlin, how after the death of 'le Roy Coveytous' the Scottish people and the Britons [that is, the Welsh], shall league together, and have full lordship and live together in accord to the end of the world.* [8]

Death of a Tyrant

Enraged that despite his best efforts, the Scottish problem was still not resolved, the elderly Edward donned his armour for yet another invasion. But in July 1307 he fell ill at Lanercost Priory in Cumbria. Sensing the end was near, he ordered that he be carried to Burgh-on-Sands on the Solway where he could see and curse Scotland with his dying breath. His instructions to his son, King Edward II, were clear. His body was to be boiled, the flesh flayed from the bones, and the bones carried before his army. Edward junior was ordered not to return to England until Scotland was completely subjugated. But Edward the son was not made from the same stamp as Edward the father. He undertook a desultory foray into Scotland then returned home, placing his father's body in a sarcophagus in Westminster Abbey bearing the Latin inscription 'Malleus Scotorum' – *Hammer of the Scots*. Having lived his life in the shadow of an angry and warlike man, the time had come for Edward II to finally focus on his own priorities. Scotland was not one of them.

The Herschip of Buchan

The death of such an implacable enemy was a massive boost to Robert's cause. With Edward I's unremitting attention gone, the Bruce was able to turn his attention to the matter of the civil war. Without the destruction of the Comyns and their allies, Bruce could never have peace. And so he crossed the Mounth, heading for Inverness. The Earl of Ross, who had captured Bruce's ladies the previous year, was intimidated into agreeing a

---

[8] Bain, *Calendar Of Documents Relating To Scotland Preserved in Her Majesty's Public Record Office, London, Vol II*, p.513.

truce:[9] Robert could turn his full attention towards Aberdeenshire, under the control of the Comyn Earl of Buchan. The struggle lasted all winter, during which Robert fell gravely ill, but at the battle of Inverurie on 23 May 1308 his forces triumphed.[10] With other nobles there could be a rapprochement, but not with this old enemy, who fled to England and died within a year. The lands of Comyn were laid waste, a horrific devastation of Scottish lands by a Scottish king. It took a lifetime for the people to fully recover,[11] perhaps the greatest waste of the northeast since the Roman battle of Mons Graupius.

Next it was the turn of MacDougall of Lorne. Around August, the Bruce's forces marched west to Argyll. As they approached the narrow Pass of Brander by Loch Awe, Robert sensed the potential for ambush. He ordered James Douglas take a detachment to climb Ben Cruachan and scout out the area. It was a wise precaution. Seeing from his elevated vantage point a force of MacDougalls waiting to ambush Robert on the track further below, Douglas fell on their rear. The MacDougalls were caught in their own trap.[12] John MacDougall of Lorne was watching the battle from his galley and fled, like Buchan, for England.

Flood Tide

The tide had turned for the Bruce. His major enemies at home were dead or exiled. Edward II negotiated a truce for most of 1309, during which the church assembled at St Andrews and issued the 'Declaration of the Clergy', which said that the people, as per Duns Scotus' advice, had chosen their king;[13] a kingship which the French now recognised.[14] Bruce made peace with the Earl of Ross, who became an ally.[15] He could ride with impunity throughout the countryside, hostile garrisons cowering in their castles. From 1310 he sought to reduce those garrisons, one by one.

---

[9] Linklater, *Robert The Bruce*, pp.80-81.
[10] Barbour and Duncan, *The Bruce*, pp.318-333.
[11] *Ibid*, pp.332-335. 'and heryit thaim on sic maner/that eftre weile fyfty yer/men menyt [bemoaned] the herschip off Bouchane.'
[12] Barbour and Duncan, *The Bruce*, pp.360-365.
[13] RPS *1309/2*.
[14] Mackie, *A History Of Scotland*, p.74.
[15] Linklater, *Robert The Bruce*, p.90.

The Black Douglas

In his fight for Scotland, Bruce's most capable lieutenant was James Douglas. Well before the king's domestic enemies were dealt with, Douglas had gone off in 1307 to recapture his own castle. Joining the garrison at prayer on Palm Sunday, his men mingled with the enemy in the church before throwing off their cloaks and slaughtering the defenceless Englishmen, who had left their swords outside. Riding to the castle they killed their remaining prisoners, ate the dinner that had been prepared for the garrison's return, then set the castle on fire. History records this gruesome incident as the 'Douglas Larder.'[16]

The castle was quickly repaired and reoccupied by the invader. Douglas returned, driving off the castle's cattle in full view of the garrison. They rode out to stop this but unbeknownst to them, a larger force of Scots waited in ambush. Most of the garrison were killed but some returned to the safety of the castle and Douglas, who had not prepared for a siege, rode off.[17]

The garrison was relieved by Sir John of Webton, whose men saw in the distance a line of hay carts led by gowned figures. As the garrison was short of hay to feed their horses, they rode out to commandeer the carts. At the point when they were most vulnerable, the hay was thrown aside to reveal carts full of armed Scotsmen, and the 'ladies' leading the carts cast aside their gowns and jumped on the horses to attack. Douglas was awaiting nearby with a larger force which simultaneously stormed the castle. As his men were rifling through Sir John of Webton's possessions, they found a letter from his sweetheart promising to marry him if he could do what no other English knight had managed, and hold for a year 'the adventuris castell off Douglas.' But Webton was dead.[18] For his ability to appear out of nowhere, wreak terror, then disappear, he gained a nickname. Contemporary Scots called him the Good Sir James. But nursemaids across the border crooned to their babies: "hush pet, the Black Douglas shall not get ye."

---

[16] Barbour and Duncan, *The Bruce*, p.206-211.
[17] *Ibid*, p.244-247.
[18] *Ibid*, p.312-317.

Cunning and Subterfuge

In the summer of 1308 Douglas captured an English patrol near Peebles. Amongst their number was Thomas Randolph, Bruce's nephew. He had initially been forced to fight for the English side, but now did so willingly, scorning Bruce as unchivalrous for his reliance on guerrilla tactics.[19] A proper knight met his fellows on a level playing field: he did not hide in forests and mountains, or dig pits hiding spikes to hobble pursuing cavalry. Randolph was taken to Bruce and placed in custody. Upon observing the realities for the heavily outnumbered Scots, Randolph became one of Bruce's most valued and trusted allies. Douglas had already proven adept at the cunning and subterfuge Randolph had initially despised. Randolph would find he had a talent for it too.

In 1310 Edward II was finally stirred into doing something about Scotland, and arranged an invasion. Hearing the English were coming, Bruce burned the land and retreated before the invaders. Edward was discomfited to find nobody to fight, no cattle to capture, not even any fodder for his horses to eat. He reached as far as the Forth and then retreated. English barons now started to look to the future, anticipating the day they might need to do deals with the Bruce, who was threatening to gain complete control of the Borders. Isabella MacDuff and Bruce's sister Mary were removed from their cages and imprisoned in greater comfort, MacDuff with the Carmelites in Berwick[20] and Mary exchanged for a Comyn hostage.[21] In August and September 1311 Bruce sent two chevauchées, or cavalry raids, into England with a force large enough to overwhelm any local resistance, raiding Northumbria, burning Corbridge, and extorting blackmail to keep him away until Candlemas in February 1312.[22]

The English barons had had enough.

They passed a law putting 'Lord Ordainers' in effective control of England, their first move towards removing power from Edward, who failed to react

---

[19] Linklater, *Robert The Bruce*, pp.91-92.
[20] ODNB, *Buchan [née Macduff], Isabel, countess of Buchan.*
[21] *Foedera Vol I*, p.160.
[22] Sadler, *Border Fury*, p.113.

decisively towards this warning.[23] In 1312 Bruce attacked England again, this time as far as Durham. His mounted infantry moved fast and avoided sieges, bringing not conquest but extortion, sucking the economy of the English border dry. In the North of England law and order began to break down, the people's pleas to Edward going unheeded.[24] King Edward had become besotted with a handsome Gascon called Piers Gaveston, who unwisely goaded the English aristocracy, believing the king's favour made him immune from danger. He was wrong: the Lord Ordainers had Gaveston executed. Yet Edward still did not move against the Bruce, even as his people in the north were forced to pay extortion for a third year and his garrisons in Scotland were reduced one by one.

The Last Garrisons

In the summer of 1312, garrisons loyal to Edward still held the castles of Berwick, Perth, Linlithgow, Roxburgh, Edinburgh, Stirling, Bothwell, Lochmaben, Caerlaverock, Dumfries, and Jedburgh; and English forces could be sure of a welcome at Dunbar. Lacking the means and experience for sieges, and not wanting to be exposed in the field for any length of time, the Scots relied on cunning for a series of audacious captures. Berwick was attempted on 6 December 1312 when grappling hooks and rope ladders were heaved over the town walls, but the barking of an alert dog warned the defenders. Berwick would have to wait.[25]

In January 1313, Perth was held against Bruce by Oliphant. He had held Stirling against Edward I in 1304 but had since defected to the English side. Bruce made a show of abandoning a siege, dismantling his siege engines, levelling his trenches, and departing. But secretly, he returned a few nights later, waded the moat, and scaled the walls in sufficient numbers to open the gates. As a strategic asset, Perth's value was too great, and it was razed to the ground, town, castle, walls and all.[26]

In the same year, a fellow named Bunnock delivered hay to the garrison of Linlithgow Castle. As the haycart passed underneath the portcullis, Bunnock

---

[23] Encyclopædia Britannica, *Ordainer | English History*.
[24] Sadler, *Border Fury*, p.116.
[25] Barrow, *Robert Bruce And The Community Of The Realm Of Scotland*, p.253.
[26] Linklater, *Robert The Bruce*, pp.106-108.

halted the horses and armed patriots jumped out. Hiding nearby were more men who swarmed through the gate, stuck open due to the haycart jamming the entrance.[27]

By the end of 1313 Roxburgh Castle found itself under siege by James Douglas and Walter Stewart. In order to get close enough to storm the castle, in February 1314 they disguised an advance party as cattle. The fake cows approached in the darkness on all fours, carrying siege ladders, which they laid against the castle walls, clambering quickly up the side of the castle to the garrison's total surprise.[28] On the orders of the king, the castle was razed to the ground. Every castle the Bruce captured was destroyed, even Douglas' own. The strategy was sound. Robert now had total command of the countryside, and he would not have this advantage threatened by a hostile garrison holed up in a castle.

Dundee fell. Dumfries fell. Lochmaben and Caerlaverock fell. The Isle of Man, a Scottish possession since 1266, was recaptured.[29] By the spring of 1314, only three castles apart from Berwick remained in English hands: Bothwell, Edinburgh, and Stirling.

Edinburgh's Back Door

By now a convert to underhand tactics, Thomas Randolph discovered a back door into Edinburgh Castle unknown to the garrison. A lad called William Francis approached the Scots, and informed them that he could show them a safe route up the seemingly impregnable crags on which the castle stood. He knew this route, had traversed it many times, because he had used it to secretly woo a girl in the town when he was son of the castle's keeper. One night in March, while a diversionary attack was made on the east gate, Francis led Randolph's party of 30 commandos up the crag. They scaled the wall with rope ladders, killed the sentry, burst open the gate and so captured the castle, which like the rest, had its walls dismantled so it could no longer be used against the Scots.[30]

---

[27] Barbour and Duncan, *The Bruce*, pp.366-373.
[28] *Ibid*, pp.378-387.
[29] Mackie, *A History Of Scotland*, p.74.
[30] Barbour and Duncan, *The Bruce*, pp.386-401.

One more castle remained: Stirling. Its situation between a marsh and the sea on the only crossing of the Forth led to it being described as the brooch of Scotland: 'whoever held Stirling,' the saying went, 'could split Scotland in two.' This impregnable fortress was not going to fall by the tactics that had captured every other castle. Only a long, drawn-out siege to starve out the defenders would do. Robert's impatient, last remaining brother Edward Bruce couldn't wait. In the spring of 1314, by the rules of chivalry, he made an arrangement with the castle's commander. Should English reinforcements not arrive by 24 June 1314, Philip de Mowbray would surrender the castle. In return, his garrison would be given safe passage back to England. Satisfied with the arrangement, Edward Bruce rode off to tell his brother.[31]

Robert was not happy.

---

[31] Barbour and Duncan, *The Bruce*, pp.402-3. Traditionally the agreement between Bruce and Mowbray was made in the summer of 1313, but that conflicts with other evidence.

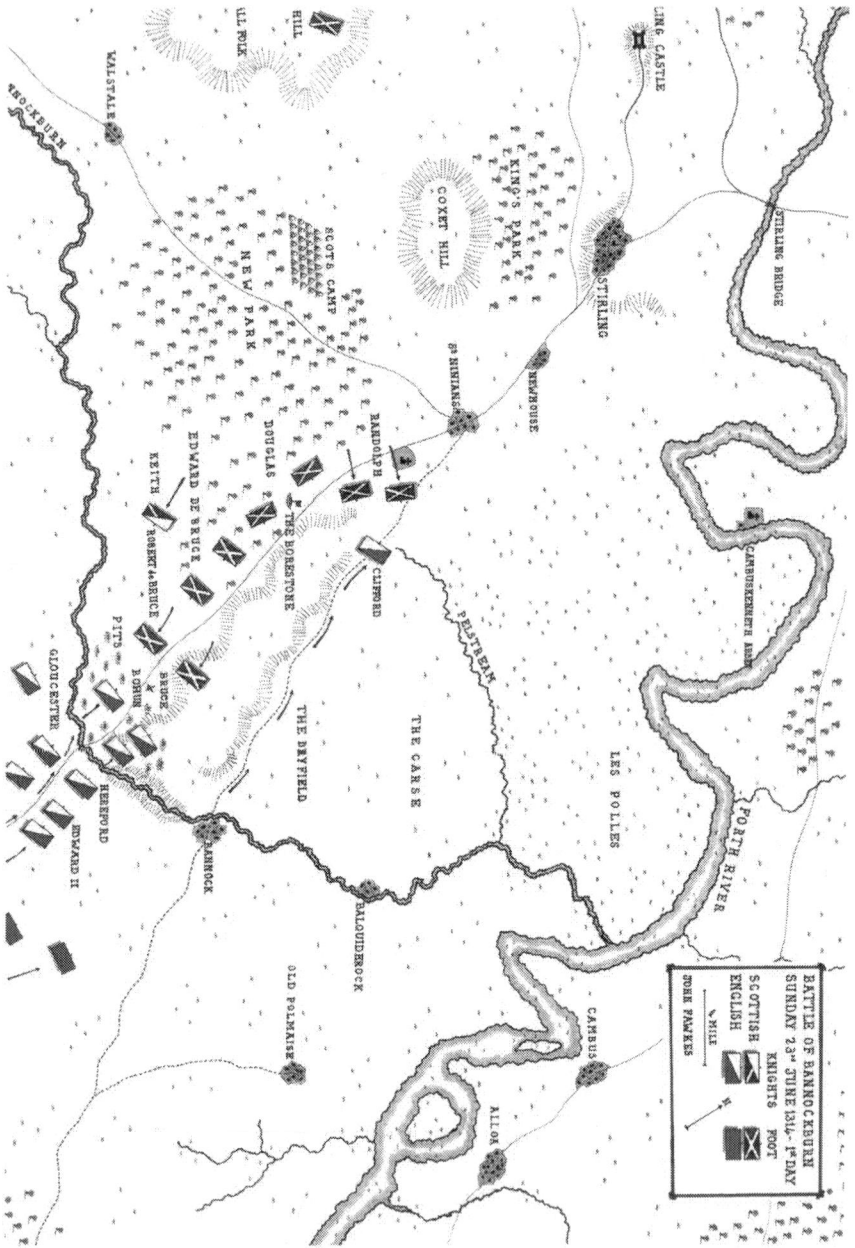

Figure 12: Battle of Bannockburn, Day 1. © Britishbattles.com

CHAPTER NINE

The Battle of Bannockburn

The Bruce had learned a hard lesson from his reverses before 1307. He had taken great care to hit, run and harry; ambush and retreat; use the local terrain to his advantage; waste the land before an invader's advance; wear down the enemy through attrition; destroy fortresses that could be used against him; extort and blackmail the North of England; never commit all his forces to an action. He had become a master of asymmetric warfare, letting the landscape of Scotland fight on his behalf. He knew that in men and material he could not match the resources of the King of England. Should he be forced into battle in the open field, all his painstakingly achieved gains could be reversed in a single morning. But now it seemed that was inevitable. Bruce set about drilling an army and choosing a battle site.

But Edward II wasn't pleased either. His attention towards Scotland had been intermittent, and the English lords had grumbled over the cost of the Scottish wars, but something now had to be done unless he wanted to lose Scotland entirely; especially as the Bruce had given an ultimatum to the remaining Scots loyal to the English crown.[1] And so he set about raising funds and appointing commanders. Edward Bruce's arrangement had precipitated a battle royale that would decide Scotland's fate.

On 10 June 1314, Edward marched his army of around 20,000[2] from Wark into Scotland, arrived in Edinburgh without opposition, and reached Falkirk on 22 June.

---

[1] Barbour and Duncan, *The Bruce*, p.376.
[2] *Ibid*, p.410. Nobody really knows the size of the army. Barbour, for effect, says 100,000; A.A.M. Duncan suggests that with no-shows and desertions, it may be as low as 10,000.

Robert had prepared his force of around 8,000[3] a mile or so from Stirling Castle, at a point where the road from Falkirk was constricted between marshland leading to the Forth on one side, and a forest called Torwood and escarpment called New Park on the other. They dug caltrop pits to hobble cavalry and took up position. On 23 June the two armies came in sight of one another.

Now's the day and now's the hour
See approach proud Edward's power
Chains and slaverie![4]

Edward immediately ordered a frontal assault by the Earls of Hereford and Gloucester, while a flanking party under Clifford rode to relieve Stirling Castle. Randolph's schiltron engaged with the flanking knights, and a hard battle ensued.[5]

As Randolph locked arms with Clifford in a side battle, the Bruce rode in front of his main army to address them.

Wha for Scotland's king and law
Freedom's sword will strongly draw,
Freeman stand, or freeman fa',
Let him follow me!

As he did, a knight in Hereford's vanguard called Henry de Bohun saw that the Bruce was alone and undefended. It was an opportunity to win the battle with a single blow. Couching his lance, de Bohun thundered towards Scottish king. Calmly the Bruce faced the oncoming juggernaut. His horse was not the impressive *destrier* of the English knight but the nimbler palfrey of the Scottish guerrilla. Side-stepping at the last second, he parried de Bohun's weapon and brought his axe down on de Bohun's head. A fatal blow was served, and not the one de Bohun had anticipated. The Scots cheered at the great omen they had just witnessed, then advanced on the

---

[3] Barbour and Duncan, *The Bruce*, p.416; Lynch, *Scotland: A New History*, p.124. Again, the size is unknown. Barbour says 30,000; other historians place it as low as 3,500.
[4] Burns, *Scots Wha Hae*.
[5] Barbour and Duncan, *The Bruce*, pp.430-439.

disorganised English front who retreated to regroup.[6] Randolph also won his engagement, and as the afternoon turned into evening, the Bruce offered his leading men outright the opportunity to stay, or to go home in honour.[7]

> *Scots, wha hae wi' Wallace bled,*
> *Scots, wham Bruce has aften led;*
> *Welcome to your gory bed,*
> *Or to victory!*

The day's encounters had done more to bolster the Scots' morale than any number of eloquent words. That night Bruce received more good tidings, when a defector brought news of poor morale in the English camp.[8] Edward had ordered his entire army to flank the Scots, which had taken them off the dry road and into less suitable ground between the Forth and the Bannock Burn. They spent the night bridging the 'evil deep boggy stream' and preparing for a night attack.[9] Even at this late stage, the Bruce had contemplated the possibility of a tactical retreat in the face of the superior force before him, but the defector's news crystallised the decision. There would be a fight next day.

---

[6] Barbour and Duncan, *The Bruce*, pp.448-453.
[7] *Ibid,* pp.456-465.
[8] Linklater, *Robert The Bruce*, p.127.
[9] Barbour and Duncan, *The Bruce*, pp.466-469.

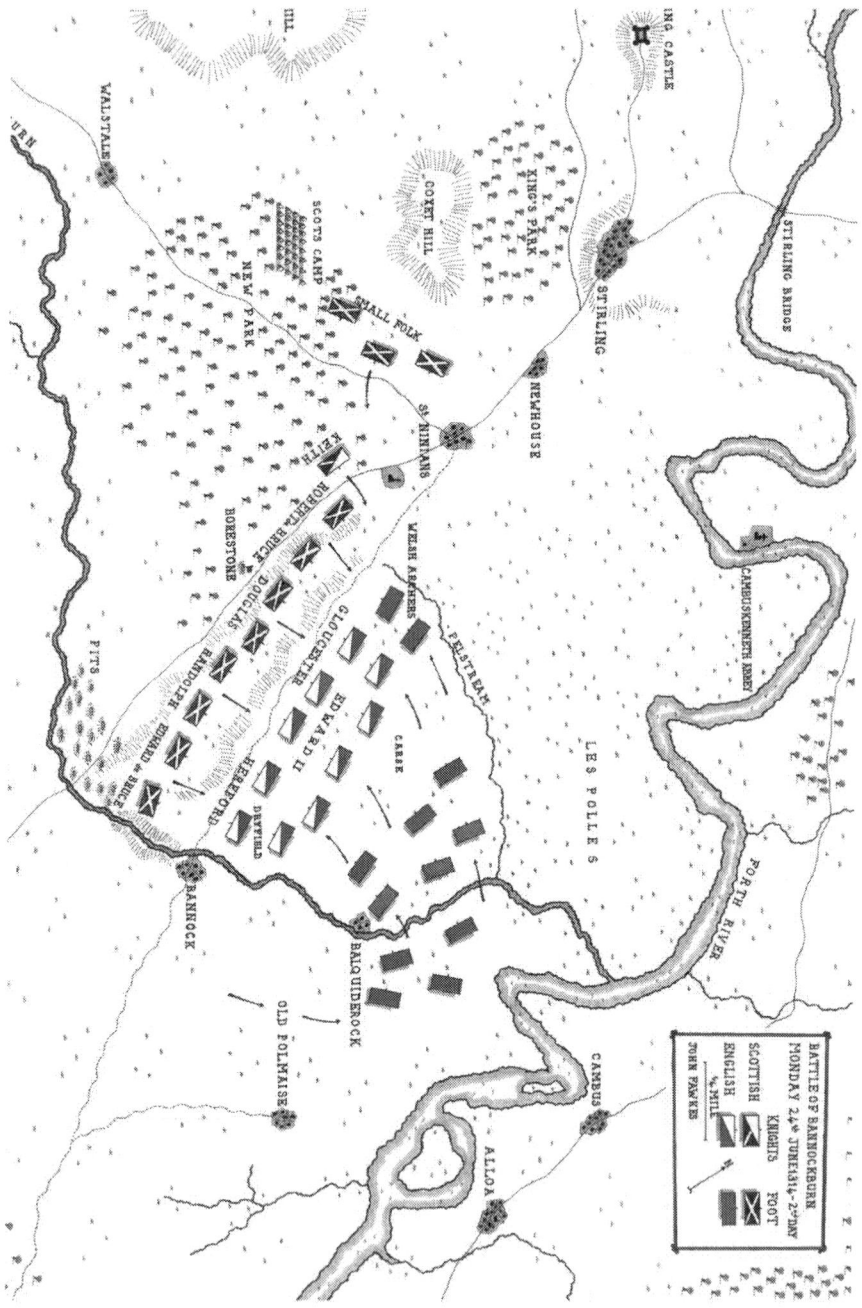

Figure 13: Battle of Bannockburn, Day 2. © Britishbattles.com

On the morning of 24 June the Scots heard mass early, kneeling on the ground in front of their priests. "Look," Edward II is reported to have said, "they ask for our mercy!"

"Nay sire," came the reply, "they seek the Lord's forgiveness for what they are about to do..."[10]

> *By oppression's woes and pains!*
> *By our sons in servile chains!*
> *We will drain our dearest veins,*
> *But they shall be free!*

Bruce's army then rolled downhill in three divisions. Edward Bruce led the front division, Randolph the next, King Robert the rear, three Scottish divisions against Edward II's nine.[11] By the time Randolph's brigade arrived the English knights were already being pressed back onto their men who, thanks to their disposition on the field, had no room for manoeuvre. Edward had also failed to deploy his archers effectively. Those bowmen who did manage to take up a strong position against the Scottish left flank were mown down by light cavalry led by Keith.[12]

For an hour the two lines remained locked in a desperate struggle. But then the English rear started to retreat. Seeing how the day was going, Edward's household bodyguard dragged him from the field.[13] As the English king's standard departed the field, the Scots auxiliaries and baggage handlers appeared, intent on joining the fray.[14] It was the last straw, and defeat turned into a rout. Edward was chased all the way to Dunbar where he boarded a ship for England.[15] Some fled to Bothwell which immediately surrendered to the Scots.[16] So many English nobles were captured that their ransom brought riches to the victors: an especially welcome bounty, as eighteen years

---

[10] Barbour and Duncan, *The Bruce*, pp.472-3.
[11] *Ibid*, pp.474-479. Barbour describes four Scottish divisions, with the fourth commanded by Douglas and Walter Stewart; other sources mention only three.
[12] *Ibid*, pp.482-5.
[13] *Ibid,* pp.494-5.
[14] *Ibid,* pp.490-493.
[15] *Ibid,* pp.508-513.
[16] *Ibid,* pp.500-501.

of scorched earth policy from both sides had wreaked havoc on Southern Scotland. Robert swapped the Earl of Hereford, Edward II's brother-in-law, for Bishop Wishart and the ladies who had been captured after Kildrummy – Bruce's wife Elizabeth, daughter Marjorie, and sister Christina.[17] And amongst the captured Englishmen was Sir Marmaduke Tweng, who had made a remarkable fighting escape from Wallace at the Battle of Stirling Brig seventeen years earlier. The Bruce treated him to a banquet and safe passage home.[18]

Edward had brought the bigger army, but the Bruce's well-drilled men and skilful use of ground had carried the day. For the Bruce this was to be the most significant victory of his life, and for Scots ever since, Bannockburn would become totemic. They had proven they could, at least once, beat the English in the open field, a result that meant the Scots would no longer be subject to English rule. As John Barbour wrote:

> A! Fredome is a noble thing
> Fredome mays man to haiff liking;
> Fredome all solace to man giffis:
> He levys at es that frely levys.[19]

The Irish Front

Bruce had won a famous victory, but the war would not be won until Edward withdrew his claim on Scotland, and acknowledged the Bruce and his successors as King of Scots. And so the fight was taken to the enemy.

By land, the North of England had already suffered and would continue to suffer Scottish raids. English borderers, particularly from Tynedale, compounded the misery by falling on their fellow countryfolk. By sea, privateers were active, and by 1314 both Scots and Flemish privateers preyed on English shipping, which had to travel in convoy for protection.[20]

---

[17] Barbour and Duncan, *The Bruce*, pp.514-517; *Foedera Vol I*, p.184.
[18] *Ibid*, pp.506-509.
[19] *Ibid*, p.57.
[20] Davidson, *Scots and the Sea*, p.23.

Diplomatically, the offensive was renewed at the court of the Pope. And Ireland too would suffer the aftermath of Edward's defeat at Bannockburn.

Anglo-Norman land grabbers had been in Ireland since 1169, when Diarmaid MacMurrough invited them to help defeat his enemy, the High King of Ireland. Now Domnall O'Neill of Tyrone saw a similar chance. He wrote to Robert the Bruce with an irresistible offer: O'Neill support, in return for removing the English from Ireland. Fine words were talked of a pan-Celtic alliance. The Bruce family may have been part Norman in origin, but they were part Gael as well, and Robert looked even further into the future, imagining Ireland as a stepping stone for a Scottish invasion of Wales. Robert's only surviving brother, Edward Bruce, was nominated High King of Ireland. Supported by O'Neill and Randolph, he landed at Larne in 1315.[21] The Normans in Ireland had not yet had to deal with a commander experienced in the Scottish wars; and Edward Bruce defeated them at Carrickfergus, Coleraine, Dundalk and Kells.[22] Dublin was only saved by the Governor ordering houses and churches be razed to build a defensive wall. [23]

But though the Scots ran rampant across the countryside, they neglected to dislodge the Anglo-Normans in their castles, who simply retook their lands after the Scots passed through. Worse was to follow. A great famine passed through Europe between 1315 and 1317.[24] At home the hungry Scots raided the North of England, magnifying their enemy's woes: but in Ireland, Bruce's army ate itself to defeat. The Scots sustained themselves from the local countryside, leaving Irish peasants to starve. This was not how a High King would act towards his people: what was Edward Bruce to the Irish, but just another half-Norman adventurer seeking to exploit them? Bruce's support melted away and his army shrank. At Faughart in Louth, on 14 October 1318, he decided to engage a superior force and was defeated and killed.[25] A small strategic victory had been won: no more was Ireland used as a

---

[21] Sadler, *Border Fury*, pp.140-141.
[22] Barbour and Duncan, *The Bruce*, pp.520-563.
[23] McNamee, *The Wars of the Bruces*, p.182.
[24] Lucas, "The Great European Famine of 1315, 1316, and 1317" *Speculum*, 5(4), pp.343-377.
[25] Barbour and Duncan, *The Bruce*, pp.666-677.

springboard for English attacks on Western Scotland. But Robert the Bruce had lost his last brother. They had all been killed in his fight for the throne.

And there was plenty more fighting to be done.

Berwick Regained

The last Scottish town in English hands was Berwick. It was besieged and retaken in April, 1318, and Berwick Castle in June.[26] King Edward immediately started planning Berwick's recapture, and in 1319 he arrived with the Earl of Lancaster to attack the newly installed Scots. But rather than face an English army directly, Bruce sent Randolph and Douglas across the border to harry and burn down to Yorkshire, despoiling the home territories of many of the lords present at the siege of Berwick. As Edward's Queen Isabella was in York, rumour spread that the Scots intended to capture her. She was moved further south to Nottingham, and the Bishop of York raised a force to check the Scottish advance. But all the proper soldiers were at the siege of Berwick. The Bishop met the Scots at Myton, ten miles north of York, where his makeshift army was massacred. When news of this defeat came to Berwick, the Earl of Lancaster and other northern lords immediately headed south to succour their own lands and relieve York.[27] The Scots slipped back over the border by a different route, their plan to relieve the siege of Berwick successful.

The Declaration of Arbroath

By the end of the 1319, a two-year truce was agreed, and the Scots could focus their attention on reclaiming support from the Pope. In the spring of 1320, the nobility gathered at Arbroath, where they added their seals to a magnificent document composed under the supervision of Abbot Bernard. This stirring document put King Robert on a warning: should he go against the people of Scotland and submit to the rule of the English king, they would find another champion. In an age of feudalism, of personal loyalty to a distant monarch of a different race, such national, and democratic sentiments appear on the surface to be surprisingly advanced:

---

[26] Barbour and Duncan, *The Bruce*, pp.616-629.
[27] Sadler, *Border Fury*, pp.147-149.

Yet if he should give up what he has begun, seeking to make us or our
kingdom subject to the King of England or the English, we shall exert
ourselves at once to drive him out as our enemy and make some other
man who was well able to defend us our King. For so long as one
hundred of us remain alive, we shall in no way submit to the dominion
of the English. In truth it is not for glory, nor riches, nor honours that
we are fighting, but for freedom alone — which no honest man gives up
but with life itself.[28]

But the Declaration had a hidden purpose: it was as much a justification of deeds already done, as a manifesto for the future. Robert the Bruce was only on the throne because he himself had deposed a king. With the Declaration, the Scots were letting the Pope know that this was how things were going to be from now on.

In England, the Earl of Lancaster was frustrated at his king, and he was not alone in thinking like Duns Scotus: if the English king would not protect their interests, they would overthrow him. In 1321, Lancaster raised the northern Earls. But those who answered his call were beaten at Burton-on-Trent, and as they retreated north to Boroughbridge in Yorkshire, Andrew Harcla cut off their retreat route. With Edward's royal army coming up from behind, Lancaster gave battle to Harcla and was defeated on 16 March 1322, then executed. Harcla was reported to have faced Lancaster 'in the Scottish fashion', using an army of mobile light horse and schiltrons, and was promoted to Earl of Carlisle for his loyalty to Edward.[29]

Edward's Nightgown

His enemy's blood in his nostrils, Edward II mustered a large army at Newcastle with the intention of building on the momentum against the Earl of Lancaster. The Scots, who had been raiding the north of England since the start of the year, would be taught a lesson too. On 12 August 1322 he entered Scotland, plundering Holyrood and Melrose Abbeys and burning Dryburgh.[30] Bruce called an army together at Culross and repeated his

---

[28] NRS, *Transcription And Translation Of The Declaration Of Arbroath.*
[29] Sadler, *Bannockburn: Battle For Liberty*, p.116.
[30] Skene and Skene, *John of Fordun's Chronicle of the Scottish Nation*, p.342.

scorched earth policy in the Borders and Lothian to deny forage and sustenance to the English, while their seaborne supplies were plundered by Flemish and Scottish privateers.[31] On coming across a lame cow near Tranent, the only thing they had found in a hundred miles they could eat, the Earl of Surrey remarked it was the dearest beef he had ever yet seen.[32] The formidable but slow-moving English army retreated, suffering from hunger and dysentery, having achieved nothing but a large bill of expenses. They were harried over the border by Douglas, while Bruce marched down by the Solway and Eden to Yorkshire. His army moved fast and carried little, with no great baggage trains, no siege engines; for sustenance they cooked animals in their own skins and carried bags of oatmeal, making oatcakes when they stopped for the night.[33] The Scots arrived in Northallerton to learn that Edward was resting only 20 miles away at Rievaulx; they advanced to find a detachment of the English army standing in their way on the Hambleton Hills. On 14 October 1322 Douglas and Randolph conducted a frontal assault while Bruce directed his Highlanders to climb a precipitous slope and charge the surprised English on their flank; they then ran, according to a contemporary source, 'as a hare before greyhounds.'[34] Simultaneously Bruce sent Walter Stewart with 500 horsemen to capture Edward, who was alerted of the danger in the nick of time. Not even having time to dress he fled for the safety of the walled city of York clad only in a nightshirt, leaving behind a rich haul of baggage and ransomable nobles.[35] The Scots took Edward's booty and, not having siege engines for an attack on York, extracted blackmail from North Yorkshire before heading home.[36]

This was the final straw for the new Earl of Carlisle, who was as concerned as the Earl of Lancaster had been about his king's ability to protect him and his tenants. Before long Harcla entered into negotiations with Bruce,

---

[31] Sadler, *Border Fury*, p.152.
[32] Barbour and Duncan, *The Bruce*, pp.680-1.
[33] *Ibid*, pp.710-711.
[34] Maxwell, *Scalacronica*, p.69.
[35] Barbour and Duncan, *The Bruce*, pp.690-697.
[36] Barrow, *Robert Bruce And The Community Of The Realm Of Scotland*, p.318.

concluding a treaty on 3 January 1323. For this he was arrested by Edward and executed for treason.[37]

A Woman Scorned

And now Edward's deadliest enemy of all plotted against him: his wife Isabella. She was as wounded by the liberties taken by his male favourites as his earls were by his lack of leadership ability. When Charles IV of France insisted Edward II travel to France to do homage for Aquitaine, Edward demurred. Isabella suggested that he send their son instead, also Edward. The king agreed to this and Isabella travelled with young Edward, setting up court at Hainaut. Taking Roger de Mortimer for a lover, she promised her son in marriage to the daughter of the Count of Hainaut in return for assistance in overthrowing her husband. English lords started to cross the Channel, publicly as emissaries, but privately to join her side. The Count of Hainaut gave Isabella an army and when she landed in Suffolk in 1326 Edward was caught unawares.[38] The London mob showed favour to Isabella, and Edward fled with his favourites to Wales where he was captured. The King of England was eventually killed: a grisly legend claims it was through 'a red hot-poker being thrust up into his bowels.'[39]

The new king Edward III was only fourteen. Isabella and Mortimer took charge of his affairs: and dealing with Scotland was back on the agenda.

Will o' the Wisp

With the reinvigorated English refusing to acknowledge his kingship, Bruce marched to the border in 1327. Edward III moved north to greet him, fortified by men-at-arms from Hainault that alone had cost him £41,000.[40] Edward's forces outnumbered the Scots by two or three to one but the Scots were more manoeuvrable, seeming to shift around like mist. The English knew there was a Scottish army at large in northern England as they came across burned and devastated lands, yet could not pin them down. They camped for a week at Haydon Bridge in torrential rain, swords rusting and

---

[37] Sadler, *Border Fury*, pp.160-163.
[38] *Ibid,* pp.159-160.
[39] Doherty, *Isabella and the Strange Death of Edward II*, p.129.
[40] Rogers, *War Cruel And Sharp*, p.23.

horse leather rotting, their potentially deadly new weapon, cannon, rendered unusable by the terrible weather. In frustration, Edward promised a knighthood and land to any scout who could bring news of the Scots. Men fanned out in search, and Thomas Rokeby was captured by Douglas. On hearing of Edward's reward, Douglas let Rokeby return to claim it, telling him the Scots would wait for the English at Stanhope Park in Weardale.[41] Edward was delighted. At last he would bring the Scots to battle and crush them!

On 1 August 1327 the armies faced up against each other for what would be a four-day showdown. English bowmen sneaked round the rear of the Scots to catch them from behind. Douglas had anticipated this and hid a body of horse to ambush any flanking move. As the archers approached, he rode out alone intending to act as a decoy. But the English recognised the lone horseman as the Black Douglas and, such was his reputation for trickery, the archers prudently fled, Douglas' men at their heels.[42]

The Scots had taken up a strong position; Edward's heralds challenged them to come down onto the plain, but the Scots refused:[43] and on the night of 3 August they stoked their campfires to conceal a manoeuvre. Come morning the English saw they had struck camp and moved to an even better position above the English lines. Edward spent the day improving his own position. But the next night Douglas attacked the English rear with a small force, getting as far as Edward's tent, starting up the shout *'A Douglas! A Douglas!'* which caused rank panic in the camp: the king's bodyguard repelled the surprise attack and Douglas withdrew.[44]

The next day, the Scots telegraphed that there would be another attack the following night. The English dug in.

On the night of 4 August, the Scots left a few men behind to make a racket, whilst the rest of the army slipped away back home.[45] On seeing the empty

---

[41] Sadler, *Border Fury*, p.170.
[42] Barbour and Duncan, *The Bruce*, pp.716-723.
[43] Linklater, *Robert The Bruce*, p.162.
[44] Sadler, *Border Fury*, p.171.
[45] Barbour and Duncan, *The Bruce*, pp.730-739.

field before him on the fifth day, Edward screamed and cried in frustration.[46] After being kept so long in the field, his expensive army was disbanded having achieved nothing. The teenage king was learning the art of war the hard way from a master tactician.

As soon as Randolph and Douglas returned home, Bruce ordered them back over the border: his stated aim was the annexation of Northumbria, and he had arranged a pact of neutrality with Edward's Irish peers. So in September 1327, as the Scots were besieging Norham, Alnwick, and Warkworth, the English sent the flag of truce to negotiate a peace.[47] This was unexpected but welcome: all Bruce had wanted was recognition of his crown. The negotiations took place at Newcastle, and the Treaty of Edinburgh-Northampton was signed by the Scots in March 1328 in Holyrood Abbey. England formally renounced all claim on Scotland and recognised Robert I, his heirs and successors, as rightful monarchs of Scotland. It was the fulfilment of Bruce's life's work. He had a young son called David, born in 1324, and as part of the peace treaty, David was betrothed to be married to Edward III's young sister Joan.[48]

The War Won

The Bruce lived another year, his victory complete. He moved to a manor at Cardross, and spent his final year peacefully sailing up and down the Clyde.[49] When he died in 1329, the nobility ensured a smooth transition of power to his son David. Yet lurking over the border and in France were the exiled friends, family and supporters of the Balliol and Comyn families. They had been forced to flee abroad by Robert the Bruce, who had parcelled out their estates to his own loyal followers. And they didn't recognise the arguments of Duns Scotus or the Declaration of Arbroath. Because they could not get beyond the fact that by the laws of primogeniture, the legitimate King of Scots had been John Balliol.

And Balliol also had a son.

---

[46] Sadler, *Border Fury*, p.171.
[47] *Ibid*, pp.171-172.
[48] Barbour and Duncan, *The Bruce*, pp.742-749.
[49] Linklater, *Robert The Bruce*, pp.168-169.

CHAPTER TEN

The Second War of Independence

On his deathbed, Robert requested Douglas carry his heart into battle against 'God's foes' to atone for an unfulfilled ambition to go on Crusade. Douglas cut the dead king's heart out, placed it round his neck in a silver casket, and travelled to the Continent.

Brave Heart

Douglas' first chance to fulfil the king's last wish was a fight in Spain, which had been conquered by North Africans centuries earlier. At the Battle of Teba in 1330, Douglas was given command of a division. Accounts of what happens next differ; tradition says that, in his eagerness to engage the Moors, he galloped too far ahead of his supporting soldiers. Realising the situation he turned back; and saw another Scottish knight surrounded and outnumbered. Douglas went to his aid, galloping onward towards certain death.[1] A later story, almost certainly invention, has Douglas tear the silver casket from his neck, and fling it towards the enemy saying:

"Lead on, brave heart, as thou were ever wont to do!"[2]

It seems a rash act for such a cunning and experienced commander, but a violent end is surely the most fitting for Sir James Douglas.

In the same year Edward III, now eighteen and come of age, overthrew his mother to rule in his own right. There were some men very interested to gain an audience: supporters of Balliol, who believed they were owed titles and estates in Scotland. They called themselves the Disinherited. The inheritor of the old Comyn Earldom of Buchan, Henry de Beaumont, was determined

---

[1] Maxwell, *A History Of The House Of Douglas*, pp.62-63.
[2] *Ibid*, p.63.

to take possession of his lands. He put his case to Edward III and the son of the Scottish King John, Edward Balliol. A plan was agreed: Balliol would give homage to the English king as his father had done. In return, he would gain English assistance in regaining Scotland. Edward III offered an army of Welsh longbowmen and Beaumont, Balliol, David de Strathbogie, and other figures of the Disinherited prepared an invasion to regain Balliol's inheritance.[3]

Edward the First, King of Scots

Robert the Bruce's hard-won legacy outlasted him by a few brief years. James Douglas was dead; Bruce's other trusted lieutenant Thomas Randolph died at Musselburgh in 1332 making preparations to resist Balliol's invasion.[4] With Bruce, Randolph and Douglas gone, Scotland found itself in the indifferent hands of Donald, the Earl of Mar, who on 2 August 1332 was made regent on Randolph's death. Mar was a relative of the Bruce, but he had grown up in England and had not been hardened in war like his countrymen. His rapid promotion based on blood, rather than ability, would prove fatal. Henry de Beaumont sailed from the Humber in eighty-eight boats containing the Disinherited and a borrowed army. They landed in Fife and marched on Donald's army camped at Dupplin Moor near Perth, which at the crucial moment fell into disarray, quarrelling over leadership.[5] The enterprising de Beaumont had arranged his archers in an innovative funnel formation, and the leaderless Scots marched into this deadly trap on 11 August. Donald was killed and chaos and rout ensued. Parts of Galloway rose for Balliol, and a second Scottish army marching to aid Mar was diverted away to deal with the south-west.[6]

Balliol took the opportunity to crown himself King Edward I of Scots in September 1332. But except for the Disinherited, the Scots were hostile. When the Disinherited dispersed to their estates and the army lent to him by Edward III marched back south, Balliol became vulnerable. On the night of 16 December he was surprised at Annan by the new generation of Scottish

---

[3] Sadler, *Border Fury*, pp.183-185.
[4] Barbour and Duncan, *The Bruce*, pp.772-773.
[5] Brown, *The Second Scottish Wars Of Independence,* p.28.
[6] Sadler, *Border Fury*, p.188.

leaders, Robert the Stewart, John Randolph, and Archibald Douglas. They chased the Pretender over the border in his shirt-tails, 'one shank booted and the other bare,' and killed his heir, his younger brother Henry.[7]

By February 1333, the Bruce faction was fully in control again. A new Guardian was appointed, Archibald Douglas, who besieged and retook Berwick. It was clear that if Balliol was to have any further success, Edward III would have to get personally involved. The English Parliament, stung by recent defeats at the hands of Robert the Bruce, refused to grant their king money to wage a Scottish war, but Edward raised the feudal levies anyway, diverted the exchequer, and set up his capital in York.[8] His real desire was to attack France, but he couldn't risk it until the Scottish front was secured. Like a Roman Emperor of old, he ended up stuck in York for several years.

Halidon Hill

Edward III led an army in person back into Scotland, preceded by Edward Balliol who besieged Berwick. The defenders of Berwick agreed to an honourable surrender if succour did not come by 11 July. To guarantee the surrender, Berwick's defender Sir Alexander Seton was required to hand over hostages including his son Thomas. Archibald Douglas marched on Berwick, bypassed it for Northumberland, and besieged Bamburgh. But if he planned to repeat an earlier success in distracting the English from Berwick it was a vain hope. When 11 July came and the Scots hadn't surrendered, the English started to execute two hostages a day within sight of the town walls, starting with Seton's son Thomas. Douglas felt compelled to return, a move which allowed Edward III to choose his ground. It was to prove disastrous.[9]

The two armies met on 19 July 1333. It must have been obvious to Douglas that the terrain was bad: to reach the English, the Scots had to cross a bog then march uphill. Yet it was that or lose Berwick. With none of the cunning of his brother, the famous Black Douglas, Archibald chose the former action, gambling his entire army on a frontal assault of the English position.

[7] Sadler, *Border Fury*, p.189.
[8] Brown, *The Second Scottish Wars Of Independence*, p.37.
[9] Sadler, *Border Fury*, pp.190-192.

Caught in the bog, they were fatally weakened by arrows, and eventually broke and fled.[10] It was a restoration of English pride, their first victory on British soil for decades, a disaster for Scotland whose nobles largely lay dead on the field, including Archibald Douglas. Victory seemed so complete to Edward III that after accepting the capitulation of Berwick, laying waste a large swathe of Southern Scotland, and arranging the recapture of the Isle of Man, he headed back to York, confident that Edward Balliol could complete the job and run Scotland for him.

But one crushing victory in battle does not alone win a war.

Balliol held a Parliament at Edinburgh in February 1334, whose main business was the acknowledgement of the overlordship of the English king.[11] The followers of the Bruce faction did not attend. Crucially, these men were loyal not just to the young King David II, but to the concept of Scotland, or 'the Lion', as a nation in its own right.[12] The original Disinherited had no such loyalty, and once they had achieved the restoration of their estates, their interest in Balliol's cause waned spectacularly. In fact, after quarrelling over who should possess the vacant estate of the ejected patriot Alexander Mowbray, de Beaumont retired to his castle of Dundarg in Buchan and refused to entertain Balliol.[13] Balliol was losing the support of the Disinherited, ruining his chance of holding Scotland without a permanent presence of English arms.

The People vs Edward Balliol

David II remained safely locked away, but Scotland was no place for a child king with an adult rival, and so in 1334 his regents sent him to sanctuary in France. He was not needed: even without the presence of their king, the Scots rejected Balliol as a foreign body. MacDonald, Lord of the Isles teamed up with patriots in Ayrshire and Renfrewshire to deny Balliol a hold on the west coast.[14] Garrisons loyal to Balliol or Edward III remained stoppered up in their castles, expensive and ineffective. And now the Scots finally had

---

[10] Maxwell, *A History Of The House Of Douglas*, pp.74-75.
[11] RPS, *1334/1*.
[12] MacInnes, *Scotland's Second War Of Independence*, p.25.
[13] Skene and Skene, *John of Fordun's Chronicle of the Scottish Nation*, p.349.
[14] Davidson, *Scots and the Sea*, p.24.

access to siege technology. In the latter half of 1334 Sir Andrew Murray, Guardian of Scotland as his father had been in the time of Wallace, besieged de Beaumont at Dundarg. Dundarg was captured, levelled, and de Beaumont exiled to England. He would never see Scotland again. Balliol was forced to retire to Berwick, and David de Strathbogie coerced into switching sides.[15] The Scots had not been prevented from maintaining the upper hand in numerous smaller affairs despite the loss of two big battles at Dupplin Moor and Halidon Hill. Even at sea they became notorious pirates of English shipping, whose naval capability was greater, but was needed to protect the south coast against raids from France.[16]

Realising that Balliol still needed help, the English king arranged a serious invasion force for the summer of 1335. Half the army entered Scotland via Berwick with Edward I of Scots, and the rest via Carlisle with Edward III of England. They met at Glasgow, then continued together up to Perth. Well aware of the damage an English army could inflict in the field – Dupplin and Halidon were painfully recent memories – John Randolph contented himself with harrying supply lines and refused to engage in battle, burning the country as he retreated.[17] Edward III forced several nobles to surrender and give fealty: Robert Stewart did so reluctantly, David de Strathbogie enthusiastically. Randolph defeated a band of knights led by Guy, Count of Namur, who was in Scotland for no reason other than the opportunity of chivalric adventure; but on escorting his vanquished enemy to the border, Randolph was captured by English forces.[18]

The Battle of Culblean
With Robert Stewart temporarily under the obligation of Edward III, and Randolph captured, the defence of Scotland was left in the hands of Sir Andrew Murray. While the two King Edwards were at large in Southern Scotland, David de Strathbogie was active in the north, attempting to eradicate freeholders, those small landowners and farmers who were the backbone of Scottish resistance. In November 1335 he besieged Kildrummy

---

[15] MacInnes, *Scotland's Second War Of Independence*, p.19.
[16] Davidson, *Scots and the Sea*, p.24.
[17] Sadler, *Border Fury*, p.198.
[18] *Ibid*, p.199.

Castle, held by Andrew Murray's wife Christina. On hearing of this, Murray galloped to her aid with a tiny force of only eight hundred, a quarter of Strathbogie's force. But Murray was joined by a Donside man, John Craig, who led them round the side of Strathbogie's force by local ways, and by William Douglas, who approached Strathbogie's front, showed himself, and appeared to hesitate, precipitating a charge by Strathbogie. When the Disinherited force reached a burn their battle order broke and Douglas attacked while simultaneously, Murray appeared and took them on the flank. Despite Strathbogie's superior numbers, it was a rout. Refusing to surrender, he stood with his back to an oak and fought on until he was killed.[19]

The battle had been small in scale, but big in significance: Balliol's last supporter in the north was dead. The Bruce's wisdom of destroying castles now bore fruit: there was nowhere in Scotland well-enough fortified for Edward Balliol to be safe, and he saw in the New Year in Yorkshire.[20]

La Vieux Alliance

If one act had sparked the Wars of Independence, it was the 1296 pact with France of mutual support against English aggression. Now France threatened to raise sail in Scotland's cause. Edward Plantagenet rode north again in 1336 in an attempt to deny them any ports, subjecting the whole north-east coast to 'all-devouring flames,'[21] as his brother rode through the west, consuming it with fire and sword.[22] Scotland was deliberately devastated, fields burned, houses destroyed, and the castles refortified. But even as the English armies penetrated into Scotland and destroyed the harvest, a mixture of French and Scottish privateers captured and harassed English shipping off the east coast and the Channel Islands.[23] Never mind a French invasion via Scotland: English emissaries now feared a direct invasion across the Channel. They wrote to Edward, who returned to

---

[19] Laing, *The Orygynale Cronykil Of Scotland, Vol II*, pp.422-427.
[20] Maxwell, *The Chronicle Of Lanercost*, p.95.
[21] Barbour and Duncan, *The Bruce*, p.352.
[22] *Ibid*, p.353.
[23] MacInnes, *Scotland's Second War Of Independence*, pp.94-96.

England to organise its defence.[24] Without having actually landed any troops, French pressure caused Edward III to abandon Scotland.

As soon as the English king left, the Scots went on the offensive. Murray captured and levelled the castles of Dunnottar and plundered Balliol's heartland around Perth and north Fife. In 1337, St Andrews Castle fell to Murray's 'boustour' siege engine, and Murray's own castle of Bothwell in Lanarkshire was retaken and deliberately ruined. All Balliol could do was ride out from Perth and devastate Strathmore.[25] With Scotland being laid waste by both sides, famine stalked the land. Legend tells of a butcher from Perth, Christie Cleek, who along with his friends survived by ambushing passers-by and eating them.[26] Edward III found it increasingly hard to raise enthusiasm amongst his nobles for the situation in Scotland which offered neither profit, plunder nor romance.[27] His Scottish ally Patrick, Earl of Dunbar, whose support was based on entirely pragmatic grounds, had found he could not prevent hungry English garrisons devastating his lands, and had switched back to the Scottish side a couple of years earlier.[28] Scottish forces now entered England, and laid Cumberland and Coquetdale to waste.[29] With his focus taken up by France, Edward sent the Earl of Salisbury, William Montagu to attack Scotland. He achieved nothing except an expensive, drawn-out siege of Dunbar.

Black Agnes

In January 1338, Montagu initiated the siege of Dunbar Castle, a preliminary move in support of yet another invasion attempt by Edward Balliol. The castle was held by Randolph's sister 'Black' Agnes, Countess of Dunbar, in the name of her husband Patrick who was out in the field supporting Murray. She withstood the siege for nineteen weeks, before Montagu realised Dunbar Castle was too difficult to take by land and requested a fleet. The fleet brought heavy siege machinery and bombarded the castle. To mock the damage caused by the bombardment, Agnes sent the maids of the castle

---

[24] *Foedera Vol I*, p.285.
[25] Barbour and Duncan, *The Bruce*, pp.353-354.
[26] Laing, *The Orygynale Cronykil Of Scotland, Vol II*, p.455.
[27] Brown, *The Second Scottish Wars Of Independence*, p.104.
[28] MacInnes, *Scotland's Second War Of Independence*, p.55.
[29] Sadler, *Border Fury*, p,207.

dressed in their best clothes to walk the parapets and make a show of dusting the walls with white handkerchiefs. As Salisbury brought up his siege engine 'the Sow' to bear upon the castle gate, Agnes had her own counter-siege fling huge stones, shattering the Sow and all within. But behind the bravado was genuine concern: the defenders were running low on food. Up stood one of Scotland's boldest knights, Sir Alexander Ramsay, who gathered a flotilla of fishing boats, loaded them with provisions, and appeared off Bass Rock at dawn apparently fishing. Under the nose of the English blockade they made a dash for Dunbar harbour and successfully resupplied the garrison. Next morning, Agnes presented a hamper of fresh bread and wine to Montagu, who was himself running low on food. Enraged, Montagu brought Agnes' brother Randolph to the field. With a noose around his neck, the English threatened to execute him if she did not surrender. But Agnes was too smart for this. "Go ahead," she said, "kill him and I inherit his earldom!"

Montagu had one more trick to play. He bribed a castle porter to let the English in by a postern gate. But the porter was working a double bluff and had, with the connivance of Agnes, laid a trap. The Earl of Salisbury was nearly captured, and as he fled Agnes mockingly shouted:

"Adieu, adieu, Monsieur Montagu!"[30]

After six fruitless months Montagu realised the siege could continue indefinitely, and returned home.

Scotland suffered yet as Murray and Stewart ruthlessly extirpated any Balliol supporters, leaving behind a trail of destruction and hunger. The last of them surrendered at Perth in 1339, French ships beating off English reinforcements.[31]

The Hundred Years War
In the meantime, a matter of great succour to Scotland occurred. In 1337 Philippe VI of France confiscated Edward III's lands in Gascony, which he held as Duke of Aquitaine but subordinate to the King of France. Edward, a close relative of the French king, retaliated by claiming that *he* was the

---

[30] Goring, *Scotland: Her Story*, paras.10.100-109.
[31] MacInnes, *Scotland's Second War Of Independence*, pp.36-37.

legitimate king of France. He crossed the Channel in 1338 to attack France and claim its crown. For Edward III, Scotland had been a proving ground for new types of warfare that would devastate the French. The importance of the longbow; the use of combined arms; the contract system of warfare; the psychological toll of the destruction of crops and murder of civilians; the English were battle-hardened for their French wars by fighting the Scots.[32]

The focus of English attention moved decisively away from her British neighbours and onto the bigger and more lucrative challenge of conquering France. This titanic battle occupied English kings on and off for over a hundred years, with periods of looting by English mercenaries on a scale not seen in France since the days of the Vikings. An important early naval encounter at Sluys in 1340 meant that the war would be fought on French rather than on English soil. Scotland would still come under occasional attack; but the persistent, unremitting attention that had conquered Wales and had nearly done for Scotland between 1296 and 1305 was now focused on France. The Scots had gained some breathing space.

The Battle of Neville's Cross

In 1341, David II reached his majority at the age of seventeen. It was time to return in glory to his kingdom that had been so doughtily defended by Murray, Stewart, Douglas, and hundreds of nameless freeholders. It seemed that the tide had turned for the Scots. In 1342 Stirling Castle was re-taken, and with only Berwick and Lochmaben remaining in English hands;[33] David raided Northumberland.[34] In 1345 he raided Northumberland again.[35] 1346 was shaping up for more of the same.

David had been back in Scotland for five years when he answered a cry of assistance from France. The siege of Calais was going badly for Philippe VI, who requested the Scots king open a second front to distract Edward III's attention.[36] From David's point of view, it was an opportunity to increase his influence in Northern England. The English garrisons in Southern

---

[32] Sadler, *Border Fury*, p.218.
[33] Lynch, *Scotland: A New History*, p.130.
[34] Sadler, *Border Fury*, pp.209-210.
[35] Sumption, *The Hundred Years War, Volume I*, p.499.
[36] Sadler, *Border Fury*, p.220.

Scotland, beleaguered as they were since 1335, had performed a valuable service to their countrymen by keeping war out of Northern England. If David wanted to stamp his authority over both his nobles and his southern neighbours, then a successful invasion and victory in a set-piece battle would do the trick.

So David obliged Philippe by leading an army of 12,000 into Northern England in October 1346.[37] He expected to encounter no serious organised resistance, but Edward III was no fool, and an army had been given time to prepare in Yorkshire. While at Durham, the Scots were surprised when Sir William Douglas hot-footed back from a raid to inform them of the imminent English approach.[38] David's lack of military experience now told. Rather than mobilise his force to maximise their ground, the King of Scots dallied. His army's position was poor: hemmed in by walls and a gorge of the River Wear, the arriving defenders realised they could command better ground. The two armies faced off. David's division engaged, but at the crucial moment, Patrick Dunbar and Robert Stewart withdrew from the field, a decision possibly coloured by the fact Stewart had been named David's successor should the king die childless. The king's division was left to face the brunt of the action. Randolph was killed and Douglas and the king captured.[39] David had already spent eleven years in exile in France, and was about to spend even more time as the unwilling guest of a foreign king.

Checkmate.

With their king in his power, Edward knew the Scots would not dare move against him. And there was a silver lining for the Scots. David was only a useful hostage if the English recognised his legitimacy. This recognition undermined Balliol's claim on the Scottish throne, and his campaign of 1347 accomplished nothing lasting.[40]

David's capture had come at a good time for Edward Plantagenet. He had captured Calais too. It would prove a beachhead for English attacks on

---

[37] Sadler, *Border Fury*, p.220.
[38] *Ibid*, p.222.
[39] *Ibid*, pp.224-227.
[40] Brown, *The Second Scottish Wars Of Independence*, pp.139-140.

France for the next 200 years, but the war had left England penniless. Peace with Scotland was guaranteed by his possession of their king, and a truce with France allowed England to rebuild its reserves, partaking in the far more profitable chevauchées than all-out warfare of conquest.

Though ambassadors shuttled to and fro to negotiate David's release, the Scots refused the offered terms that David should do homage for his kingdom to Edward III.[41] David would spend a further eleven years in captivity.

The Scots took their comforts where they could. The death of a third of England in a terrible plague called the Black Death proved one thing: God was punishing them for their king's wickedness.

The Black Death

The plague had entered Europe from the Mediterranean in 1347, brought by a ship fleeing a Mongol siege of Caffa in Crimea. Nobody knew how it spread. The answer, only discovered centuries later, was infected rat fleas: and the cramped, dirty conditions in which most Europeans lived, *the clartier the cosier*, were ideal breeding grounds. Historian John of Fordun wrote that 'nearly a third of mankind were made to pay the debt of nature.'[42]

Can you imagine the horror of that? One third of the whole of Europe dropping dead of a disease nobody knew how to prevent? In Siena in Italy, Agnolo di Tura wrote:

> *Giant pits are being excavated for the multitudes of the dead and the hundreds that die every night. The bodies are thrown into these mass graves and are covered bit by bit. When those ditches are full, new ditches are dug. And I, Agnolo di Tura, have buried five of my sons with my own hands... So many have died that everyone believes it is the end of the world.*[43]

---

[41] Duncan, "Honi Soit Qui Mal y Pense: David II and Edward III, 1346-52" *The Scottish Historical Review*, vol. 67, no. 184, 1988, pp.113–118.
[42] Skene and Skene, *John of Fordun's Chronicle of the Scottish Nation*, p.359.
[43] Aberth, *The Black Death*, p.81.

By 1348 it was England's turn. Priests in Scotland gloated from their pulpits about 'the foul English pestilence,'[44] which was clearly God's vengeance for English wickedness. With England ripe for invasion, a Scottish force assembled at Caddonlee near Selkirk intending to loot what they could from their prostate neighbour. But as the army gathered, disease broke out. Men panicked and dispersed. Instead of booty and slaves and captured nobles to ransom, the Scots returned to their local communities carrying the plague. It seemed that the Scots themselves were not immune from God's wrath.

So many peasants died in the Black Death that their scarcity changed the nature of feudal society. Where peasants were paid, the scarcity of labour increased their wages. Where they were paid in kind, they were able to move to find work with better conditions elsewhere.[45] Obligations to feudal lords became replaced with cash rents.[46] For the first time, in some parts of Europe at least, the use of money reached into every part of society.

Burnt Candlemas

In the midst of this great social change, David II was temporarily released from captivity to continue negotiating his release. He met Scottish ambassadors at York, at Newcastle, and in 1351, even travelled to Scotland.[47] Edward's demands of suzerainty had already been rejected, and David, perhaps knowing his Parliament would not accept, counter-offered his kingdom. The kingdom would remain intact and independent, but should David die childless, went the deal, Edward's younger son John of Gaunt would become King of Scotland. The Scottish delegation rejected these terms out of hand, and the hapless King of Scots remained in captivity.[48] Edward, alarmed at the stiffening effect French payments may be having on his northern enemies, prepared to invade again.[49] The Scots had recaptured Berwick, but fell back, burning the town, driving their cattle before them and

---

[44] Moffat, *The Borders: A History Of The Borders From Earliest Times*, p.219.

[45] Routt, *The Economic Impact Of The Black Death*, [online] Eh.net.

[46] Mackie, *A History Of Scotland*, pp.84-85.

[47] Duncan, "Honi Soit Qui Mal y Pense: David II and Edward III, 1346-52." *The Scottish Historical Review*, vol. 67, no. 184, 1988, p.121, 125-126.

[48] *Ibid*, p.128–132.

[49] Skene and Skene, *John of Fordun's Chronicle of the Scottish Nation*, pp.360-361.

laying waste their own fertile lands of the Merse and East Lothian.[50] Edward Balliol, childless and now in his seventies, arranged to meet Edward Plantagenet at Roxburgh Castle on 20 January 1356. In a dramatic gesture conveying utter defeat, he snatched off his crown, grabbed a sod of earth, and thrust them both into the English king's hands, abdicating, according to Fordun, with these words:

> *'I yield unto thee all right I have to the throne of Scotland... so that thou avenge me of my enemies, the Scottish nation; who have always cast me aside.'*[51]

Edward Balliol retired to France as his father had done before him.

Taking advantage of this unexpected development Edward III now claimed the crown of Scotland, marching north towards Scone intending to conduct his own coronation. He got as far as Haddington when news came that his provisioning fleet had been shipwrecked off North Berwick in a storm. The chroniclers reckoned this storm a divine intervention, the wrath of God smiting the English after a party of troops had desecrated a particularly sacred site dedicated to the Virgin Mary at Whitekirk.[52] The brutal scorched earth strategy of the Scots now proved its effectiveness. In losing his fleet Edward had lost the means to feed his army or any easy means of escape. With continued guerrilla resistance and bad winter weather hampering progress, and nothing for his army or the local inhabitants to eat anywhere in South-east Scotland, he elected to retire, burning anything the Scots had missed. This invasion became known as the 'Burnt Candlemas'.[53] It was Edward's fifth and final invasion of Scotland, as he became completely preoccupied with France where he was having more luck. In a stunning victory at Poitiers in September 1356, English forces captured French King

---

[50] Rankin, "Whitekirk and 'The Burnt Candlemas'" *The Scottish Historical Review*, vol. 13, no. 50, 1916, p.133.

[51] Skene and Skene, *John of Fordun's Chronicle of the Scottish Nation*, p363.

[52] Rankin, "Whitekirk and 'The Burnt Candlemas'" *The Scottish Historical Review*, vol. 13, no. 50, 1916, p.134.

[53] Skene and Skene, *John of Fordun's Chronicle of the Scottish Nation*, pp.363-365.

Jean II.[54] Edward III now had the pleasure of holding captive both the Scottish and French kings.

Double checkmate.

Edward III was at the height of his powers. These wars had cost him the immense fortune of 1.5m gold florins.[55] He had dealt with this problem by refusing to pay his bankers, and his creditors ended up in jail.[56] But now, along with ownership of the western side of France, he got 3m gold crowns for the release of Jean.[57] It was time to release the Scots king too.

A Royal Ransom

The Scots and English delegations met one final time at Berwick. Finally, on 7 October 1357, they agreed a price for David: 100,000 merks, payable over the next ten years, and a ten-year truce.[58] David II came home, and English garrisons remained in Berwick and Roxburgh castles.

The Scots had shown little urgency in arranging David's return, and the nobles, led by Robert Stewart, would actively rise against him: but the rebellion was not serious, and David reaffirmed his grip on the kingdom.[59] In 1363 David visited London as an ally, and was pressed by Edward III that the Scottish crown should pass to his son in return for waiving David's ransom fee.[60]

Once again, in 1364 the Scottish Estates rejected this arrangement, and made a determined decision to pay David's ransom in full,[61] which due to defaults had been increased to £100,000.[62] In order to assist this aim the value of Scottish land was reassessed. Thanks to decades of war, plague, and

---

[54] Skene and Skene, *John of Fordun's Chronicle of the Scottish Nation,* pp.365-366.
[55] Hunt, "A New Look at the Dealings of the Bardi and Peruzzi with Edward III" *The Journal of Economic History,* vol. 50, no. 1, 1990, pp. 149–162, says the exact amount is disputed.
[56] Freedland, *The Long View, Sovereign Debt And Default.* [online] BBC.
[57] *Foedera Vol I,* p.408.
[58] *Ibid,* p.392.
[59] Skene and Skene, *John of Fordun's Chronicle of the Scottish Nation,* pp.369-370.
[60] *Foedera Vol I,* p.430.
[61] RPS, *1364/1.*
[62] Mackie, *A History Of Scotland,* p.82.

deliberate destruction by both English and Scots armies, it became apparent that the land was worth only half of what it had been in the 13th century.[63] The third estate of Parliament, the royal burghs, were leaned upon to raise more money.

Compared to the 13th century, Scotland was a poorer place. It was the price she had paid to remain a sovereign nation in the face of English attack. And stirring as the story of Robert the Bruce at Bannockburn may be, it was the grinding wars of attrition fought by Randolph, Murray, Stewart and the Douglases that ensured Scotland's independence. Despite the absence and ineptitude of David II, despite the attentions of Edward Balliol and his band of Disinherited, despite the ravages of Edward Plantagenet, despite the Black Death, the nobles, burghers and commoners of Scotland had shown they could pull together in common cause. As in the old days of tanistry, when one regent or guardian fell, another immediately took his place. The Scots had lost some big battles in the open field; but their enemies had found Scotland impossible to govern, and had finally abandoned the war. But the cost of victory was immense. Cordiality with England had been replaced with mutual hostility, as the border counties, on both sides, became a semi-permanent warzone. Scottish nobles were barred from holding land in England. Scottish scholars were excluded from Oxford and Cambridge Universities. English privateers harassed Scottish shipping, making trade difficult, and fewer foreign merchants visited Scotland in the middle of the 14th century: at the start of David's reign, Scots exported 5,700 sacks of wool and 36,100 leather hides; by the time of his return from France in 1341, those figures had slightly more than halved.[64]

The Scots had earned their independence. It had come at a price.

The Last Bruce

When David returned in 1357 his Queen Joanna decided to remain in her homeland. Her death in 1362 was the trigger for the king to marry his mistress Margaret Drummond; and it had been the fear of a royal baby that caused Robert Stewart's rebellion. Yet eventually David tired of Margaret

---

[63] Mackie, *A History of Scotland*, p.82. Half secular; two-thirds clerical.
[64] Jillings, *Scotland's Black Death*, p.71.

and obtained a divorce, hoping to marry his latest mistress Agnes Dunbar.[65] Before this could happen, in February 1371 he died, childless, at the age of forty-seven.

Robert Stewart, who had been nominated in his infancy as stand-in for the throne as far back as 1318, finally became King of Scots. He founded the long-lived Stewart dynasty with whom Scotland's story, and eventually all of Britain and Ireland's, is intimately woven.

But first, the Stewarts had some barons to fight.

[65] Cannon and Hargreaves, *The Kings And Queens Of Britain,* pp.144-145.

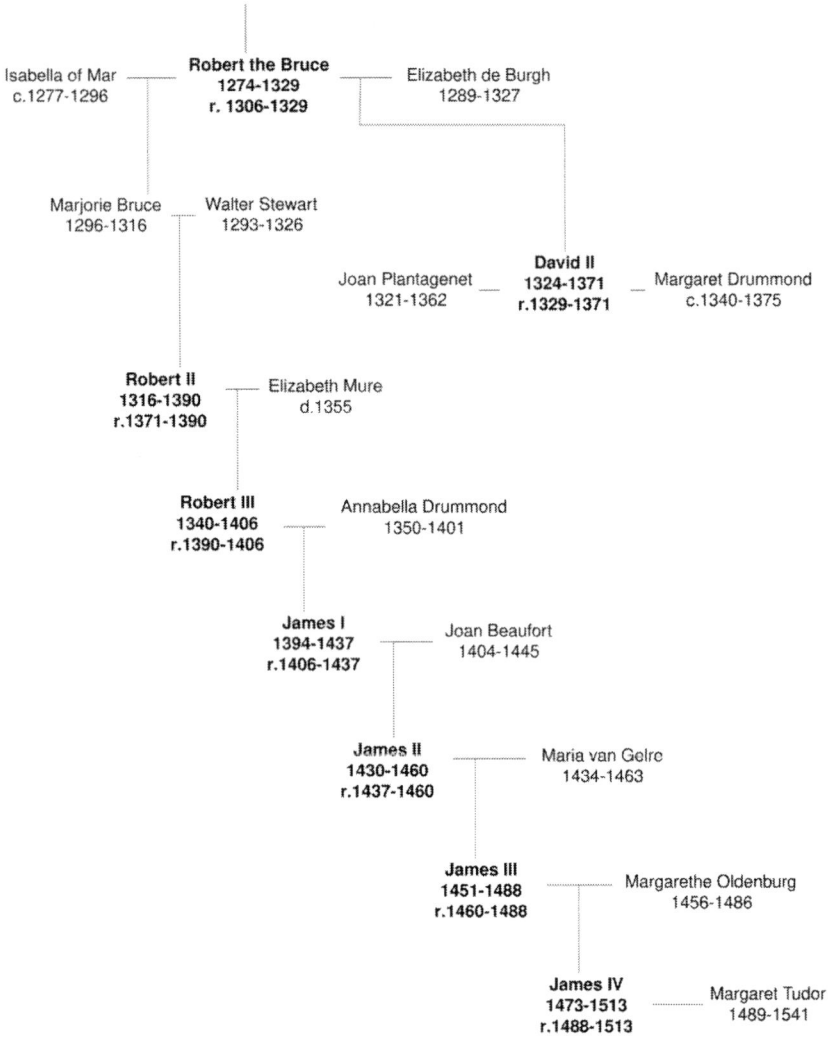

Isabella of Mar
c.1277-1296

Robert the Bruce
1274-1329
r. 1306-1329

Elizabeth de Burgh
1289-1327

Marjorie Bruce
1296-1316

Walter Stewart
1293-1326

Joan Plantagenet
1321-1362

David II
1324-1371
r.1329-1371

Margaret Drummond
c.1340-1375

Robert II
1316-1390
r.1371-1390

Elizabeth Mure
d.1355

Robert III
1340-1406
r.1390-1406

Annabella Drummond
1350-1401

James I
1394-1437
r.1406-1437

Joan Beaufort
1404-1445

James II
1430-1460
r.1437-1460

Maria van Gelre
1434-1463

James III
1451-1488
r.1460-1488

Margarethe Oldenburg
1456-1486

James IV
1473-1513
r.1488-1513

Margaret Tudor
1489-1541

Figure 14: The Stewart Dynasty

118

CHAPTER ELEVEN

Enter the Stewarts

Robert Stewart had waited a long time to ascend to the throne. As an infant he'd been named heir presumptive after Edward Bruce died in 1318. He'd been Guardian of Scotland in David's absence and youth. Now David was dead without issue.

His time had finally come. At the age of fifty-five, Robert Stewart was now King Robert II. His house would rule Scotland and then England and Ireland right up to 1714: even today, British monarchs bear his DNA.

The new Stewart dynasty would not suffer the same lack of heirs as the Bruces. From his mistresses and two wives Elizabeth Mure and Euphemia Ross, at least *twenty-three* of Robert's children reached adulthood.[1] John of Carrick, two Walters, Robert of Menteith, Alexander of Buchan, two Margarets, a Marjory, Johanna, Isabella, Katherine, two Elizabeths, David of Caithness, Egidia, and Thomas Bishop of St Andrews... The Stewarts were the veritable one-family football team. The Bruces had been a small family who sought support from other nobles. The Stewarts alone could fill most of the senior leadership positions within Scotland; within a generation, Robert's children controlled twelve of Scotland's sixteen Earldoms, either in their own right or by marrying men such as MacDonald of the Isles, the Earl of Douglas, or the Earl of March.[2]

Robert's approach was to promote peace with England. He avoided the Anglo-French wars and renewed truces each year to 1383. Meanwhile, the work of managing his kingdom and reclaiming those parts still held by the English was delegated to his sons and earls. The wars in France had turned sour for Edward III, who lost all his gains in France save the cities of Bordeaux, Bayonne, and Calais. The Scots followed the French example, and

---

[1] Weir, *Britain's Royal Families: The Complete Genealogy*, pp.216-228.
[2] Lynch, *Scotland: A New History*, p.138.

steadily reduced the English pale. In 1371 when Robert II took over, the castles of Berwick, Jedburgh, Roxburgh and Lochmaben remained in English hands, controlling the surrounding areas of Berwickshire, Teviotdale, and Annandale. Annandale was retaken in 1376 by Scotland's most able general, George Dunbar, the 10th Earl of March, and the rest of Southern Scotland followed; by 1381, parts of England such as Redesdale, Wark, and the contested town of Berwick were paying blackmail to the Scots. In 1377, 1381 and 1384, Berwick itself briefly fell, and Teviotdale came under Scottish control. In all Scotland, only Roxburgh Castle retained an isolated English garrison.

These efforts were assisted by Edward III's death in 1377. His son and heir Richard II was ten years old and unable to control the kingdom, having to face a peasant's revolt in 1381. With an absence of English attacks on Scotland, for the last had been 1356's Burnt Candlemas, the economy flourished. Scotland's exchequer stabilised and improved throughout the 1370s and 80s due to a recovery in trade to levels last seen in the 1320s, and the end of ransom payments for the release of David.[3]

To the contemporary chroniclers Wyntoun and Bower there was no doubt. Robert II was a king whose rule encouraged tranquillity and prosperity,[4] and who defended the integrity of his territory; for during his rule:

> *Off Scotland wes na fute off land*
> *Owte off Scottis mennys hand.*[5]

First Amongst Equals

But Robert II faced stirrings of revolt of his own. Not from peasants; rather, from those nobles who saw him as just another one of them. Douglas made a tentative bid for the crown in 1371.[6] His family had been as close to governing Scotland as the Stewarts were during the Bruce years. Robert II

---

[3] Lynch, *Scotland: A New History*, p.132.
[4] *Ibid*, p.138.
[5] Laing, *The Orygynale Cronykil Of Scotland, Vol III*, p.45.
[6] Mackie, *A History Of Scotland*, p.89.

faced no further coup attempts during the 1370s, but his large and unruly family would prove a source of trouble.

The king's son Alexander, Earl of Buchan, was a particular nuisance. The nobles felt this Stewart, sallying forth from his impregnable island fortress of Lochindorb in Badenoch, was a law unto himself. His private army of Highland caterans terrorised the Lowlands of Moray and Angus, and he gained the nickname *The Wolf of Badenoch.'* The king made no move to check his excesses. An entirely new strain of prejudice entered Scottish thought, one whose effects echo down to this day: the demonisation of Highlanders by Lowlanders. In the 1380s chronicler John of Fordun claimed that though the people of the Highlands were 'faithful and obedient to their king and country', they were also:

A savage and untamed race, rude and independent, given to rapine.[7]

If raiding fellow Scots was unacceptable, attacks on England were good form: but here again the king tried the patience of his nobles, trying to prevent his eldest son John of Carrick raiding Northern England.[8] A policy of improving trade and avoiding foreign wars was not enough for the hot-blooded knights of the 14th century. Contemporary chronicler Jean Froissart was certainly unimpressed, who saw Robert in 1385 when he was 69, grown weak and with bad eyesight:

[He had] red bleared eyes, the colour of sandalwood, which clearly showed he was no valiant man, but one who would rather remain at home than march to the field: he had, however, nine sons who loved arms.[9]

Scottish commanders went ahead with their planned attacks on England anyway,[10] captured Berwick[11], and in November 1384, John of Carrick led a

---

[7] Skene and Skene, *John of Fordun's Chronicle of the Scottish Nation*, p.38.
[8] Boardman, *The Early Stewart Kings*, p.119-120.
[9] Johnes, *Sir John Froissart's Chronicles of England, France, Spain, and the Adjoining Countries, Vol II*, p.48.
[10] Sadler, *Border Fury*, p.270.
[11] Though it was sold back to the Earl of Northumberland for 2,000 merks. Sadler, *Border Fury*, pp.270-1.

Parliamentary coup to replace his father.[12] The king remained on the throne, but in name only. Management of the kingdom was placed in John of Carrick's hands. It gave him a free hand to do what the nobles dearly wanted: invade England.

Scorched Earth

In the winter of 1384-5, 240 French ships landed an army in Scotland.[13] They came with the intention of attacking England from the north. On 23 July the combined Franco-Scottish force crossed the border, destroyed castles in Northumberland, and burned the surrounding countryside. In response to this aggression Richard II mustered 14,000 men at Newcastle under the banner of St Cuthbert and led them into Scotland in person on 6 August. The Franco-Scottish army retreated and Richard burnt Edinburgh and destroyed the abbeys of Dryburgh and Melrose. The French were galled at the Scots' ignoble retreat in the face of the English army: it robbed them of the opportunity for chivalric glory.[14] But the tactic was borne out by results. As formidable as an English army could be, it was an expensive beast, and the Scots knew the invasion could not last. The unpaid English army soon fell out with itself. They were back in Newcastle by 19 August.[15] The Scots marched south, burned the Eden Valley around Carlisle, and besieged Roxburgh Castle, which was spared due to a stupid argument between French and Scottish generals over whether it should be captured in the name of Robert II of Scotland or Charles VI of France.[16] The French now openly disdained the poverty of Scotland, incredulous at the *blasé* attitude exhibited by people towards the destruction of their homes.

"Suppose the English turn us out,"

said the Borderers as they drove their cattle back from the hills to their burnt homes,

---

[12] RPS, *1384/111/1-17.*
[13] Skene and Skene, *John of Fordun's Chronicle of the Scottish Nation*, p.371.
[14] Sadler, *Border Fury*, p.272.
[15] *Ibid.*
[16] *Ibid.*

After a century of devastation, ordinary Scots had learned to live with what they could carry.

The French had outstayed their welcome. They were asked to leave, and the Scots returned alone to Cumbria and Northumberland to attack Cockermouth and Hexham.[18]

John of Carrick agreed a truce with Richard II through 1386-7. Both sides of the border had suffered much for little gain. The Scots had found their French allies wanting. Their strategy for the next century was based on local advantage rather than any action co-ordinated with events on the Continent. And the English lost their pale in Scotland, which meant it would be their own northern marches that would bear the full brunt of any future incursions.

The next was not long in coming.

The Battle of Otterburn

In 1387 the English 'Lords Appellant' followed the example of the Scottish coup of 1384. They seized control of Government but kept Richard II nominally in power.[19] The Scots prepared to take advantage of England's distraction by leading an invasion of Northumberland. But when John of Carrick became permanently injured by a horse kick at Linlithgow, his brother Robert, the Earl of Menteith, took control of preparations.

Many Borderers responded to Menteith's call to arms in the summer of 1388, congregating for a wappenschaw, or a 'weapons show', at Jed Forest so Menteith could gauge the strength of the force available to him. In July, Menteith and Archibald the Grim took a column from Jed Forest to Carlisle, burning Eden and Appleby. The Earls of Moray and March plus James, the 2nd Earl of Douglas, took a second column, 6,600 strong, over Carter Bar for Durham. They carried no baggage or siege engines and moved fast, lifting

---

[17] Mackie, *A History Of Scotland*, p.86.
[18] Sadler, *Border Fury*, p.274.
[19] *Ibid.*

cattle as far south as Durham before returning.[20] The cattle were sent on ahead while Douglas camped outside Newcastle for two days to delay any pursuit. On the morning of 4 August the Scots were gone. The Earl of Northumberland, ensconced in Alnwick Castle, sent his son Sir Harry after them. The Scots rested again at Otterburn on a hot and dusty August evening when, with daylight fading, 8,000 men under Sir Harry arrived.

By attacking immediately, Sir Harry would not have the opportunity to deploy his archers to best advantage; but if he waited till morning, the Scots may slip away. The man nicknamed Hotspur chose to dive straight in.

The Scots had expected a chase, and reacted by getting in battle order. In the chaos, Hotspur lost the battle and was captured. In the morning the Bishop of Durham approached with 10,000 reinforcements, who were spooked so much by fugitives fleeing Otterburn that they joined in the rout. Durham rallied his men and tried a second time, but the Scots had dug themselves in and taunted the Bishop from behind temporary fortifications. Durham's men retreated.[21]

It had not been a complete Scottish victory. The Earl of Douglas had been killed on the first night. His column returned to Melrose, abandoning any plan to combine with Menteith at Carlisle, and buried Douglas in the abbey.

Otterburn had three consequences. The first was the creation of two of the greatest Border Ballads: *The Ballad of Chevy Chase* told from the English viewpoint, and *The Battle of Otterburn* from the Scots.

> *It fell about the Lammas tide, when the muir-men win their hay,*
> *The doughty earl of Douglas rode into England, to catch a prey.*
> *He chose the Gordons and the Graemes, the Lindsays light and gay;*
> *But the Jardines wald not with him ride, and they rue it to this day.*[22]

The second was the discouraging effect that Otterburn had on English armies. It disproved their strategy, based on an assumed superiority in the

---

[20] Sadler, *Border Fury*, pp.274-5.
[21] Bourchier and MacAulay, *The Chronicles of Froissart*, pp.376-379.
[22] Scott, *Minstrelsy Of The Scottish Border, Vol. I*, p.34.

open field, of always trying to force the Scots into a set-piece battle. An inferior Scottish force had been taken by surprise but still won, as crucially Hotspur had failed to make the longbow count. The English marches went on the defensive, reluctant to engage the Scots, who in turn gained confidence from Otterburn. They held the upper hand for the next fourteen years in the smaller engagements that ensued.[23]

And finally, Otterburn had consequences for the governance of the kingdom. John, Earl of Carrick, had lain idle as an invalid while his younger brother Robert of Menteith planned and executed the most complete Scottish victory for many years. Menteith now plotted to take control of the kingdom for himself. John of Carrick's key ally, the 2nd Earl of Douglas, had died at Otterburn. In the legal battle that followed to appoint an heir to the earldom, Menteith supported Archibald the Grim, who was already Lord of Galloway at Threave. Archibald became 3rd Earl of Douglas and the most powerful magnate in Southern Scotland, imposing his own special legal code in the Border Marches, and his reciprocal support for Menteith led to a counter-coup against Carrick.[24] Robert II remained king but humiliatingly for the lame John, the Guardianship passed from him to his younger brother Robert of Menteith.[25] Menteith dealt with the Wolf of Badenoch's lawlessness by relieving him of his duties, replacing him as Justiciar and Lieutenant north of the Forth with his own son Murdoch.[26]

Under this more stable regime Robert II had one last farewell tour of his kingdom, then retired to Dundonald Castle in March where he died on 19 April 1390.[27] The lame John of Carrick, whom Parliament had already deposed as Guardian in favour of his younger brother, became king. Awkward.

John II
Two brothers. One cunning, clever, and possessing all the necessary characteristics of a late medieval king. The other crippled by physical

---

[23] Sadler, *Border Fury*, p.283.
[24] Boardman, *The Early Stewart Kings*, p.148-153.
[25] *RPS, 1388/12/1.*
[26] *RPS, 1388/12/3; 1389/3/12.*
[27] Boardman, *The Early Stewart Kings*, p.171.

infirmity and depression, possessing nothing, he believed, of benefit to his subjects. Only one could be king. Had the rules of tanistry held sway there would be no contest. Yet the rules of primogeniture were clear: the fifty-three year old John of Carrick was king. Everybody went along with the farce while Menteith continued the day-to-day running of the kingdom.

And there was something else peculiar about John's reign. Scotland's previous King John Balliol had surrendered his kingdom to Edward I of England. It was a name no future King of Scots could bear. So John changed his name. There never was a King John II of Scotland. Instead, John took the more illustrious name of Robert III.

The Joust

After Otterburn, a Cold War atmosphere prevailed in border relations. Scots and English knights met in brutal duels and jousting tournaments under the veneer of chivalry and sport, the end coming to the loser with a dagger through the visor. Sir William Douglas was killed by Sir Thomas Clifford in a duel in the Baltic whilst on crusade with the Teutonic Knights against the Balts.[28] The Earl of Moray was killed by the Earl of Nottingham in a tournament at York on 28 May 1390.[29] But the most famous duel of all came on 23 April 1390, held on London Bridge in front of a large crowd and the King and Queen of England. Lord Welles, ambassador to Scotland, had boasted that the English were more valiant than the Scots in battle, and he would fight any knight who disagreed. Sir David Lindsay took issue with Welles, and bested him in front of his home crowd. But instead of dispatching Welles, Lindsay showed mercy, earning him the admiration of Londoners and the favour of the English king.[30]

Battle of the Clans

In such an atmosphere, it is no surprise that the old practice of trial by combat returned. It reached its apogee in the gladiatorial Battle of the Clans.

---

[28] Sadler, *Border Fury*, p.290.
[29] *Ibid*, p.289.
[30] *Ibid*, pp.289-290.

The clans Chattan and Cameron had an intractable dispute,[31] and in 1396, King Robert agreed to let them settle the issue with a fight. An arena was set up on Perth's North Inch where thirty of each clan's best warriors fought to the death in front of the king and his court. When only one Cameron and eleven Chattans remained, the king threw down his royal baton to end the slaughter. The last Cameron fled the field, jumped into the River Tay, swam across, and disappeared into the forest on the other side. As justice it was a success; Bower reports that 'for a long time the north remained quiet,'[32] though memories were long: the feud would continue a generation later.[33]

But if the king had occasional moments of effectiveness, he had an ambitious son who would not be bound by either his father or his uncle. In a bid to reconcile these rivals, Robert created Scotland's first dukedoms. In 1398, Prince David became the Duke of Rothesay, and Robert of Menteith the Duke of Albany. Reconciliation was unsuccessful, and a series of unfortunate events fatally weakened the new Duke of Rothesay's position. His advisors and champions died within a short time of each other: first his father-in-law Archibald the Grim, then his mother the Queen, and finally the Bishop of St Andrews.[34] Without the support of his mother, the bishop, or the Earl of Douglas, Rothesay was terribly exposed, especially given his willingness to act independently as if he himself were already king;[35] and in February 1402 Albany had him arrested on a slight charge and then starved to death. In May the Scottish Parliament exonerated Albany of all blame for Rothesay's death.[36] The prince had blocked Albany from attacking England by negotiating a truce with John of Gaunt.[37] The way was now clear for Albany and the new 4th Earl of Douglas to repeat, or so they hoped, the success of Otterburn.

---

[31] The proper names of the clans aren't known for sure. Wyntoun has them as *Clachinyha* and *Clahynnhe Qwhewyl*; Boece, as *Clankay* & *Clankquehere*. Various scholars have identified the clans as Chattans, Kays, Camerons, Macintoshes, Macphersons, or Davidsons.
[32] Boardman, *The Early Stewart Kings*, p.203.
[33] The Camerons and Chattans were fighting again in 1429s Battle of Palm Sunday.
[34] Boardman, *The Early Stewart Kings,* p.232-233.
[35] *Ibid,* p.233-235.
[36] RPS, *1402/5/1.*
[37] Sadler, *Border Fury*, pp.291-292.

Homildon Hill

In August 1402 Douglas crossed the border with 10,000 men and Albany's son Murdoch. The Scots devastated England as far south as the River Wear before returning north. But Hotspur lay in wait, and he had a secret weapon: the assistance of Scotland's finest general, George Dunbar, the Earl of March. The presence of Dunbar in the enemy camp was a wound the Scots had inflicted on themselves. Dunbar's daughter Elizabeth had been betrothed in marriage to the Duke of Rothesay, but Archibald the Grim had counter-offered a bigger dowry for his own daughter, and Elizabeth had been cast aside. The king kept her dowry. It was enough to turn Dunbar's coat.[38] He had already assisted a siege of Edinburgh by new English King Henry IV in 1400.[39] And now in 1402, as the invading Scots approached the River Till and saw the English position, they climbed the slopes of Homildon Hill above and formed a defensive formation of schiltrons. Hotspur was all for charging up the hill after them, but the wiser counsel of Dunbar prevailed.[40] Familiar with the devastating effects of an archery barrage, and also how vulnerable the English were without their archers, Dunbar held Hotspur back and had the archers fire into the stationary schiltrons, which began to fall apart. Douglas hesitated to move, and eventually some of the Scots commanders such as Sir John Swinton, 14th of that Ilk took matters into their own hands, charging his men forward with the cry:

"Better to die in the melee than be shot down like deer!"[41]

His men were cut to pieces. By the time Douglas gave the order to charge, it was too late, and the decimated ranks of Scots were slaughtered. The haul of captured Scottish nobles was particularly satisfying for Percy, the Earl of Northumberland, who anticipated a rich ransom. He may have expected that Albany's son Murdoch would be kept in captivity as a guarantee of good behaviour against his father, but to the earl's anger, Henry IV refused to let him ransom the rest. If they were freed, they would just cause more trouble for England, and so Percy was instructed to entertain them indefinitely at his

---

[38] Sadler, *Border Fury,* p.296.
[39] *Ibid,* p.297.
[40] *Ibid,* pp.301-302.
[41] Maxwell, *A History Of The House Of Douglas,* pp.136-137.

own expense. With this news of a reversal in his fortunes, Percy instructed his son Hotspur to raise his banner against his own king; and his captive, the Earl of Douglas, freely offered his support for another crack at the English. But at the ensuing battle at Shrewsbury, Henry IV prevailed. For a second time, Douglas was thwarted by George Dunbar, who had confused Henry IV's enemies by dressing decoys to look like the English king.[42]

Death of a Wretch

Back in Scotland, Albany's ruthlessness in eliminating the heir to the throne preyed on the mind of the listless king. The safety of his surviving legitimate son, James, became his last great concern. Finally stirring into action, Robert made plans for James to be sent to France for safe keeping. In February 1406, a poorly-conceived plan was enacted. James was taken from St Andrews to East Lothian, where a fight broke out between local men and his escort. The prince escaped, was put in a rowing boat, and ferried to the Bass Rock in the Firth of Forth. The 11-year old heir to the throne waited a month on this impregnable cliff amongst the boiling seas, before a ship arrived to transport him to France. But it did not arrive at its destination: on 22 March, a force of Yarmouth privateers lurking off Flamborough Head intercepted and boarded James' ship, the *Maryenknyght*. James became a prisoner of the King of England.[43]

When Robert III heard of this his heart broke in grief and despair. He died on 4 April 1406 in Rothesay Castle at the age of 69, desiring earlier, so the story goes, to be buried in a midden with the epitaph:

Here lies the worst of Kings and the most wretched of men.[44]

The Kingless Kingdom

The kidnapped Prince James became James I, King of Scots. His situation as a child prisoner in English captivity sounds desperate, but he was at least safely out of the reach of his murderous uncle Albany, who could rule Scotland without rivalry. But though Albany was more ruthless and capable

---

[42] Sadler, *Border Fury*, pp.303-307.
[43] Boardman, *The Early Stewart Kings*, p.291-297.
[44] *Ibid*, p.303.

than his brother had been, he lacked the divine approval of anointed kingship, and had to handle the nobles with care. And so Albany turned a blind eye to their financial misdemeanours.[45] He didn't have much choice: the rents and customs money that had briefly revived the economy in the 1370s and 80s, and had funded Robert II's reign, had dried up: Albany was unable to pay crown officers for their work, even if he wanted to.[46]

Yet a monarch wasn't actually needed for the day-to-day running of a kingdom. Scotland had been in this situation before under David II, and from 1388, the Three Estates of Parliament met at least once almost every year. There was no general descent into chaos.

Reid Harlaw

But as Albany worked to increase his own influence, it was inevitable he would fall foul of someone else's interests. In claiming the vacant Earldom of Ross for his younger son John Stewart, Albany crossed the most important magnate in the West, Donald MacDonald, the Lord of the Isles. MacDonald had a better claim to Ross than Albany. After some legal wrangling, MacDonald decided that the most effective method of gaining the Earldom was to take possession of it by force.

Gathering his forces at Ardtornish Castle, MacDonald marched into Ross, swept aside a force of Mackays loyal to Albany, and occupied Dingwall Castle. But he overextended himself with his next move, a march on Aberdeen with the express intent of burning the city. Against him rode Alexander, the Earl of Mar, with the knights of the north-east and the representatives of the terrified burgesses of Aberdeen. The two forces met on the road from Inverness, twenty miles outside Aberdeen at Harlaw on 24 June 1411.

The two armies set up differently. Alexander's knights rode into battle on horseback, wore armour and carried lances, swords and maces. His infantry carried spears and battle axes and formed up in schiltrons. The Highlanders wore quilted jackets and carried targes for protection, and swords, bows, dirks and pole-axes for offence. They were almost entirely infantry and

---

[45] Lynch, *Scotland: A New History*, p.143.
[46] *Ibid*, p.137.

formed up in a wedge shape.[47] As the armies faced up, MacDonald's bard Lachlan Mór MacMhuirich stood before the Highlanders to recite the genealogy of the Lord of the Isles, harking all the way back to semi-legendary 2nd century Irish king Conn of the Hundred Battles, and inciting the gathered Clan Donald to battle:

A Chlanna Cuinn Cèad-chathaich
A nois uair bhar n-aitheanta,
A chuileanan confadhach,
A bheithrichean bunata,
A leómhannan làn-ghasta,
A onchonaibh iorghaileach,
Chaoiribh chròdha, churanta
De Chlanna Cuinn Cèad-chathaich —
A Chlanna Cuinn, cuimhnichibh
Cruas an am na h-iorghaile.

O Children of Conn of the Hundred Battles,
Now is the time for you to win recognition,
O raging whelps,
O sturdy heroes,
O most sprightly lions,
O battle-loving warriors,
O brave, heroic firebrands,
The Children of Conn of the Hundred Battles —
O Children of Conn, remember
Hardihood in time of battle.[48]

The two armies fought each other to a standstill. The battle between Hector Ruadh Maclean and Sir Alexander Irvine of Drum typified the battle as a whole; they fought in single combat and each died from the wounds the other inflicted.[49] As night fell, the Earl of Mar and his men collapsed

[47] MacLean, *A History of the Clan MacLean*, pp.41-42.
[48] Carney and Greene, *Celtic Studies: Essays In Memory Of Angus Matheson*, p.152,161.
[49] Way, and Squire, *Collins Scottish Clan & Family Encyclopedia*, p.238.

exhausted on the battlefield, expecting to have to fight on at dawn the next day. To their joy they discovered that the MacDonald had retreated in the night. They had saved Aberdeen, and prejudice against Highlanders was ratcheted up another notch in Lowland minds. For John of Fordun, Lowland Scots were home-loving, civilised, trustworthy, tolerant, urbane, and peaceful: a view he had perhaps not reached by consulting the French or Northumbrians. Gaels from the mountain areas on the other hand were wild, untamed, primitive, and proud; given to an easy life, and ripe for demonisation.[50]

The Lord of the Isles remained at large: in 1412 Albany led an army into Ross, and finally cornered MacDonald at Lochgilphead where he extracted a promise of good behaviour.[51] But it wasn't the last we'll hear of the MacDonalds.

A Trickle of Trade

While a cultural gap began to open up between Lowlander and Highlander, and customs revenue was plundered by the nobility, there was at least peace over the border. The status of Albany's son Murdoch as a hostage in English hands guaranteed it. But it was a hard kind of peace. Scottish merchants depended on Continental trade, but few foreign merchantmen visited Scotland, and the Scots had to hazard the journey to Bruges themselves.[52] Meanwhile in the Borders, a hundred-plus years of warfare meant looting and cattle raiding had already largely replaced trade as a way of life.

And that wasn't all. The Scots were starting to question the very foundations of the church that had done so much to secure the country's independence.

The Scottish Inquisition

The church and the aristocracy were the two pillars of feudal society, but heretics called Lollards started to reject some of the doctrines and assumptions of church and society:

---

[50] Skene and Skene, *John of Fordun's Chronicle of the Scottish Nation*, p.38.
[51] Lynch, *Scotland: A New History*, p.143.
[52] *Ibid*, p.70.

When Adam delved and Eve span, who then was the gentleman?[53]

Their questioning had caused a short-lived peasant rising in England, and by the end of the century heretical ideas had taken root in Scotland, particularly in Ayrshire and the south-west.[54] But Albany, to the approval of chroniclers like Wyntoun, had no interest in alienating the church. He was:

> *a constant Catholike;*
> *All Lollard he hatyt and heretike.*[55]

And so Lawrence of Lindores, Abbot of Scone, was appointed *Haereticae Pravitatis Inquisitor*: the first religious inquisitor in the Kingdom of Scotland.[56] He enthusiastically persecuted his duties. In 1408, James Resby was brought before an ecclesiastical court in Perth, charged with promoting heresies. Forty points of doctrine were argued over between Resby and Lindores. Claiming that the clergy should live saintly lives, or that there was no Biblical authority for the Pope, would get anyone in hot water.[57] Resby was condemned and taken by the civil authorities to be burned at the stake. He was the first man in Scotland to be executed by the state for his religious beliefs.

But Lindores was not just a religious enforcer: his efforts resulted in a major contribution to scholarship. For two centuries, Scottish scholars had travelled to Oxford, Paris, and Bologna for their higher education. The Wars of Independence had put England out of bounds, and now English pirates and blockades made the journey to the Continent chancy. Above all, the local Lollard problem needed weeded out. And so between 1410 and 1413, St Andrews' University was founded and recognised by the Pope, with Lawrence of Lindores as one of its earliest masters. From the start, St Andrews was a machine designed to combat dangerous thinking: by 1417,

---

[53] Freedman, *Images Of The Medieval Peasant*, p.60.
[54] Mackie, *A History Of Scotland*, p.145; Lynch, *Scotland: A New History*, pp.186-7.
[55] Laing, *The Orygynale Cronykil Of Scotland, Vol III*, p.100.
[56] Stevenson, *Power And Propaganda*, p.143.
[57] *Ibid*, p.142.

graduates had to take an oath that they would remain vigilant against heresy.[58]

Meanwhile in England...

... King James was left to stew in impotence. In 1412 he wrote letters to his earls accusing Albany of stalling his release.[59] He was right. And it would get worse. After Henry IV died in 1413, the half-hearted negotiations halted completely. The new King of England, Henry V, decided he wasn't going to release James at all. It seemed to James, trapped in gilded captivity, that those he was reliant upon had deserted him. Like many a frustrated youth he turned to poetry. But in the depths of despair something wonderful happened. Every day he saw a young lady walking beneath his window in Windsor Castle and was smitten. James was moved to write:

> *Beautee eneuch to mak a world to dote.*
> *A, suete, [sweet] ar ye a warldly creature*
> *Or hevinly thing in liknesse of nature?*
> *Or ar ye god Cupidis owin princesse*
> *And cummyn ar to louse me out of band?*[60]

He dropped a plucked rose where he knew she would be walking and the next night at dinner, saw she was wearing it on her dress.[61] The romance proved enduring. The young lady was Joan Beaufort. James published *The Kingis Quair*, a long poem inspired by her. Its composition was a necessary distraction from the knowledge that Albany, who had successfully secured the freedom of his son Murdoch, had no intention of securing the release of his monarch.

In 1420, at the age of 80, Albany died. His son Murdoch inherited the Dukedom of Albany and Governorship of Scotland. It seemed that the Albany Stewarts had no intention of loosening their grip on power. But where the first Duke of Albany had managed to keep a lid on the Scottish

---

[58] Stevenson, *Power And Propaganda*, p.143.
[59] Lynch, *Scotland: A New History*, p.142.
[60] Mooney and Arn, *James I Of Scotland, The Kingis Quair*. [online] Robbins Library Digital Projects.
[61] Connolly, *Heroines Of The Medieval World*, p.222.

nobles, Murdoch was nowhere near as practiced. The demands for the return of the king were rekindled. The opportunity came on Henry V's death in 1422. The regency of his nine-month old son proved more accommodating to negotiations, and a ransom for James of 60,000 merks was demanded and accepted.[62] His freedom imminent, James married his sweetheart Joan Beaufort on 12 February 1424 at Southwark Cathedral in London, and the royal couple entered Scotland on 5 April.

James was nearly thirty. He had spent eighteen years in English captivity, and an angry man was he.

An Antidote to the English

James pointed the finger of blame for his captivity at the Albany Stewarts who had betrayed him then left him languishing. James had signed a non-aggression pact with England and promised not to fight them in France, but when Murdoch had been released, Albany had sent an army to France anyway: they formed the *Garde Écossaise*, gained a reputation as swaggardly wine-bibbers,[63] but then beat the English at the Battle of Baugé, at which the Pope quipped:

"Truly the Scots are an antidote to the English!" [64]

James had been humiliated at the siege of Melun when, still in English captivity, Henry V told him to order the Scots to surrender: they had refused, and mocked their monarch from the battlements.[65] But on James' return home, the Scots in France were destroyed as an effective force by an Anglo-Burgundian army at the Battle of Verneuil.[66] Sensitive of their martial reputation,[67] the Scots, unlike their French allies, had refused to run or surrender, and been slaughtered to the last man. With James on the throne, no more reinforcements would be coming to aid France.

---

[62] Mackie, *A History Of Scotland*, p.91.
[63] Skene, *The Book Of Pluscarden, Vol II*, p.265,368.
[64] Watt, Scotichronicon, Volume 8, pp.120-121.
[65] Sadler, *Border Fury*, p.320.
[66] *Ibid,* pp.321-323.
[67] MacRitchie, "FRENCH INFLUENCE IN SCOTTISH SPEECH" *Transactions of the Glasgow Archaeological Society*, vol. 2, no. 4, 1896, pp. 433–440.

Murdoch's position was weakened by the loss at Verneuil, and James made his move. Between April and May 1425, Parliament had Murdoch and his family arrested. The subsequent trial found them guilty of robbery and extortion, and they were beheaded on 24 May. Nineteen years after the first Duke of Albany had taken control of Scotland, his family had finally paid the price.

And the king had gained not just revenge: in a foretaste of things to come, he also gained their estates.[68]

---

[68] MacQuarrie, *Medieval Scotland: Kingship And Nation*, pp.215-216.

Figure 15: James I

CHAPTER TWELVE

The King of Parliaments

As James and his new wife had set off for his kingdom from London he vowed:

> *"Let God but grant me life, and there shall not be a spot in my dominions where the key shall not keep the castle, and the furze-bush the cow, though I myself should lead the life of a dog to accomplish it."*[1]

He now upheld his vow to bring order to Scotland, using Parliament as his preferred instrument. The nobility and senior clergy had been holding Parliaments since at least 1235: and from 1357, the representatives of royal burghs were included as permanent participants too. But the nature of these Parliaments was about to be transformed. They had previously met to administer justice, arbitrate on territorial disputes, appoint Guardians, discuss ransoms, ratify international treaties, or occasionally award money for an embassy to the Pope. But the sinews of state had withered through Albany's neglect, and James used Parliament to help repair them. In 1424 his legislation-making machine began. James passed laws banning war amongst his lieges, riding through the countryside with unnecessarily large retinues, and rebellion against the king. He banned the catching of salmon outside of season, and the purchase of church benefices without royal approval.[2] He banned begging,[3] and slapped a 9 o'clock curfew on drinking in taverns.[4] He asserted the crown's mineral rights in silver and gold mines.[5] He raised ordinances for the organisation of fire-fighting and regulated the location of brothels.[6] He banned football.[7] Yes, football... because Scotsmen were

---

[1] Ross, *The Stewart Dynasty*, p.125.
[2] RPS, *1424/2a-1424/17*.
[3] RPS, *1425/3/22*.
[4] RPS, *1436/10/9*.
[5] RPS, *1424/15*.
[6] RPS, *1427/3/7-16*.
[7] RPS, *1424/19*.

gathering for the supposed aim of practicing archery for the defence of the realm, and playing football instead. James legislated on football, archery, beggars, lepers, wolves,[8] industry, agriculture, weights & measures, coinage, inns, ferries, and an Act of 1425 ordered that judges must obtain an advocate for any poor creature on trial unable to provide counsel for himself.[9]

And there was one other thing James wanted above all from Parliament.

Money.

A Scotsman's Purse

James had a ransom of 60,000 merks to pay to Henry VI, and to collect the tax to pay this he made a list of all lands, charters and rents pertaining to the king at the time of David II, to whom they belonged to at present, plus a census of the inhabitants of towns and the value of their goods.[10] This 'domesday book' was controversial even at the loyal parliament of 1424, which took a month and a half to agree the exact method of raising the tax.[11] James, raised in the English court, did not see the problem. But there was a fundamental difference in the attitude to money between English and Scottish Parliaments. English parliaments were called almost annually. They usually granted the king tax for his wars, which, provided they were to pillage the fat of France rather than the gristle of Scotland or Ireland, could prove profitable for all involved. Their power came in the threat of a refusal to grant money. Scottish parliaments after 1424 were called as frequently. But their power came instead from the tantalising prospect of a rare approval of tax to the king. Because Scottish Parliaments were not in the habit of doing so. The last before 1424 had been the grant in 1326 to the elderly Robert the Bruce of a life income of 2s in the pound, or 10%.[12] When David II paid his English ransom, he paid it not from a general tax, but from customs duty that accrued directly to the royal purse.[13] But customs revenue had plunged

---

[8] RPS, *1428/3/6,9.*
[9] RPS, *1425/3/25.*
[10] Tanner, The Late Medieval Scottish Parliament, p.10-11.
[11] *Ibid,* p.13.
[12] *Ibid,* p.12.
[13] *Ibid.*

during Albany's custodianship, and what little was left had been plundered by great nobles.

After paying the first tranche of James' ransom, Parliament dug in its heels and refused to authorise the rest.[14] James' continued insistence on raising more tax sowed the first seeds of discontentment at his rule.

To modern eyes, James I's legislative vigour seems admirable. His contemporaries saw it differently. The chronicler Walter Bower, reflecting the opinion of the people at large, thought that taxation was a last resort. It was acceptable only for defence, crusade, sending an ambassador to the Pope, and royal poverty.[15] It was unacceptable for the king to take tax and spend it on elaborate manor houses, surplus horses, sumptuous garments, gambling debts or parties: and James was spending the money he raised on just that, building and furnishing a grand palace at Linlithgow.[16] His attempts to raise more tax between 1425 and 1431 were rebuffed, and in return he confiscated land from the nobility. In the contemporary chronicle *The Dethe of the Kynge of Scotis*, John Shirley wrote:

> *The people of the land sore grutched, and mowrnid; seying that thay suppoised and ymagynd that the Kyng did rather that vigorious execucion upon the Lordes of his kyne for the covetise of thare possessions and goodes, thane for any other rightfull cause.*[17]

Shirley said people accused James of killing the Albanys not in revenge, but because he coveted their possessions. The King of Scots had gained an ill reputation amongst his parsimonious lieges.

Ri Innse Gall

Having alienated the burghers and Lowland nobles with demands for money, James turned his attention to the Highlands. Since the start of the century, the Duke of Albany had plotted against the Lords of the Isles over

---

[14] Tanner, The Late Medieval Scottish Parliament, pp.13-14.
[15] *Ibid,* p.23.
[16] *Ibid,* p.53.
[17] Shirley, The Dethe Of James Kynge Of Scotis, p.7.

possession of the Earldom of Ross. Blows had been traded at Harlaw over the issue. The new Lord of the Isles, Alexander MacDonald, had therefore been a natural ally of James against their common enemy Albany. But with the Albanys destroyed, James turned on MacDonald to grab Ross for himself. In 1428 he called Parliament to Inverness Castle for late August.[18] The location was deliberate: James wanted as many Highland chiefs as possible in attendance. Those who came, discovered too late they had been summoned in bad faith. Once safely inside Inverness Castle and disarmed, James arrested fifty chiefs, including MacDonald. Some were executed. After setting this example of his royal might, James freed the rest and headed south. For this insult to his honour, in the spring of 1429 MacDonald returned in force and razed Inverness to the ground.[19] It was all the provocation James needed.

Around midsummer James marched into Lochaber and confronted MacDonald near Inverlochy. MacDonald had little choice but to capitulate: having gathered an army of 10,000 men, half of them, the clans Chattan and Cameron, switched sides when James unfurled the royal banner.[20] MacDonald escaped, but James sent an artillery-armed fleet into the Hebrides to capture him. The Lord of the Isles was imprisoned in Tantallon Castle to await his fate. In March 1430 Parliament persuaded James to spare his life.[21] In the summer of 1431 MacDonald was joined in jail by the Earl of Douglas. Parliament became uneasy at Douglas' imprisonment for what they saw as a minor infraction, and both men were released through Parliamentary pressure in September 1431.[22]

But the MacDonalds had not been idle while their chief languished in jail. Alexander's cousin Donald Balloch had raised an army and confronted the king's forces in September 1431 at Inverlochy Castle. This time, the MacDonalds were victorious. Balloch ravaged the lands of Chattan and

---

[18] RPS, A1428/8/1.
[19] Brown, *James I*, pp.96-101.
[20] Gregory, History of the Western Highlands and Isles of Scotland, pp.36-37.
[21] RPS, *1430/30*.
[22] Tanner, The Late Medieval Scottish Parliament, p.52-53.

Cameron in revenge for their treachery in 1429, but James sent a counter-force to chase Balloch out of Scotland. Balloch's friend in Ireland, Hugh Buy O'Neill sent James a head pickled in a jar. The king called off the hunt. The head belonged to some other poor soul, and Balloch was safe.[23]

James called another Parliament at Perth for October 1431 to raise money and men to return to the Highlands, but as he had spent the money he raised earlier on palaces, guns, furniture, and tapestries, Parliament didn't trust him not to do the same again. They grudgingly granted James tax, but only on the condition it was held by his political opponent, the Bishop of St. Andrews.[24] James suspended Parliament and when they re-met six days later, he abandoned his attempts to invade the Highlands. It was the last Parliament he would call for two and a half years.[25] Scotland's representatives were already voting with their feet: the burgers of Aberdeen and Montrose had refused to attend Inverness, and had been fined for the crime of 'contumacy,' or refusing to attend the royal summons.[26]

The Stormclouds Gather

At the Parliament of January 1435 in Perth, James had the Earldom of March forfeit and George Dunbar, 11th Earl of March, left for England. George's land was parcelled out to his rivals in the south-east... plus some for King James himself, which only furthered his covetous reputation.[27] In ten years, James had executed the Duke of Albany and Earl of Lennox and forfeit their lands, had exiled the Earls of Strathearn and March and forfeit their lands, and imprisoned the Lord of the Isles and the Earl of Douglas, the latter without just cause. Who, wondered the nobles nervously, would be next? On 15 January 1435, James required all members of Parliament to write letters of fealty to the Queen, who was busy increasing her own estates in

---

[23] Gregory, History of the Western Highlands and Isles of Scotland, pp.37-39.
[24] *RPS, 1431/10/2.*
[25] Tanner, The Late Medieval Scottish Parliament, pp.54-56.
[26] *Ibid,* p.42,
[27] *Ibid,* p.60-63.

central Perthshire at the expense of Walter, the Earl of Atholl.[28] Perhaps, Atholl thought, it would be him?

Atholl decided to do something about it. His chance came at an Assembly at Edinburgh in October 1436. The king had renewed the alliance with France and marked this with a failed siege of Roxburgh, running away on the approach of an English army as he had become afraid his own generals were plotting against him.[29]

James was right about a plot, but it wasn't his generals in the field. It was the 1436 Parliament that gave his opponents a chance to band together. The three estates chose a speaker to make a speech against James' plans. Their choice was a former servant of Albany's called Sir Robert Graham, who now supported Walter of Atholl due to James' treatment of his family: their estates had been forfeit and his kinsman Malise Graham languished in English captivity as security for James' unpaid ransom.[30] But Graham went further than just speaking against the king's plans. He set his hands upon the royal person and in an extraordinary scene said:

> *'I arrest you yn the name of all the thre astates of your reume, here now assemblid yn this present parliament, for right as youre liege peple be bundun and sworne to obeye your Majeste noble riall, yn the same wise bene ye sworne and ensurid to kepe youre peple, to kepe and guverne youre lawe.'*[31]

Arrest the king?! The assembled worthies looked at the floor and held an uncomfortable silence. In a fury, James ordered his personal bodyguard into the chamber, and only on this threat of force did Parliament accede to the king's latest demands. Graham was arrested.

Sir Robert Graham had seriously miscalculated. Parliament had legitimised coups against the first two Stewart kings, but these were affairs of royal rivals replacing each other. The concept that the estates themselves were owed

---

[28] Tanner, The Late Medieval Scottish Parliament, p.63-64.
[29] Tanner, The Late Medieval Scottish Parliament, p.67.
[30] *Ibid,* pp.69-70.
[31] Shirley, The Dethe Of James Kynge Of Scotis, p8.

duty by the king was not one that a feudal country like Scotland was ready for. But James failed to heed the warning of this attempted coup. Graham was exiled, only to take himself off for sanctuary in 'the cuntreis of the Wild Scottis.'[32]

Dying for a Game of Tennis

It's not surprising that a man who grew up being held against his will in castles had an aversion to stout fortresses: James preferred domestic surroundings. But this was a fatal preference for a man who had made so many enemies with his land grabs and demands for money. As he relaxed with the Queen in his nightclothes in Blackfriars in Perth on the night of 20 February 1437, undefended except for a royal guard in a different room, James' nemesis Graham suddenly burst in with his followers. The king fled for his privy and leapt into the sewer underneath, from where, covered in shit, he would be able to crawl to safety. But this route to life was blocked. Just three days earlier, fed up with his tennis balls disappearing down the same sewer when he was playing on the court next door, he had ordered it to be covered over.[33] Graham cornered the king in the sewer and stabbed him to death. The noise of this commotion roused the king's servants. They failed to catch the fleeing Graham, but he and his co-conspirators were quickly hunted down and brought to justice. Joan's retribution was savage. Walter of Atholl and the rest of the plotters were arrested and tortured by methods recounted in gruesome detail in *Dethe of the Kynge of Scotis*.[34] Atholl, according to Buchanan, was 'crowned' with a red hot band of iron inscribed with the words 'King of Traitors.'[35]

Graham was tracked down to the Highlands. He died unrepentant to the last, stating at his trial that:

> "...Yit doubt y nat that ye shall se the daye and the tyme, that ye shall pray my soule, for the grete good that I have done to you, and to all this

---

[32] *Ibid*, p.9.
[33] Shirley, The Dethe Of James Kynge Of Scotis, pp.15-16.
[34] *Ibid*, pp.22-28.
[35] Sutton, *Rerum Scoticarum Historia*, Book X, Chapter 41.

reaume of Scottland, that I have thus slayne and delyveryd you of so cruell a tirant...'[86]

The nobility and burgess had been upset with James and his land-grabbing avarice. Their grumbling had persuaded Graham and Atholl of the justice of their cause.

But to kill the king...?

Battle Regent

With James' six-year old son James II now king, the race was on to run the regency. The king's mother Joan was first out the lists. But she was given her head only as long as retribution lasted for her husband's murder. Medieval Scots considered her unsuited to run the kingdom on three counts: one, she was a woman, two, she was English, and three, she was deeply associated with the covetousness that led to her husband's assassination. The Three Estates met in March 1437 and gave her 4,000 Merks for the upkeep of young James.[37] But to run the Kingdom they appointed Archibald, the 5th Earl of Douglas. In Scotland he was Earl of Douglas, Lord of Galloway and Annandale, Lord of Lauderdale, Bothwell, Selkirk and the Ettrick Forests; in France he was Comte de Longueville, Duc de Touraine and lord of Dun-le-roi. Douglas was easily the most senior noble in Scotland.[38] But he was quiet by nature, and trod carefully with the other nobles. Two castellans, Sir Alexander Livingston the keeper of Stirling Castle, and Sir William Crichton the keeper of Edinburgh, found themselves in a position to increase their own power and influence.

The Conniving Castellans

Sir William Crichton moved first. After the king's coronation at Holyrood Abbey, Crichton held James and his mother as effective prisoners in Edinburgh Castle. But Joan believed she had allies. With Sir Alexander Livingston's help, she smuggled James out of Edinburgh Castle, hidden in a large chest of her belongings. Crichton had given her leave to visit the shrine

---

[36] Shirley, The Dethe Of James Kynge Of Scotis, p.25.
[37] Tanner, The Late Medieval Scottish Parliament, p.80.
[38] *Ibid,* p.78.

of the Virgin at Whitekirk in East Lothian: but on leaving Leith, the ship's captain sailed not east but west towards Stirling and into the hands of Livingston, who proved no more a friend to the queen than Crichton had been.[39]

Only the Earl of Douglas had the power to shake Crichton and Livingston from their perches, but the 5th Earl was content to leave things be. The castellans came to an agreement, mutual advantage trumping mutual distrust. Livingston kept possession of the king at Stirling and gained influence as Guardian; Crichton was appointed Lord Chancellor of Scotland and gained control of the country's purse-strings.[40] But the death of Archibald Douglas on 26 June 1439 threatened this arrangement: William, the new 6th Earl of Douglas, was ready to make his mark. Joan sought an alliance with the vigorous young lord.

The conniving castellans struck first. The queen was seized on 3 August by Livingston and confined to a chamber. Parliament ordered her release, but on the condition, insisted upon by Livingston, that Joan declare before Parliament that she sanctioned her arrest as for the good of the king, herself and realm. She was freed, after publicly promising that she would not attempt to recover the boy king, now firmly in Livingston's grip.[41]

The Black Dinner

With the queen neutralised, Crichton and Livingston turned their attention to the Earl of Douglas, who alone could threaten their position. They approached James the Gross, who would inherit the earldom of Douglas should anything happen to the new earl. If such a scenario came to pass, James the Gross confirmed with a nod and a wink, he would not obstruct Crichton and Livingston in their sterling work running Scotland.[42]

On 24 November 1440, William Douglas and his brother David were invited by Crichton to dine with the king at Edinburgh Castle. Only sixteen and fourteen years old, the Douglas boys suspected nothing. According to

---

[39] Ross, *The Stewart Dynasty*, p.136; McGladdery, *James II*, pp.135-6.
[40] Tanner, The Late Medieval Scottish Parliament, p.88.
[41] *Ibid*, pp.91-92; RPS, *1439/9/1*.
[42] Ross, The Stewart Dynasty, p.138.

legend, as the dinner drew to its end, a platter was brought in and placed on the table. Its cover was removed and the head of a black boar was revealed. It was the traditional symbol of death, and signalled the last moment of the Douglas boys' short lives. The earl and his brother were seized and summarily beheaded in the teeth of protest by the horrified ten-year old king.[43] Unlike the death of David, Duke of Rothesay in 1402, there was no Parliamentary inquiry, no opprobrium, no contemporary censure for Crichton or for James the Gross, the new 7th Earl of Douglas. No public justification or apology was forthcoming.[44] But the people took note, and again, according to legend, a popular song arose from the street:

> *Edinburgh castle, toune, and towre,*
> *God grant thou sink for sin;*
> *And that e'en for the Black Dinner,*
> *Earl Douglas gat therein.*[45]

With James the Gross in charge of the earldom, there was no retaliation from the Douglas clan. But when he too died in 1443, the fundamental weakness of Livingston and Crichton's position was revealed. The new 8th Earl of Douglas, James the Gross' son William, was a more vigorous player in high politics than his father, and to protect himself, Livingston made himself Douglas' man. Crichton was 'blown out', or declared a rebel,[46] and Joan, who had sided with Crichton in desperation to see her son once again, was besieged in Dunbar Castle where she died.[47] The rule of Scotland had coalesced decisively around the figure of William Douglas.

Douglas packed the 1445 Parliament with his supporters. Since the death of James I, the lack of senior adult nobility worried Scotland's leaders. And so an old expedient of 'Lords of Parliament' was re-created: men without

---

[43] Maxwell, *A History Of The House Of Douglas*, pp.155-156.
[44] Tanner, The Late Medieval Scottish Parliament, pp.98-99.
[45] Maxwell, A History of the House of Douglas, p.156.
[46] Thomson, The Auchinleck Chronicle, p.36.
[47] Connolly, Heroines Of The Medieval World, p.226.

extensive lands were given extensive legal powers. Douglas ennobled his relatives this way, entrenching his own position.[48]

But two developments would eventually propel the House of Stewart far ahead of their rivals. If Douglas could create Lords of Parliament, the king could too, and these legislators who owed everything to the king would one day rival the great landowners.

The second development was a deliberate marriage policy of widening the Stewart net beyond Scotland. James' delicate elder sister Margaret was betrothed to the heir to the French throne: she was herself heir to Scotland should anything happen to young James. She died young, unhappy with the boorish Prince Louis who went on to destroy all her poetry.[49] But this would not stop the Stewarts from trying again. European thrones were becoming concentrated in fewer and fewer hands, including those of the Stewarts.

Back in 1371, Robert Stewart faced competition for the throne from the 1st Earl of Douglas. As late as the 1420s, the Stewarts were merely first amongst equals. But by 1450, the dynasty had arrived: as even the 8th Earl of Douglas would discover.

In 1449 James was married to Maria, daughter of the Duke of Gueldres. He was ready to take charge of his kingdom.

But first there would be a reckoning with those who had hounded his mother to death.

[48] Tanner, The Late Medieval Scottish Parliament, pp.114-118.
[49] Connolly, Heroines Of The Medieval World, pp.240-243.

CHAPTER THIRTEEN

James of the Fiery Face

By 1448 James was eighteen: no longer a boy. In preparation for his personal rule, Parliament sent Crichton, who was back in favour, to the Continent to find the king a bride.[1] He returned in 1449 with the fifteen-year old niece of Philip of Burgundy, daughter of the Duke of Guelders – Maria van Egmont-Gelre. They married on 3 July 1449. King James was now a man: a man with scores to settle. Raised a virtual prisoner in Stirling Castle, he had reached his majority safe from harm. But he resented his jailer Livingston. He'd been deprived of his father's counsel and his mother's love, and had turned out thin-skinned and headstrong. A red birthmark covered half his face: a visible warning, people said, of a quick temper.[2]

In 1448 the Earl of Northumberland had tested Scotland's defences but found them sound, being beaten by the Douglases at the Battle of Sark. As a result, Livingston was sent to Durham in 1449 to negotiate a truce with England. With Livingston out the country, the king exercised his new power by combining with Douglas and Crichton to arrest his enemies. Livingston was declared an outlaw, his family executed, and the lands they had gained during James' minority were forfeit.[3] Livingston's position had been sustainable only for as long as he held the king's person; now that James was old enough to command loyalty and make his own decisions, Livingston's fall was sudden and brutal.

And he wouldn't be the last nobleman James had a score to settle with.

---

[1] McGladdery, *James II*, p.54. Crichton had provided practical support to James in the form of loans.
[2] ODNB, *James II (1430-1460), king of Scots*.
[3] Tanner, *The Late Medieval Scottish Parliament*, pp.122-124.

Tae Ding Doon a Douglas

At the height of his powers and confident of his relationship with the king, William, the 8th Earl of Douglas, left Scotland in October 1450 for a pilgrimage to Rome. He was recognised as a major European player in his own right: he met the Duke of Burgundy, gained an audience with the Pope, and was welcomed at the courts of the French and English kings on his way back.[4] It couldn't have gone better. Until he heard the news from Scotland.

James had used Douglas' absence to do as he'd done to Livingston. He appropriated the Lordship of Galloway to the crown and moved against Douglas' strongholds in January 1451. He used his authority as king to persuade Douglas' allies to drop their links to him, offering grants of land and offices to buy their compliance.[5]

Douglas may have sought help from the English king.[6] But it was to James' advantage that the English, normally eager to keep the Scots at each other's throats, were preoccupied with the hammering they were taking in France as the Hundred Years War drew to a close with a decisive French victory.

When Douglas returned to Scotland in April, a rapprochement was brokered by the Scottish nobility. James called Parliament to meet in June. The king gave ground, reconfirming Douglas in almost all his lands,[7] and 'all gud scottismen war rycht blyth of that accordance,' according to the Auchinleck Chronicle.[8]

But the Douglas family realised the precariousness of their situation. They had been cast outside the king's circle of trust. The Douglas relatives who had been influential during the latter years of James II's minority now avoided attending Parliament,[9] and the Earl cast around for allies. He contacted John MacDonald, Earl of Ross and Lord of the Isles, a man who had been active in his own cause against James. The two magnates, along with the Earl of Crawford, signed a band of mutual defence against the

---

[4] Brown, *The Black Douglases*, p.287.
[5] Lynch, *Scotland: A New History*, p.150.
[6] Brown, *The Black Douglases*, p.290.
[7] RPS, *1451/6/5-11*.
[8] Thomson, *The Auchinleck Chronicle*, p.45.
[9] Tanner, *The Late Medieval Scottish Parliament*, pp.130-131.

king.[10] Perhaps William Douglas came away from this feeling secure for the first time since his return from Rome. It was then the king sent a summons to meet him at Stirling Castle, accompanied by a letter promising safe conduct.

On the night of 22 February 1452 at Stirling Castle, Douglas was treated to a banquet by the king. But afterwards, having drunk too much wine, James started asking questions about Douglas' mutual protection band with MacDonald. The king ordered him to break the agreement. Douglas replied he "mycht nocht, nor wald nocht."[11] James snapped, drew a dagger, and stabbed his guest. His courtiers piled in. William Douglas suffered twenty-six stab wounds and had his head smashed in with a pole-axe.[12] Once again, an Earl of Douglas had dined with James II and not seen the night's end.

Scotland was in uproar. On 17 March William's brother James, now the 9th Earl of Douglas, marched into Stirling in force, looted and burned the town, had the king's worthless safe conduct letter dragged through the mud tied to the tail of a horse, and cried 'richt slanderfully of the king' for 'the foule slauchter of his brother'.[13] But James moved fast. He was already at Lochmaben and Morton in early March, consolidating promises to former Douglas allies who were amenable, and neutralising those who were not.[14]

The murder raised eyebrows across Europe: James wrote to the French king seeking his confidence and support.[15] Monarchs routinely eliminated powerful subjects, but the correct way to do it was via the courts. It was one thing to set in motion the wheels of justice against your enemies. To lose your temper in an argument with a man you'd promised safe conduct, then stabbing him in the neck when you'd drunk too much claret was something else entirely. James of the Fiery Face was well named.

Once James was sure of his support, a Parliament was called for 12 June 1452 to absolve him of blame. That evening, Douglas supporters pinned a

[10] Lynch, *Scotland: A New History*, p.148.
[11] Thomson, *The Auchinleck Chronicle*, p.46.
[12] *Ibid*, p.47.
[13] *Ibid*, p.47.
[14] Brown, *The Black Douglases*, pp.294-295.
[15] *Ibid*, pp.294-295.

letter to the door of Parliament House in Edinburgh withdrawing allegiance to the king and calling the King's Council traitors.[16]

But the 9th Earl of Douglas had little room for manoeuvre. His ally in the North-east, the Earl of Crawford, had been defeated in battle by the Earl of Huntly. By August 1452, Douglas had submitted to the king,[17] and Parliament had reassured James that the 8th Earl was responsible for his own death due to resisting the king's 'flattering persuasions.'[18] But with James busily undermining him and isolating him from any allies, Douglas fortified his strongholds. Various crimes were laid at his door in 1455: burning Dalkeith, abetting Robert Douglas in depriving the king of the succession to Strathbrock, harrying the royal functionary Lawrence, Lord Abernethy.[19] It was all the excuse James was looking for to openly declare war on Douglas.

Figure 16: Threave Castle

---

[16] Thomson, *The Auchinleck Chronicle*, p.48.
[17] MacQuarrie, *Medieval Scotland: Kingship And Nation*, p.223.
[18] RPS, *1452/6/1*.
[19] McGladdery, *James II*, pp.85-86.

Arkinholm

Douglas was supported by MacDonald, who burned the royal fortresses in the Highlands and, in an echo of Haakon of Norway's expedition of 1263, sent Donald Balloch up the Clyde in July 1455 to attack royal land on Inverkip and Arran.[20] But the issue would be settled on land, not by sea.

In March 1455, James launched his attack. Douglasdale and Avondale were burned, Douglas castles cast down, and the lands harried of Lord Hamilton, Douglas' major supporter. Hamilton was in England trying to drum up support. By the time he returned, Douglas' main fortress of Abercorn Castle was under siege. Douglas dithered. He didn't have the inclination or support to depose the king, so what course of action could he take? In the face of this indecision, the glamour of royalty and the promise of a complete pardon was more than Hamilton could resist: he switched sides. This betrayal was too much for Douglas who fled for England.[21]

Douglas' three brothers remained and made a last stand against the king in the Borders. But at Arkinholm in May 1455, two brothers were killed and the third fled to England.[22] Finally in June, the Earl's great keep of Threave in Galloway was besieged, surrendering two months later.[23]

Douglas' lands were annexed to the crown. The peerages in the possession of the Douglas family were parcelled out to James' supporters, and the great Earldom of Douglas was made forfeit. The family who had shaped and captained Scotland since the Wars of Independence was destroyed, their punishment for approaching too close to the king's power. But the Douglases were not quite gone. The irony was that the king's forces at Arkinholm were led by the Earl of Angus, descended from another son of William, the 1st Earl of Douglas. This branch of the family was known as the Red Douglas, to differentiate from the vanquished Black Douglas. So the

---

[20] Thomson, *The Auchinleck Chronicle*, p.55.
[21] McGladdery, *James II*, pp.86-87.
[22] *Ibid*, pp.129-130.
[23] Sadler, *Border Fury*, pp.331-332; HES Editors, *Threave Castle: History*. [online] Historic Environment Scotland.

Black Douglases were gone... but the *Red* Douglases would continue to thrive as loyal servants to the king.

Mair Curious than was Becoming of a King

For his 25th birthday on 16 October 1455, Parliament granted James II his head. He immediately pursued territorial claims over Roxburgh & Berwick, which were rightfully part of Scotland; Orkney, Shetland & the Isle of Man,[24] which weren't really; and the Duchy of Saintonge in France, a substantial area north of Bordeaux, which definitely wasn't Scottish, but had been promised to the previous King of Scots in a treaty that included the marriage of James' unfortunate sister Margaret.[25]

James' territorial ambitions were significantly aided by England's woes. Since the siege of Orleans was lifted in 1429 by Joan of Arc, English armies had suffered defeat after defeat at the hands of the French and their Scottish allies, going in to battle to the tune of *Marche des soldats de Robert Bruce*,[26] until being finally kicked out of France for good in 1453. The long connection between the English and French crowns that was established with the Norman Conquest of 1066 was finally over. The repercussions of this loss rumbled on. Henry VI lost his mind and was deposed in 1455. England turned in on itself. The Hundred Years War had ended; what Sir Walter Scott would call the War of the Roses had begun.

This was haymaking weather to James. In 1455 he wrote to Charles VII of France to organise an attack on the last English toehold in Calais whilst he simultaneously besieged Berwick.[27] In 1456 he revived the ancient pastime of Scottish kings by leading a successful raid on Northumberland.[28] Parliament made plans for war, mandating quarterly wappenschaws, where

---

[24] Ross, The Stewart Dynasty, p.149.
[25] Ibid.
[26] Bagad de Lann-Bihoué, *Marche des soldats de Robert Bruce*, [online] YouTube.
[27] McGladdery, *James II*, pp.96-97. James' attack on Berwick was averted by some quick-thinking Englishmen, who persuaded him they were ambassadors from the Pope come to negotiate a peace.
[28] Sadler, *Border Fury*, p.333.

Scotsmen were to gather and parade their weaponry, practice archery, and not use the excuse of a gathering to play football or golf:

Anent wapinschawingis [weaponshows]

Item it is ordanyt and decretyt that wapinschawingis be haldin be the lordis ande baronys spirituale and temporale foure tymis in the yere, and at the futbawe ande the golf be utirly cryit doune and nocht wsyt, ande at the bowe merkis be maide at all parrochkirkis, a paire of buttis, and schuting be wsyt ilk Sunday.[29]

In England, the Wars of the Roses were heating up, and James sought to take advantage from their troubles. War had broken out on the border during Richard of York's brief ascendancy in 1455. In 1456 Henry VI was back in control, and the King of France asked James to send an embassy to England. Yet even as he did so, James announced the truce over due to English aggression. Parliament preferred a more cautious and less expensive approach, leading to a two-year truce.[30] But James was keeping his options open, and by the summer of 1459 his ambassadors were negotiating with Lancastrians in England, whilst simultaneously swapping envoys with Richard of York who was in Ireland planning his own invasion. In the summer of 1460 rumours of a Scottish invasion of England swept Bruges, rumours with a basis in fact: James was spending large sums importing cannon and arms from Flanders. When forces loyal to Richard defeated Henry VI's doughty wife Margaret of Anjou in battle at Northampton and captured her husband, James immediately swung into action.[31]

But summer was to be cut short for the King of Scots. James thrilled to the roar of cannon fire and loved to get as close as he could to the action, 'mair curieous,' said Lindsay of Pitscottie, 'nor becam him or the maiestie of ane king.'[32] On 3 August, while laying siege to the English garrison in Roxburgh Castle, James in his enthusiasm was standing too close to one of the cannons,

---

[29] RPS, 1458/3/7.
[30] McGladdery, *James II*, p.98-99.
[31] *Ibid*, pp.110-111.
[32] Pitscottie, The Historie And Cronicles Of Scotland, Vol. I, p.143.

which burst and killed him.[33] He was 29. Scotland found herself without an adult king again.

This was becoming a habit.

A Woman's Hand

The bereaved Scots buried their grief in action, concluding the siege of Roxburgh by bringing England's last stubborn outpost in Scotland to its knees. The queen was summoned to Roxburgh with the heir to the throne, who at Kelso was crowned James III.[34] As the Scots celebrated their new king, they destroyed Roxburgh so that it could never again be used by hostile forces: one of Scotland's most impressive fortresses was razed completely to the ground.

Maria's first priority was stabilising affairs for her son's future. She was fortunate: the Douglases, who would have otherwise challenged her authority, had been eliminated five years earlier. Across Europe similar power struggles had erupted between kings and barons. England itself, Maria's other source of potential trouble, was in the middle of a civil war over the very same issue. But in England, as in Scotland, a pragmatic foreign woman was in charge. In the winter of 1460, Margaret of Anjou visited Scotland to raise support for her mentally incapacitated husband Henry VI.

The native noblemen resented a woman running the country:

> *The lordis said that thai war littil gud worth bath spirituale and temporall that gaf the keping of the kinrik [kingdom] till a woman.*[35]

But for once, government was dominated not by squabbling aristocrats or self-aggrandising kings, but by a stability-seeking mother and a wife. Through Maria's skilful negotiation, in April 1461 the Scots regained Berwick without a drop of blood shed.[36] She gained agreement on the important topic of possession of the boy king, holding him herself while the

---

[33] Macdougall, *James III*, p.35.
[34] *Ibid*, p.35. Though the *Extracta E Variis Cronicis Scocie* has James firing the cannon in honour of the arrival of his queen. McGladdery, *James II*, p.112.
[35] Thomson, *The Auchinleck Chronicle*, p.59.
[36] Macdougall, *James III*, pp.44-46.

Earl of Orkney was appointed official Guardian. Unlike Joan Beaufort before her, Maria van Gelre's grip on government seemed firm.

But reversals of fortune came almost immediately. After a battlefield defeat by the man who had newly crowned himself Edward IV of England, Margaret of Anjou fled with her family to sanctuary in Maria's Scotland. With Margaret's Lancastrian cause seemingly dead, Maria opened negotiations with Edward of York. At this, the first cracks in her regency appeared. The influential Bishop Kennedy of St Andrews was an enthusiastic supporter of the Auld Alliance and whoever opposed the English government of the time: and that meant supporting Margaret and Lancaster.[37]

Meanwhile, the Lord of the Isles took advantage of James II's death to harry Caithness and Orkney. He was summoned in February 1461 to attend Parliament to account for himself, but arrived with such an intimidating entourage that he was left unchallenged.[38] Then, with the exiled 9th Earl of Douglas and the new King Edward IV, MacDonald made a secret and treasonous pact. Their treaty divided Scotland in two: when the moment was ripe, MacDonald and Douglas would support Edward IV in conquering Scotland. They would rule half of Scotland each, in Edward's name: MacDonald north of the Forth, and Douglas to the south.[39] There were no plans to put the treaty into action, but its very existence showed how powerful forces at home and abroad had readied themselves to take advantage of any slip-ups by Maria.

Maria died three years after her husband, in 1463. She was only 29. Bishop Kennedy of St Andrews had already wrested control and invaded England in the summer of 1463, but had been forced to retired and seen the Borders burned.[40] Though he was a Francophile, pragmatism brought him to a 15-year truce with England.[41] But Kennedy too died in 1465.

James III was thirteen. With echoes of Crichton and Livingston's treatment of his father, the king was seized when out hunting from Linlithgow Palace

---

[37] Macdougall, *James III*, p.48.
[38] *Ibid*, p.43.
[39] *Ibid*, p.51.
[40] *Ibid*, pp.52-56.
[41] *Foedera Vol I*, p.694.

and transported to a guarded chamber in Edinburgh Castle. The keeper of the castle was Sir Alexander Boyd, whose brother Lord Robert had engineered the coup. A risky move for Lord Robert, but it paid off. He persuaded Parliament to make him sole Governor of the Realm, Great Chamberlain, and Lord Justice General. But he went too far when he married his own son Thomas to James' sister Princess Mary, and gave Thomas the title of Earl of Arran. It was the gift of kings to confer titles, not guardians, and an insult to the teenage monarch to arrange a royal marriage without his consent. This affront to the royal dignity would not long be tolerated. When Boyd was away in Denmark in 1468 preparing to return with the king's bride-to-be Princess Margarethe, sixteen-year old James seized power for himself. His first act was to have the Boyds charged with treason. James' younger sister Princess Mary, loyal to her husband Thomas, warned him and they managed to flee.[42] Lord Robert escaped too, fleeing to Bruges for safety.[43]

But he had left behind in Scotland something important: a Danish princess.

Norðreyjar

Thanks to the diplomatic skills of a remarkable Danish queen called Margrete,[44] the crowns of Norway and Denmark had been united in 1380, and the Danish monarch inherited Norway's international agreements. In 1426, the Scots stopped paying the annual stipend for the Hebrides that had been agreed with Norway in 1266 and renewed in 1312,[45] and the King of Denmark agitated for his Scottish stipend.[46] Meanwhile in another Norwegian territory, the fate of the locals and the Scots had become ever more entwined. The Jarls of Orkney had long held a stake in Scottish affairs – Jarl Magnus was at Arbroath to append his seal to the famous Declaration, and Jarl Malise, in his other guise of Earl of Strathearn, supposedly led a division against Edward III at Halidon Hill.[47] In 1379 Henry Sinclair of Roslin was confirmed by Haakon VI as Jarl. In the 1460s King Christian of

---

[42] Mackie, *A History Of Scotland*, p.100.
[43] Macdougall, *James III*, p.93.
[44] Encyclopædia Britannica, *Margaret I*.
[45] Bricka, *Dansk Biografisk Lexikon, tillige omfattende Norge for Tidsrummet 1537-1814. XI. BIND*, p.122; McGladdery, *James II*, pp.101-102.
[46] RPS, *1320/4/1*.
[47] Balfour Paul, *The Scots Peerage, Vol VIII*, pp.252-253.

Denmark accepted that the Earl of Orkney would answer to the King of Scots and not to him, and appointed Bishop Tulloch as his main representative in the Norðreyjar, or Northern Isles. The Earl's family promptly put the Bishop in prison.[48] The Orkney situation, and the Scottish debts for the Hebrides had to be resolved.

What better way of doing so than a dynastic marriage?

That was the winning proposal put forward by the King of France in an international arbitration to resolve Denmark's grievance with the Scots.[49] And so in July 1469, a teenage marriage was conducted between King Christian's daughter Margarethe and the King of Scots at Holyrood Abbey. The Danish claims on historic debts were dropped. Even better from the Scottish point of view, the direction of the debt was reversed. Not only did their king get a wife, but the Scots had negotiated a dowry for Margarethe of 60,000 florins. Christian discovered he could not pay, and first Orkney, then Shetland, were pawned in lieu of the dowry.[50] When it became clear the money would never be forthcoming, James declared the Earldom of Orkney forfeit to the Scottish Crown. On 20 February 1472, the Northern Isles were annexed permanently to Scotland by Act of Parliament.[51] Scotland's modern-day territorial extent was more-or-less complete.

---

[48] Macdougall, *James III*, p.79.
[49] Bricka, *Dansk Biografisk Lexikon, tillige omfattende Norge for Tidsrummet 1537-1814. XI. BIND*, p.122; McGladdery, *James II*, pp.101-102. The agreement was first made at Chinon in 1459, but the death of James II had halted negotiations.
[50] Cannon and Hargreaves, *The Kings And Queens Of Britain*, p.158.
[51] RPS, *1472/14*.

CHAPTER FOURTEEN

The Stewart Empire

Though his marriage to Margarethe had come right at the start of his reign, it was one of the last politically astute moves James III made. His ambition fatally outstripped his ability. His maternal grandfather, the Duke of Gueldres, fell out with his son & heir, and wrote to Edinburgh asking if one of his three Scottish grandsons would take control of the duchy. The duke eventually sold Gueldres to Charles the Bold of Burgundy instead. It marked the end of any chances of a Stewart running Gueldres, but undeterred, James sent an ambassador to Burgundy to press his claim.[1]

At the same time Charles the Bold of Burgundy, Duke Francis of Brittany, and Edward IV of England plotted an alliance against Louis XI of France. Sensing a chance for glory, James offered a mercenary army to Louis XI in return for 60,000 crowns a year.[2] James, who had rarely left Edinburgh since his kidnap from Linlithgow, gave the impression of wanting to lead the Scottish army into Brittany himself, and annexe it to Scotland.[3]

Parliament viewed these developments with alarm. They wanted James to spend his time travelling around the country, making royal authority visible and dispensing justice.[4] They wanted him to stop pardoning murderers in return for money.[5] They considered his plans of European conquest as dangerous folly.

But instead of disagreeing outright with the king, the Parliament of July 1473 put in place conditions that appeared to flatter James, yet were impossible to attain. They insisted that if he did travel abroad, he should not take an army to Brittany, but set out instead pre-conditions to France and Burgundy:

---

[1] Tanner, *The Late Medieval Scottish Parliament*, p.201.
[2] *Ibid,* p.201-202.
[3] RPS, *1472/33.*
[4] RPS, *1473/7/9.*
[5] Tanner, *The Late Medieval Scottish Parliament*, p.204.

James would arbitrate their dispute, and the price for submitting to the Scottish king's judgement was possession of the Duchy of Gueldres from Burgundy and the Duchy of Saintonge from France. Only once France and Burgundy had agreed to these unlikely demands, should James leave Scotland and act as wise ambassador.[6]

James was flattered at the thought of the key role he would play in matters of high state on the Continent, and promised Parliament he'd do nothing until these conditions were met. But the Scots knew neither Louis XI nor Charles the Bold would ever accept such terms. For the time being, their king was safe in Scotland.[7]

The satirical poem *The Buke of the Howlat* describes the situation. The howlet, an owl, felt naked and appealed to the Pope to be made more handsome. The Pope called a council of birds who all agreed to sacrifice a feather each for the howlet: but the howlet begun to vainly strut around, and the other birds stripped him of his donated plumage. The satire illustrated the dependence any king had on his nobles and his Parliament.[8]

It was not a lesson James was minded to heed.

A Cultured King

For there was more. Born in the same year as Leonardo da Vinci, James III patronised the arts and science in a manner proper to a king of the renaissance. He promoted talented courtiers to central place in his court. Men such as the musician William Rogers, tailor James Hommyl, and two particular sources of the nobles ire, the unsavoury Robert Cochrane and the low-born but talented William Sheves, who rose to become Archbishop of Saint Andrews.[9] In making these men advisors and counsellors, claimed later chroniclers, his major nobles were displaced from the royal household.[10] If this is true, then for the governance of the realm, James would have been

---

[6] RPS, *1473/7/4-8*.
[7] Tanner, *The Late Medieval Scottish Parliament*, p.203.
[8] *Ibid*, p.274; McGladdery, *James II*, p.53. *The Buke of the Howlat* is thought to have been composed in the 1450s, and though the sentiments pertain well to James III, it was more likely to have been written with the Livingstons in mind.
[9] Ross, *The Stewart Dynasty*, pp.161-162; Macdougall, *James III*, pp.245-246.
[10] Sutton, *Historia Gentis Scotorum*, Appendix, Chapter 30.

better consulting with Machiavelli than with musicians. Queen Margarethe grew disillusioned with his behaviour and the pair eventually became estranged. The queen and her eldest son the Duke of Rothesay relocated to Stirling while James remained in Edinburgh.[11] The situation could not last: the king was able to run daily affairs without recourse to his major nobles, but he still depended entirely upon their loyalty to raise an army. Alienating them was not a good long-term strategy.

And there was an alternative focus for the nobility: James' more vigorous, warlike brother, Alexander, the Duke of Albany, who 'loved nothing so well as able men and good horses'.[12] He had been named Lord of the Isle of Man as an infant. Could he now, some nobles wondered, be persuaded to become King of Scots?

The Brothers' Plot

Yet again, in March 1479, James promised Parliament he'd tour the country and fix the broken justice system.[13] Instead, suspicious of plots, he had his youngest brother John the Earl of Mar arrested. Mar was imprisoned in Craigmillar Castle, then moved to Canongate where he died.[14] Rumours of conspiracy quickly circulated, that John had been murdered by Robert Cochrane at James' order. To the outrage of his nobles, James then sold his dead brother's Earldom to Cochrane.[15] James besieged his remaining brother Alexander, the Duke of Albany in Dunbar castle between April and May, before Albany fled to France. James wanted Albany charged with treason, but when the Three Estates of Parliament met again in October they refused.[16]

James was about to become victim of events. Because in the middle of his family dispute, Louis XI of France took advantage of the situation to break

[11] Ewan, Pipes, Rendall and Reynolds, *The New Biographical Dictionary of Scottish Women*, pp.299-300.
[12] Ross, *The Stewart Dynasty*, p.165.
[13] RPS, *1479/3/17*.
[14] Macdougall, *James III*, p.169.
[15] *Ibid*, pp.150-151.
[16] Tanner, *The Late Medieval Scottish Parliament*, pp.223-225.

the growing peace between Scotland and England and play one against the other.

In the Web of the Universal Spider

Louis had been the self-entitled prince whose behaviour had contributed to his Scottish wife Margaret's death: but now he had become the supreme diplomat of Europe, nicknamed *l'universelle araignée* (the universal spider), for his ability to weave plots and conspiracies. He made peace with England in 1475 and captured Burgundy for France in 1477. In 1480 he sent Sorbonne scholar John Ireland back home to Scotland to discuss the Auld Alliance. For despite making a truce with England, if Louis could keep Scotland and England at each other's throats, all to the good for France; it would keep England's attention away from interfering with Burgundy.[17] John Ireland arrived in his homeland to put the French position. Though France received mercenary soldiers and military aid from Scotland, John Ireland argued, Scotland was more than compensated in return with the gift of culture from France.[18] A blood sacrifice in exchange for learning manners: a fair trade according to the French mind.

James had pursued a sensible, if domestically unpopular policy of peace with England,[19] but continued border raids and the threat of the renewal of the Auld Alliance saw Edward IV of England make his move. He planned war on Scotland and mustered an army.[20] James raised his own host, and then disbanded it. He announced that this was because the Pope had sent a letter requesting peace,[21] but the real reason was an inability to inspire confidence in his military leadership. Fortunately for James, Edward also had issues with rebellious nobles, and the entire affair petered out into nothing.[22]

James' exasperated nobles had had enough. In the spring of 1482, the Earls of Angus and Buchan went on an embassy to France. Officially they were there to talk to Louis XI, but secretly they approached Alexander, Duke of

[17] Sadler, *Border Fury*, p.388.
[18] Mackie, *A History Of Scotland*, p.95.
[19] Ross, *The Stewart Dynasty*, p.163.
[20] Sadler, *Border Fury*, pp.392-393.
[21] RPS, *1482/3/44*.
[22] Macdougall, *James III*, pp.-174183.

Albany, and exhorted him to overthrow his brother. Louis refused to provide assistance, but when the Earls tried again in England, they found Edward IV more amenable.[23] In June 1482 Albany was proclaimed Alexander IV of Scotland by Edward, on terms similar to those accepted by Edward Balliol. The pretender to the Scottish throne marched an English army into Scotland.[24]

Crisis for the king.

The Black Money

The situation in Scotland was grave enough. There was already in the land:

Baitht hungar and derth and mony pure folk deit of hunger.[25]

thanks to a disastrous lack of trust in the Scottish currency.

Gold and silver coins were acceptable everywhere, but you could not exchange such high value coins for everyday items such as ale or bread or a day's labour. Instead, European monarchs issued copper coins of nominal value. Like modern coins and banknotes they had no value in their own right, and worked as a medium of exchange only when people trusted the issuer. The trouble was nobody trusted James III. To people's outrage, he had Cochrane order the old copper coins in circulation to be recalled and his new 'black coinzhe' be given in exchange at half the value of the old ones. People refused to use them and the economy clogged up.[26] Poor people started dying of hunger. With his people dying, the nobles rebelling, and his brother approaching from the south with an English army, James was forced to act, taking his courtly retinue out of Edinburgh to their day with destiny.

Wha Daur Bell the Cat?

At Lauder, the nobles commanding the Scottish army caught up with the king's court, and a conference was held in the kirk. Cochrane had been made commander of the artillery, which was the last straw for the nobility. They

---

[23] Tanner, *The Late Medieval Scottish Parliament*, pp.228-231.
[24] Sadler, *Border Fury*, p.394.
[25] Gemmill and Mayhew, *Changing Values In Medieval Scotland*, p.126.
[26] *Ibid*, pp.125-128.

declared they would proceed no further until low-born favourites were dismissed from positions of authority, but James refused. In the king's absence, the nobles conferred again. If Cochrane was not going to be dismissed, then he had to be eliminated.

"Aye tis well said,"

said Lord Gray who had already surrendered the town of Berwick to Albany and his English army without a fight,[27]

"but wha daur bell the cat?"[28]

"I shall," replied Archibald Douglas, 5th Earl of Angus. The nobles summoned Cochrane, who swaggered into their presence wearing a heavy gold chain. In a rage Douglas tore the chain off Cochrane's neck. He was seized and tied. A party of hereditary nobility went out to the tents and arrested the rest of James' low-born favourites. They were summarily hanged from Lauder Bridge, mercy being shown only to an eighteen-year old called Ramsay who clung to the king's leg, sobbing in terror.[29] James himself was seized. The plan to place Albany on the throne suddenly changed. Rather than waiting for him to march over the horizon, the nobles retired to Edinburgh, where they swore allegiance to James then imprisoned him in Edinburgh Castle. A bizarre situation: yet Scotland's ruling class had, since the days of David II, been perfectly comfortable with a king who ruled in name only.

When Albany arrived in Edinburgh, he found James inaccessible except by a major siege and the Earl of Angus in charge of the situation. Alexander was informed that he was welcome to remain in Scotland as Duke of Albany, but that King Alexander IV wasn't a thing any more. Unable to gain advantage, Albany's army returned home without a fight, though they did loot and burn the countryside as they went and put a garrison in Berwick Castle, which has remained in English hands ever since.

---

[27] Macdougall, *James III*, p.194.
[28] *Ibid*, p.205. It's a nice quote, but was supposedly invented by Hume of Godscroft in his 1664 *History of the House of Douglas and Angus*.
[29] Macdougall, *James III*, p.198.

Albany had lost his shot at the crown, but with James rendered a paper monarch by the coup, the nobles were keen for a counterweight to the Earl of Angus' power. It was arranged for Albany to become Lieutenant-General of the Realm. The king was released, the unstable power-sharing arrangement lasting until James attempted to arrest Albany in January 1483. Albany fled, tried his hand once more in July 1484, and returned again to France, where he was killed a year later in a joust.

James III had fought off his challengers. But his realm remained discontented, waiting for the right opportunity to eject him.

The King is Dead: Sorry About That

Through the 1480s, James' enemies simply refused to turn up to Parliament.[30] One final time in October 1487, Parliament reiterated its requirement for the king to take an interest in justice.[31] James may have had the subsequent Act of Parliament suppressed from the official report, but one of the lords present, Lord Drummond, recorded Parliament's grievance for his personal archive:

> *Our soverane lord hes considderit and understandin that his realme is greitlie brokin in the self, his liegis troublit and heryit throw tresoun, slauchter, reif, birning, thift, and oppin herschip throw default of scharpe execution of justice and over commoun granting of grace and remissiounis of trespassouris.*[32]

Too late, James realised that even his allies had turned against him. In January 1488 he created a rash of new Lords of Parliament:[33] legislators who had neither great estates nor loyal tenants to fall back on, and who owed their position entirely to the king. But James was in a weak position. His eldest son the Duke of Rothesay had been raised by his mother Margarethe in Stirling independent of influence from the king in Edinburgh.[34] James had instead showered new titles and attention on his second eldest son, and

30 Tanner, *The Late Medieval Scottish Parliament*, p.243.
31 RPS, *1487/10/5-10*.
32 Tanner, *The Late Medieval Scottish Parliament*, p.255.
33. *Ibid,* p.260.
34 Macdougall, *James IV*, p.1.

planned a glittering arranged marriage for him.[35] Scunnered with their sovereign lord, influential sections of the nobility began to plan for a future based around the Duke of Rothesay. It would only take a spark for the flames of rebellion to be rekindled.

It was James' love of music which did it.

He had a vision of founding a School of Music with a Chapel Royal in Stirling Castle, and appropriated the revenues of Coldingham Priory to pay for it. But the person who already collected those revenues, Lord Home of Berwickshire, considered them his personal gouge.[36] Home raised the lairds whose lands had been forfeited by James for failing to attend Parliament. They felt the time was now ripe to overthrow the king. Margarethe's son Rothesay had turned fifteen. Old enough, for the nobility, to replace his father.

The first act of the rebel lords was to secure Prince James, the Duke of Rothesay. He took no part in the coup, but did not object either; his father was a remote figure more interested in his younger brother, and his mother had recently died. Who else was on his side? A series of manoeuvres through 1488 brought the two sides together on 11 June at Sauchieburn south of Stirling. The king was supported by representatives from the royal burghs and by some northern lairds. But against him stood the future: his son the blameless Prince, in whose name fought the swollen ranks of nobles whom James III had alienated throughout his reign. At first contact, the king's forces were scattered and he fled, taking refuge at Beaton's Mill. A passing knight recognised the king's horse and stabbed him to death.[37] Rarely has a Scottish monarch's death been less lamented.

But killing a king had consequences. It was an offence against God, a rupture of the established order. The barons of Scotland wrote long letters of apology to the Pope,[38] whilst simultaneously spreading scurrilous libels

---

[35] Macdougall, *James IV*, p.13.
[36] Tanner, *The Late Medieval Scottish Parliament*, p.257-258.
[37] Macdougall, *James III*, pp.348-349.The identity of James' assassin will forever be unknown, but rumour abounded.
[38] *Ibid*, pp.349-350.

about James around Europe intended to excuse their rebellion.[39] Their ancestors had gladly signed the Declaration of Arbroath, which claimed it was their duty to depose a monarch who submitted to English domination. But James hadn't done that: he had made justice impossible by pardoning convicted murderers in return for cash, entertained vainglorious proposals to annexe Brittany as the price for Scottish assistance in French wars, overseen famine and starvation as people refused to use his coins, held the unsavoury character of Cochrane too close, and attempted to endow a Chapel Royal.

Prince James, now King James IV, learnt lessons from this. For his part in his father's death, he vowed in penance to wear an iron chain round his middle. As he grew fatter in older-age, Treasury Accounts itemised extra links to his chain.[40]

And James IV wasn't going to allow Parliament or his nobles to dictate terms. He was vigorous, curious, sexually magnetic, and constantly travelling around the country encouraging justice, science and culture. James IV would mould a country in his image through sheer force of personality.

Here was a *real* renaissance king.

---

[39] Macdougall, *James III*, p.328. James was a victim of propaganda designed to libel his reputation and justify his attackers: letters accusing James of murdering his Danish wife were sent to King Hans of Denmark; of murdering his brother the Earl of Mar to Phillipe de Commynes in France; and in the Holy Roman Empire, it was even rumoured he had slept with his sister Margaret.
[40] Balfour Paul, *Accounts Of The Lord High Treasurer Of Scotland, Vol III*, p.250.

CHAPTER FIFTEEN

A True Renaissance Prince

Brother Damien, the court alchemist, claimed he could build a flying machine. James IV cleared the battlements of Stirling Castle to witness the wonder of the world's first human flight. Damien launched himself with home-made flappable wooden wings covered in feathers and, to the great amusement of the poet William Dunbar who wrote scathingly about Damien in *Ane Ballat of the Fenyeit Frier, How He Fell in the Myre*,[1] broke his bones landing in the dung heap below. The fault, claimed Damien, lay in the construction of his wings which had an excess of hen and a lack of eagle feathers.[2]

When James learned of twins whose mother had died giving birth, the opportunity to resolve a dispute he was engaged in with his scholars was too great to pass up. He was deep in discussion with the professors over whether or not Hebrew was the language spoken in the Garden of Eden, and here was a chance to find out. The unfortunate twins were banished to the uninhabited island of Inchkeith, along with a mute wet nurse. In the absence of any other language, the theory went, the infants would spontaneously begin speaking Hebrew to each other. According to the historian Lindsay of Pitscottie, 'Sum sayis they spak goode hebrew bot as to my self I knaw not'.[3]

This was the nature of the man who was crowned King of Scots at Scone on 24 June 1488. John Ireland had begun writing a book of advice for James III, and presented it to his son and successor.[4] The *Meroure of Wysdome* (or, *Mirror of Wisdom*), was an early example of a new fashion for royal self-help books, such as the later *Basilik Doron* or Machiavelli's *Il Principe*. But James

---

[1] Dunbar, and Laing, *The Poems Of William Dunbar*, p.39.
[2] Lesley and Thomson, *The History Of Scotland, From The Death Of King James I In The Year MCCCCXXXVI To The Year MDLXI*, p.76.
[3] Pitscottie, *The Historie And Cronicles Of Scotland, Vol. I*, p.237.
[4] Gosman, MacDonald, and Vanderjagt, *Princes And Princely Culture, Volume One*, p.155.

IV had less need for it than his father. To the delight of his nobles he immediately toured the country, acting as a figurehead in justice ayres.[5] James was the first Scottish king since Robert Stewart to be comfortable in the Gàidhealtachd, and his tour included the Highlands. He was the last King of Scots fluent in Gaelic: a language that he spoke along with Latin, French, German, Italian, Spanish, Flemish, probably Danish, English, and finally Scots, which Spanish ambassador Pedro de Ayala describes 'as different from English as Aragonese from Castilian.'[6] It was just as well. A strong presence in the Highlands was required.

No Joy Without Clan Donald

In 1474, Edward IV of England had concluded a peace treaty with Scotland. A year later, James III had taken advantage of his improved position to move against John MacDonald, who had signed an earlier, secret pact with Edward to divide Scotland between them. John was summoned to Edinburgh to be tried for treason, avoiding a trial by quitting his claim on the Earldom of Ross.[7] But his son Angus Og disagreed with his father's actions: first he fought on the mainland to regain Ross, and in 1480 or 1481 fought for control of the Lordship of the Isles against his father in a naval action at Bloody Bay off Mull. John, supported by the MacLeans, MacNeills and MacLeods, who supposedly unfurled to no avail *am Bratach Sith,* the Fairy Flag, their magical guarantor of victory,[8] was defeated by Angus Og, who then beat the king's army on the mainland and took possession of Dingwall Castle and Easter Ross. The nobles of the rest of Scotland were preoccupied with the coup at Lauder. Angus Og remained unopposed until 1483, when the Earls of Atholl and Huntly ousted him from Ross. In 1488 he was back, taking Inverness while the Lowland lords were again distracted in dispatching their king at Sauchieburn. But the end was in sight for the Lordship of the Isles. Angus Og's harpist slit his throat while he slept. James IV launched a new campaign against the MacDonalds, and Angus Og's baby son was captured by his maternal grandfather, Colin Campbell, the 1st Earl of Argyll. After two centuries of MacDonald domination of the western

---

[5] Macdougall, *James IV*, p.62.
[6] Calendar of State Papers Spain, no.210.
[7] Macdougall, *James III*, pp.125-131.
[8] Macleod, *The Macleods of Dunvegan*, p.71.

seaboard, the clan Campbell were beginning to make their presence felt. When James IV arrived in the West Highlands in person, the elderly John MacDonald capitulated entirely. He was taken to the Lowlands to live out the rest of his life a pensioner of the king, who forfeited the Lordship of the Isles to the crown in 1493.

The loss of power of the MacDonalds on the west coast left a gap that could not be filled by either the monarch or the Campbells. MacDonald had a court at Finlaggan, and a bard, Gillecallum Mac an Ollaimh, who wrote:

Na sloigh mhòr 'us an greann,
am muirn, am meaghar s' am foghainteachd,
Ni còire bhi 'n an eugmhais,
ni h-aoibhneas gun chlann Domhnuil.

This people so great in fame
In courtesy, mind, and firmness,
there is no right without them,
there is no joy without Clan Donald.[9]

The Highlands were already turbulent. But the vacuum left by the toppling of MacDonald power would see rule of law collapse in the Gàidhealtachd: the classic era of the clan feud known in Gaelic as *Linn na Creach*, the Age of the Raids, was about to begin.

A Dialect With an Army

With the Highlands on the brink of the iconic anarchy of clan warfare, the Lowlands flowered with a lesser-known culture of its own. James III had made a play at being a Renaissance monarch, but his son proved the real deal. The language of South-eastern Scotland, originally called Inglis, descended from the language of the Angles of Northumbria: a tongue claimed well into the 14th century to be unintelligible to the Saxon ears of Southern England.[10] If a language is but a dialect with an army, then the centuries of conflict with England had led to this branch from a shared

[9] M'Lauchlan, *The Dean of Lismore's Book*, p.73,97.
[10] Wales, *Northern English: A Social and Cultural History*, pp.61-62.

Germanic root being called Scots. At James IV's court, poets and playwrights known as makars thrived in the Scots language. Robert Henryson, Walter Kennedy, Gavin Douglas, William Dunbar... Take Dunbar's most famous work, *The Flyting of Dumbar and Kennedie*, a description of the two foremost poets of the realm verbally jousting in front of the king, building insult upon insult like an early 21st century rap battle. Dunbar has the honour of being the first to get the word 'fuck' into print, in *Ane Brash of Wooing*, and an even ruder word[11] in *The Flyting*. Their language needed no army to make an impact.

And the printing press had arrived in Scotland. Invented in Germany, Scotland's first native press opened in Southgait, now called Cowgate, in Edinburgh in 1507. The king wanted them to print religious texts and Acts of Parliament, but their early print runs included chivalric romances, works by Henryson and Dunbar, and the work of Blind Harry: his patriotic *Wallace* was earthy, vital, and hugely popular:

> *Till honour ennymyis is our haile entent,*
> *It has beyne seyne in thir tymys bywent;*
> *Our ald ennemys cummyn of Saxonys blud,*
> *That nevyr yeit to Scotland wald do gud.*[12]

It wasn't all flyting and gore. Gavin Douglas kickstarted the literary renaissance with a translation of Virgil's *Aeneid*, the first classical work translated into Scots. Robert Carver produced beautiful polyphonic choral music. Renaissance architects built new palaces at Stirling, Edinburgh, and Falkland. An act was passed in Parliament in 1496 mandating all landowners send their eldest sons to school and university,[13] of which there were already three in Scotland: St Andrews, Glasgow, and Aberdeen. The Barber Surgeons of Edinburgh were incorporated as the Royal College of Surgeons in 1505. And James being James, the king himself had a go at medical procedures. He purchased a device to extract teeth and, according to the

---

[11] Strictly speaking, Chaucer was first in The Canterbury Tales, though he spelled it 'queynte'.
[12] Jamieson, *Wallace*, p.1.
[13] RPS, A1496/6/4.

Lord High Treasurer's Accounts, paid a willing victim to have his teeth extracted:

To Kynnard the barbour for twa teith drawn furth of his hed be the king, 14s[14]

Like his predecessors, he tried to have 'fut bawis, gouwf, or uther sic unproffitable sports' banned by Act of Parliament[15], but was not immune to their appeal himself: the royal accounts of 1503 itemise:

Item, for golf clubbes and balles to the King, 9s[16]

When Henry VII's representative the Earl of Somerset visited Scotland on a diplomatic mission, any southern prejudice he may have held would have been confounded on discovering just how civilised and cultured James IV's court was.[17]

But there was good reason for the court to put on a show when Somerset visited. James was getting married.

The Thistle and the Rose

The Plantagenets, that line of English Kings with half a foot in France, were dead. Their Lancastrian and Yorkist branches had fought each other to extinction in the War of the Roses, and a new family with a Welsh tinge, the Tudors, came through the middle to take the crown of England. The Tudor Henry VII's main foreign policy was the avoidance of wars. English monarchs had finally given up trying to enforce their claim on the crown of France, and Henry sought peace with Scotland. What better way of doing so than a state marriage? James had already supported a pretender to the English throne, Perkin Warbeck, and had amused himself in 1496 and 1497 with desultory invasions into England on Warbeck's behalf. No more of this

---

[14] Balfour Paul, *Accounts Of The Lord High Treasurer Of Scotland, Vol IV*, p.332.
[15] RPS, *1491/4/17*.
[16] Balfour Paul, *Accounts Of The Lord High Treasurer Of Scotland, Vol II*, p.418. James is buying golf clubs again in 1506: Balfour Paul, *Accounts Of The Lord High Treasurer Of Scotland, Vol III*, p.206.
[17] Hearne, *Joannis Lelandi Antiquiarii, De Rebus Britannicis Colleactanea. Vol IV*, pp.258-300 for the Earl's full account of his visit.

nonsense for Henry VII. In 1502 Henry and James signed the Treaty of Perpetual Peace, the first such treaty between Scotland and England, as opposed to a temporary truce, since 1328.[18] This opened the door for Henry's daughter Margaret to marry the Scottish king. She arrived in great state in the summer of 1503. She was given ownership of Linlithgow Palace and several Scottish castles. Songs and poems were written in her honour, such as William Dunbar's *The Thrissil and the Rois*:

> *The commoun voce uprais of birdis small*
> *Apone this wys: "O blissit be the hour*
> *That thow wes chosin to be our principall;*
> *Welcome to be our princess of honour,*
> *Our perle, our plesans, and our paramour,*
> *Our peax, our play, our plane felicité:*
> *Chryst thee conserf frome all adversité!"*[19]

As the cavalcade approached Edinburgh, James rode out to meet his bride-to-be, jumping up and down off his horse without touching his stirrups to impress her with his athleticism and virility. He gave her a kiss and rode back to Edinburgh to await her arrival in the city which was marked by a joust.[20] They married on 8 August 1503. James was thirty years old, in the prime of his life, with a beard *'somthynge long'*.[21] He already had five surviving children from four different mistresses.[22]

Margaret was thirteen.

---

[18] Mackie, *A History Of Scotland*, p.123.
[19] Dunbar, and Laing, *The Poems Of William Dunbar*, p.10.
[20] Hearne, *Joannis Lelandi Antiquiarii, De Rebus Britannicis Colleactanea. Vol IV*, pp.283-288.
[21] *Ibid* p.285.
[22] Weir, *Britain's Royal Families: The Complete Genealogy*, pp.241-242.

Figure 17: Margaret Tudor

James was courteous and kind to his new wife when they were together, but he was not going to give up his mistresses for a girl who was too young to share his bed. James' favourite was Janet Kennedy, red-haired and spirited, nicknamed Flaming Janet and less flatteringly, 'Janet bair ars'.[23] She had already been mistress to the middle-aged Archibald Douglas, 5th Earl of Angus: the man who had belled Cochrane's cat at Lauder Bridge. But to the earl's jealousy, Janet's head was turned by the king, who took her as mistress for himself. Shortly before Margaret Tudor arrived in Scotland, Janet was

---

[23] Macdougall, *James IV*, p.286.

discreetly moved to Darnaway Castle in Moray,[24] whose possession she was guaranteed provided she remained 'without another man.'[25] James would still visit her on his frequent pilgrimages to St Duthac's sanctuary in Tain, or to Whithorn, where Janet's possession of Bothwell formed a convenient stopover point.[26]

When Margaret Tudor arrived in her castle of Stirling, she was appalled to discover that its palaces were used as a nursery for James' children by his various mistresses.[27]

The Scottish Crusade

Having killed his father, the nobles stepped more lightly with James IV. Parliament had remonstrated with James I and James III over tax and justice, but it was in the king's gift whether or not to call a Parliament at all. James was lucky to have ways of raising money other than general taxation, such as the vacant Archbishopric of St Andrews or his future wife's dowry, and he increasingly found he could rule Scotland in the French style without calling Parliaments at all:[28] an attractive prospect to a king who, in the words of Don Pedro de Ayala, 'esteems himself as much as though he were lord of the world'.[29] The Stewart monarch was no longer first amongst equals, and James IV had the energy and charisma to carry his nobles along with him.

For James was not content with Scotland alone: his great enthusiasm was Holy War. The Ottoman Empire based in Turkey had rolled into the Holy Land and the Balkans, and Christian Europe seemed powerless to prevent them. A crusade against the Ottomans was just the cause for a vigorous man like James. To fight the Turks, he built Europe's biggest warship, the *Great Michael*. *'There is nothing else like it in Christendom'* wrote the French

---

[24] Macdougall, *James IV*, p.180; money grants in Balfour Paul, *Accounts Of The Lord High Treasurer Of Scotland, Vol II*, p.297.

[25] Ewan, Pipes, Rendall and Reynolds, *The New Biographical Dictionary of Scottish Women*, p.228.

[26] Macdougall, *James IV*, p.197.

[27] Balfour Paul, *Accounts Of The Lord High Treasurer Of Scotland, Vol II*, pp.294-298, detail several pages of expenses for the royal nursery in Stirling.

[28] Macdougall, *James IV*, pp.150-156.

[29] Calendar of State Papers Spain, no.210.

ambassador.[30] Too big to berth at any existing Scottish port, Newhaven had to be built to accommodate it.[31] Scottish knights weren't going to invade Turkey alone: that would be absurd, but James found an ally in Louis XII of France, who advocated peace in Europe so they could combine and undertake 'la guerre contre les Infidelles.'[32] For Louis, the crusade was a diplomatic smokescreen: he was at war with the Pope. The Pope wasn't going to be distracted from his fight with France by calls for Christian unity: instead of supporting a crusade against the Ottoman Empire, he called on the rest of Europe to help him out. And one man in particular was keen to have a go at France: England's new king, Henry VIII.

England's Nero

Henry VII of England died in 1509. He died with a country at peace, the warring nobles pacified. He had avoided foreign wars, made a strategic alliance with Scotland, and through prudent expenditure and deeply resented taxation, built up his exchequer to its healthiest ever state, with £1.25m in the royal coffers.[33] No English monarch would ever again operate such a surplus. In Henry VII's hands, boring governance had been good governance. But the old king had declined into bullying in his final years, and his son, observing, came to assume that ruling a kingdom required a violent temper and the indulgence of personal whims.[34] Insecure and self-entitled, the new king 'could not abide to have any man stare him in the face when he talked to them,'[35] and 'loved nothing worse than to be constrained to do anything contrary to his royal will and pleasure.'[36]

His first act at the age of eighteen, to the general joy of the nobility, was to execute his father's two leading tax collectors. He held his own advisors close, all the easier to dispose of them in future when occasion demanded.[37]

---

[30] Goodwin, *Fatal Rivalry*, p.118.
[31] Macdougall, *James IV*, p.187.
[32] Setton, *The Papacy And The Levant, Volume III*, p.87.
[33] Weir, *Henry VIII: King and Court*, p.13.
[34] Matusiak, *Henry VIII: The Life and Rule of England's Nero*, p.49.
[35] *Ibid.*
[36] *Ibid*, p.79.
[37] Sir Thomas More and Thomas Cromwell went the way of Henry VII's tax collectors.

The new king spent England's money like water. He craved influence abroad through vainglorious schemes on the Continent. He married six women and killed two of them. He started his own religion and set himself up as its Pope. He would grow corpulent, paranoid, and dangerous. He was Henry VIII. And he was bad news for Scotland.

Though his sister had married James, Henry was no friend of his brother-in-law. He reactivated the ancient claim of English suzerainty over Scotland, infuriating and alarming the Scots.[38] When the Pope called on European powers to form an alliance with him against Louis XII, Henry VIII saw an opportunity to gain land in Northern France. He attacked Calais in 1512. The Scottish reaction was frantic diplomacy, still advocating James' dream of a pan-European alliance to fight the Turks.[39] But with England, Spain, and the Holy Roman Empire, the old name for Germany, joining forces with the Pope against him, Louis XII of France needed allies. In the rounds of diplomacy England and the Pope had offered James nothing but threats, but in May 1513 Louis offered James 50,000 francs, seven galleys for his navy, and the services of France's best admiral.[40] This was more like it. French queen Anne de Bretagne sealed the deal when she sent James the ring from her finger, along with a letter begging him to be her champion and:

Come three fute on inglis ground for hir sake.[41]

This was catnip to the King of Scots.

Having put off a showdown with England as long as he could, James now committed himself. After all, he had invaded Northern England before in support of Perkin Warbeck. He would break the Perpetual Peace and throw in his lot with France.

What could possibly go wrong?

---

[38] Macdougall, *James IV*, p.259.
[39] Ellis, *Original Letters, Illustrative Of English History*, pp.76-78.
[40] Macdougall, *James IV*, pp.259-263.
[41] Pitscottie, *The Historie And Cronicles Of Scotland, Vol. I*, p.256.

Flodden

James' magnetic personality swept his nobles and people along with him. Bishop Elphinstone alone publicly considered the invasion a mistake: he was shouted down when he raised his concerns in council.[42] But caution was understandable. The Wars of the Roses were long since resolved, and England was no longer the weak and divided country that James II had been able to take advantage of. Instead, Henry VIII had been preparing for a battle on his northern frontier for over two years.

James gathered a huge host at Boroughmuir on 17 August 1513, and met the Berwickshire muster at Ellemford. The largest Scottish army to ever invade England marched southeast via Duns and Coldstream, crossing the border on 22 August. Despite the size of the army the invasion was intended as a token gesture, without a clear plan beyond diverting English attention away from the front in Northern France. The Scots besieged and took the castles of Norham, Wark, Ford and Etal. James then tarried for twenty days in Lord Heron's castle of Ford. Lord Heron was a prisoner in Fast Castle in Scotland, and James set about seducing his wife, which was:

> *against godis commandementis and against the order of all goode captanis of weir to begin at huredome and harlotrie befoir ony goode success of battell or wictorie.*[43]

James' army tarried so long that half of them returned home through a lack of victuals, something Lady Ford was sharp enough to notice. She requested, and was granted, leave to go visit her friends.[44]

For all Henry VIII's flaws, idiocy was not one of them. He had charged the defence of Northern England to the capable hands of Thomas Howard, the Earl of Surrey. Surrey was seventy years old, but the wily campaigner intimately knew James' weaknesses. Not only had Lady Heron travelled

---

[42] Macdougall, *James IV*, p.266.
[43] Pitscottie, *The Historie And Cronicles Of Scotland, Vol. I*, pp.262-3.
[44] *Ibid*, pp.263-4.

directly to York to inform him of the shrunken size of James' army,[45] but he had faced the Scottish king in battle before.

When James had last invaded England in 1497, he had besieged Norham and personally offered single combat to the man arriving to defend the castle: the Earl of Surrey. His offer was declined, and James retired home in the face of Surrey's army.[46] Surrey knew that James honoured chivalry, and sent messages to James insulting his honour, offering to meet him in battle on 9 September.[47] James agreed, and set up a defensive position on the rise of Flodden Hill across the River Till from Ford Castle. Excellent! He'd get a fight from Surrey at last.

But when Surrey arrived on the battlefield on 7 September, he had no intention of facing the larger, better defended Scottish army directly, instead sending another letter accusing James of cowardice for not lining up on the plain.[48] Surrey marched past them unmolested as the Scots looked on in concern. What were the English up to? They appeared to be heading for Scotland. It was a risky manoeuvre, but a battle-winning one. Hidden from view by the Northumbrian landscape, Surrey doubled back and took up a better position to the north of James.[49] The Scots had stayed put during this outflanking manoeuvre. James' determination to fight is well-documented. Earlier, the nobles remaining in the field had considered that they had done enough for France, and appointed Sir Patrick Lyndsey as their spokesman to tell the king so: James reputedly swore to hang Lyndsey on his own gate.[50] Another chronicler says that as the senior noble, the Earl of Angus approached the king: and viewing his caution as cowardice, James had ordered Angus home in tears of humiliation.[51]

---

[45] Pitscottie, *The Historie And Cronicles Of Scotland*, *Vol. I*, pp.263-4.
[46] Sadler, *Border Fury*, p.412.
[47] Ellis, *Original Letters, Illustrative Of English History*, pp.85-87.
[48] *Ibid.*
[49] Sadler, *Border Fury*, p.426.
[50] Pitscottie, *The Historie And Cronicles Of Scotland*, *Vol. I*, pp.267-269.
[51] Macdougall, *James IV*, p266.

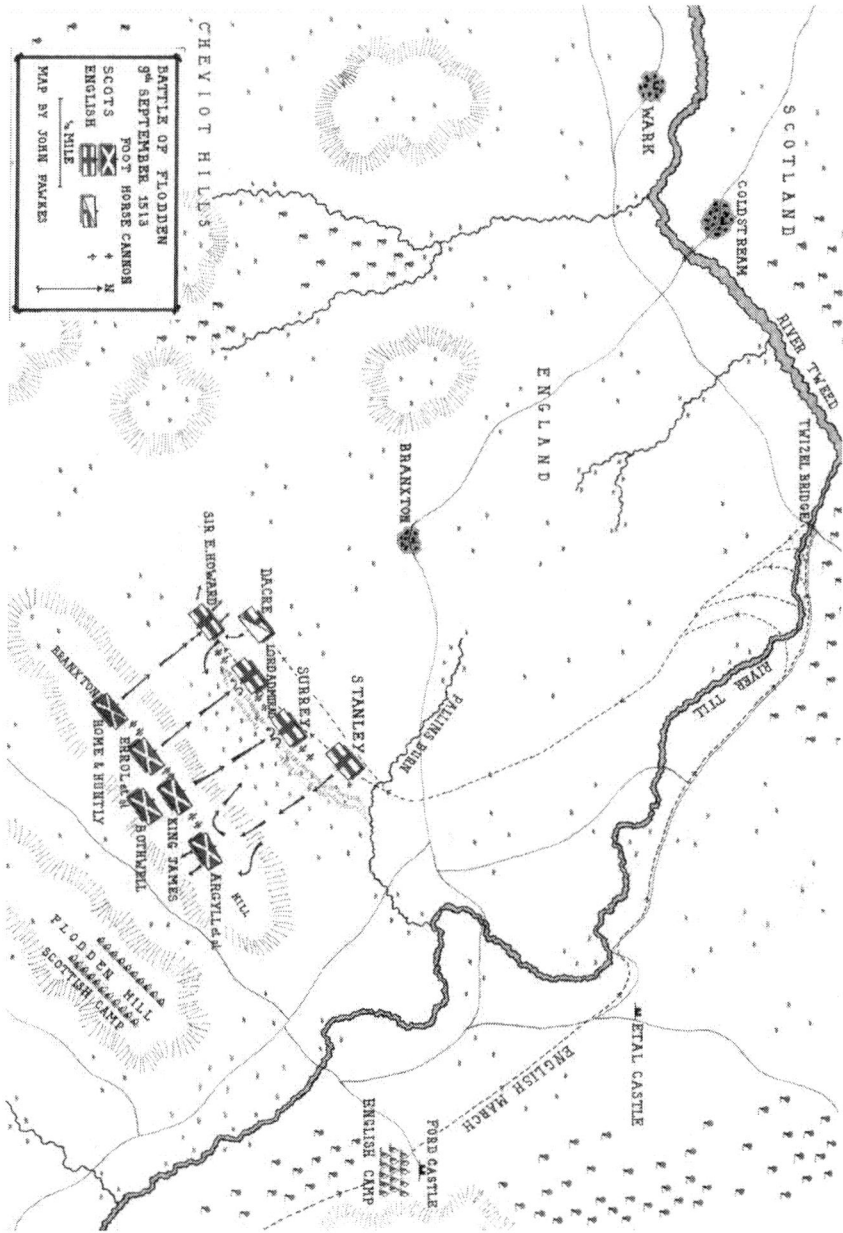

Figure 18: Battle of Flodden. © Britishbattles.com

But now the fight had come.

The Scots' northern flank was undefended, and on the morning of 9 September James ordered a rapid redeployment of his troops. His best gunners were away with the navy, and his guns at Flodden were not brought to bear down low enough to damage the English position. By contrast, English artillery played havoc with the Scots.[52] But then the Scots moved forward in good order. It was 4pm. The left flank of Borderers under Lord Home engaged first. They routed their English opponents, but the Scottish centre, with James in the thick of it, was in trouble.

As an aid to war, Louis XII had sent the Scots a fashionable new weapon: Swiss pikes, pointed lances between 16ft and 20ft long. Well-drilled Swiss infantry had proved their worth with these weapons in battles on the Continent by perfecting the art of the mobile schiltron. But the absolute key to success with pikes was the momentum generated by a disciplined mass of moving men.[53] And just in front of the English position, the Scots centre became trapped in an unexpected and treacherous bog. The English carried halberds and chopped the stationary pikes to bits. Next to be chopped up were the immobile Scottish soldiers themselves.[54] On being called on to assist, Lord Home supposedly refused, replying:

'He dois weill that dois for him self.'[55]

Unopposed by Home's horse, the English left flank marched a decoy force up the hill towards the Highlanders on the Scottish right flank, while their larger mass, hidden by the terrain, surprised the Highlanders and took them by the side.[56] The carnage continued hot and hard until the confusion of nightfall caused the sides to disengage.

Surrey braced himself for further fighting next day, but when dawn broke it was clear he had won the day. Lord Home had also remained near the field

---

[52] Sadler, *Border Fury*, p.431.
[53] *Ibid*, pp.416-418.
[54] *Ibid,* pp.434-435.
[55] Pitscottie, *The Historie And Cronicles Of Scotland, Vol. I*, p.271.
[56] Sadler, *Border Fury*, p.436-437.

of battle, but now rode home to protect his own lands of Berwickshire from the coming storm, abandoning the Scottish camp and its valuable artillery.[57]

Men armed with knives picked over the battlefield to loot and kill any wounded Scotsmen. The butcher's bill reported back was incredible. Ten Scottish earls had died. Most astonishingly of all, the body of King James was found. It was taken south, displayed as a trophy, neglected, and finally buried in an anonymous grave somewhere in England.[58]

Don Pedro de Ayala had gauged well the character of the Scottish king. Way back in 1498 he reported home that James was:

> *Courageous, even more so than a king should be... he is not a good captain because he begins to fight before he has given his orders.*[59]

The defeat stunned Scotland. One of the most haunting laments ever written, *The Flooers o' the Forest are a' wede awa'*, commemorates the battle.[60] The citizens of Edinburgh hastily erected a defensive wall in anticipation of English attack, the women of the city told to stop wailing and muck in.[61] But the country was fortunate. Henry VIII had specifically commissioned Surrey to defend England only: there would be no advantage pressed.[62] The English king was more interested in the main front in France than an invasion of Scotland. But that did not stop the raids of enterprising English Borderers as Lord Dacre, Warden of the Western March, reported to Henry VIII:

> *There never was so mekill myschefe, robbry, spoiling, and vengeance in Scotland than there is nowe, without hope of remedye; which I pray our Lord God to continewe.*[63]

The town of Selkirk remembers the return of just one local man from Flodden. The town of Hawick remembers Hornshole, where post-Flodden,

---

[57] Pitscottie, *The Historie And Cronicles Of Scotland, Vol. I*, pp.272-273.
[58] Sadler, *Border Fury*, p.438.
[59] Calendar of State Papers Spain, no.210.
[60] The Scots Guards, *Flower of the Forest*, [online] YouTube.
[61] Marwick, *Extracts from the Records of the Burgh of Edinburgh*, pp.143-144.
[62] Pitscottie, *The Historie And Cronicles Of Scotland, Vol. I*, pp.265,279-280.
[63] Ellis, *Original Letters, Illustrative Of English History*, p.93.

the Prior of Hexham led a band burning, raping and looting up Teviotdale. They camped at Hornshole with the intention of attacking Hawick next day. But that night the youths and boys of Hawick attacked the dozing Northumbrians, returning in triumph with the gold on blue saltire of the Priory of Hexham.[64]

The boys of Hawick had saved their town, but the same could not be expected from the new King of Scots.

Once again God's law of primogeniture had left Scotland in the hands of an infant: and chaos reigned supreme.

---

[64] Taylor, *Hornshole*, [online] Hawick Callants Club.

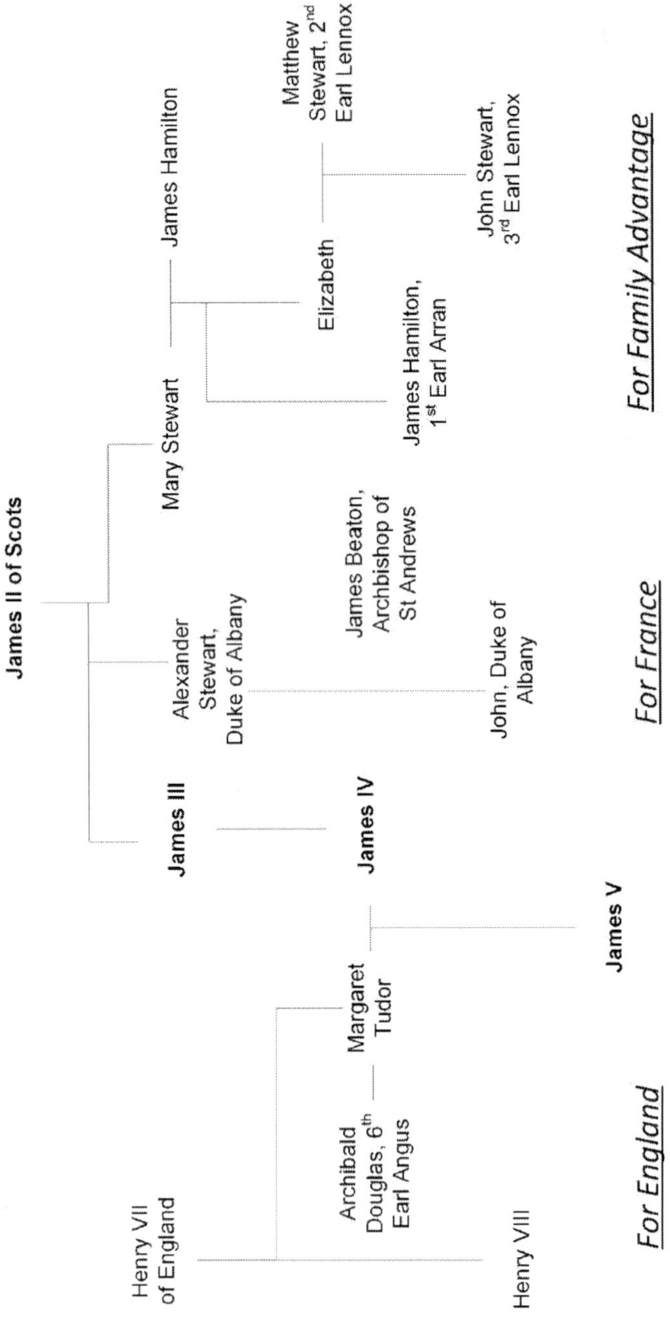

Figure 19: The main players in the minority of James V

CHAPTER SIXTEEN

Order from Chaos

After the Battle of Flodden, where King James IV fell alongside ten of his earls, the Border was in a state of lawless uproar. Bands of English Borderers roved across Southern Scotland, terrorising and pillaging the unfortunate Scots. They did not stop there: Lord Dacre, warden of the English Marches, came off worst in a skirmish in Redesdale trying to prevent his own countrymen preying on their neighbours,[1] and the Bishop of Carlisle complained:

> *There is more thefte and extorycyon by English theffes than there is by all the Scottes of Scotland.*[2]

Further north in Scotland, the Highlands weren't much quieter: the era of the clan feud had arrived. It would only grow more intense as the century evolved. The Mackenzies fought the Munros,[3] the Chattans opposed the Camerons,[4] the MacKays the Rosses,[5] the Forbes the Gordons,[6] the MacGregors and MacFarlanes raided the Colquhouns,[7] and the MacDonalds fought everyone – the MacLeods,[8] the Macleans,[9] the Mackenzies,[10] and of course, the Campbells…[11]

---

[1] Sadler, *Border Fury*, p.445.
[2] *Ibid.*
[3] Battle of Bealach nam Broig.
[4] Battle of the Shirts, the Fords of Arkaig.
[5] Battles of Tarbat, Altcharrish, Torran Dubh.
[6] Battle of Tillieangus, Craibstane.
[7] Battle of Glen Fruin.
[8] Battle of Glendale, Massacre of Eigg, Battle of Trumpan Dyke, Battle of Coire na Creiche.
[9] Battle of the Western Isles, Battle of Traigh Ghruinneart.
[10] The Raid of Ross, Battle of Blar Na Pairce, Battle of Drumchatt.
[11] MacColla's personal anti-Campbell crusade with Montrose.

With the new King of Scots James V only a year old, and his country in the hands of a new and inexperienced generation of nobility, more dependent on experienced clerics than ever before, Parliament met at Stirling to decide on the regency.[12] James IV's will ordained that his wife Margaret Tudor was to be Guardian of Scotland,[13] but the widowed queen was not welcome in the role: sister of Henry VIII of England, she sought to align Scottish policy with Henry's. Though stating in public that she had only the young king's interests at heart, in private letters to her brother she wrote:

I shall never do without your counsel, as long as I have a groat to spend.[14]

Ties with England were set to become closer still when she married Archibald Douglas, the 6th Earl of Angus and a confirmed Anglophile. But Angus was not short of enemies, and Parliament took action. By taking a husband, they said, Margaret forfeited her right to the Guardianship.[15] Angus' opponents needed no other reason to appoint a new regent, and the call went out to France for the most eligible male candidate. It was the beginning of a decades-long battle royale between French and English interests for control of Scotland.

The French Regency

In the heart of France lived John Stewart, Comte d' Auvergne & Lauraguais, master of a large part of the Auvergne, a pastoral region that today is a source of volcanic water and speciality cheese. He would give away in marriage his sister-in-law Madeleine de la Tour to Lorenzo de Medici, nephew of Pope Leo X, a lavish occasion hosted by the King of France.[16] In the Comte d' Auvergne, the Scots had a man plugged into the central current of European affairs. Because, despite growing up in France, he was also Duke of Albany, the nearest adult male relative of the infant king James V.

---

[12] RPS, *A1513/1*.
[13] Sadler, *Border Fury*, p.443.
[14] Dawson, *Scotland Re-formed*, p.93.
[15] *Ibid*, p.92.
[16] Knecht, *Catherine de' Medici*, p.7.

Albany arrived in Scotland in 1515 and faced a tussle with the dowager queen for possession of the boy king. Margaret had Edinburgh castle's portcullis lowered in Albany's face and 'more like a fishwife than a queen' shouted at him through the bars.[17] She retired to Stirling Castle, but the Scots feared she might plot with Angus to smuggle the young king to England. Stirling was besieged, and Margaret persuaded to give up the king and the castle. She was confined to Linlithgow and though heavily pregnant with Angus' baby, made a daring escape to her homeland with the assistance of Alexander, 3rd Lord Home.[18]

Angus, his rival the Earl of Arran, and Lord Home then made a bond to overthrow their common enemy: Albany.[19] Despite raising an army this came to nothing, Arran declining armed confrontation when Albany unfurled the royal standard against his army at Kittycrosshill in January 1516.[20] Angus, prudently, was in England with his wife during this rebellion: when he re-crossed the border he was pardoned. Home, however, entered into treasonable new correspondence with Dacre on the English side. He was executed in October 1516 for his trouble.[21] Scotland was finally stabilised, and Albany returned home in 1517 to negotiate the Treaty of Rouen. The Auld Alliance was renewed, and a royal French bride promised for the young James V. Scotland was left in the hands of a joint regency, whose most active member was Albany's French compatriot, Antoine D'Arces.[22]

But this Gallic regency would not last.

To and Fro

The family of Lord Home sought revenge for their kinsman's execution, and ambushed and beheaded D'Arces at Duns on 17 September 1517.[23] The Earl

---

[17] Dawson, *Scotland Re-formed*, p.96.
[18] Emond, *The Minority of James V*, pp.91-92.
[19] *Ibid*, p.96.
[20] Dawson, *Scotland Re-formed*, p.96. Also Emond p.106.
[21] Emond, *The Minority of James V*, pp.120-125.
[22] *Ibid*, p.167 & 170
[23] *Ibid*, pp.175-176.

of Arran was elected his replacement[24] and the leading factions fell out, culminating in a running battle between the Hamiltons and Douglases in the streets of Edinburgh on 30 April 1520.[25] Margaret took this as a signal to write to Albany. She was desperate to see her son again, and furious that her husband had remained in Scotland since 1516 and taken up with his mistress.[26] Albany returned to Scotland in November 1521, riding into Edinburgh at Margaret's side. Angus surrendered and was deported to France.[27]

Albany's very foreignness had proved the secret to his success. Unlike other Scottish magnates he had no eye on the throne or claim over disputed territories, and was accepted by the Scots as an honest broker, aloof from local rivalries:[28] the same could not be said of the Douglas Earl of Angus, Hamilton Earl of Arran, or Stewart Earl of Lennox. But Albany's loyalty to France could not be denied. He had returned for one particular reason: the French wanted him to recruit Scots to raise arms and invade England on their behalf. Margaret wrote to Dacre to inform him of the plans, and the Scots nobles were wary of an enterprise that offered them no personal advantage. Albany was forced to agree to a truce, and his rapport with Margaret evaporated.[29] He overwintered in France, returning with 6,000 French soldiers in September 1523.[30] Although the English had burned Annan and Jedburgh in Albany's absence, these French troops made themselves unwelcome, failing to pay properly for goods, using up stores the Scots had put aside for winter, murdering a burgess and two women in Glasgow, then rescuing the culprits when they were sentenced to execution. The Scots simply failed to attend the summons to war in any great numbers.[31] Wark was besieged for just three days and then abandoned in November 1523. The Scots peers might well court English and French influence, but they had no interest in being used as pawns in international

[24] Emond, *The Minority of James V*, p.177.
[25] *Ibid*, pp.258-259.
[26] Dawson, *Scotland Re-formed*, p.98.
[27] Emond, *The Minority of James V*, pp.298-299.
[28]: Dawson, *Scotland Re-formed*, p.95.
[29] Sadler, *Border Fury*, p.445.
[30] Emond, *The Minority of James V*, pp.353-355.
[31] *Ibid*, pp.371-372.

diplomacy.[32] By prioritising French interests, Albany had outstayed his welcome.

The tide had turned in Margaret's favour again, and she agreed a contract with Albany not to seek peace with England without first consulting the French. Albany left Scotland for good in May 1524, exhorting the lords to obey Margaret.[33] Ambassadors on the Continent refused to believe that Margaret no longer represented the English interest, but her driving motivations had become control of her son, and an enmity with Angus who she sought to divorce.[34] Margaret declared James V of age in 1524.[35] But the king was only twelve years old: with Albany off the scene, his step-father Angus returned, gathered support, and took Edinburgh in 1525.

Parliament agreed a compromise for the care of the king: he would be passed around the senior nobility every three months, starting with Angus who would then hand him over to the care of Arran.[36] Angus effected a coup by refusing to hand the king over when his time was done, and busied himself placing his Douglas kinsmen and supporters in positions of power. An attempt by the Earl of Lennox to capture the king failed in 1526, but at some point in late May or June 1528, the sixteen-year-old king announced his desire to go hunting. Once horsed and free of the gates of Edinburgh Castle, he dug in his spurs and rode directly for Stirling and his mother.[37]

James had escaped the clutches of the Douglases and was ready to rule.

In early July, he called a convention to Edinburgh to investigate Angus' maladministration. Angus was summoned for treason,[38] then charged at the September 1528 Parliament with:

---

[32] Emond, *The Minority of James V*, p.612.
[33] *Ibid*, pp.390-391.
[34] *Ibid*, p.406.
[35] *Ibid*, p.407.
[36] RPS, *1525/7/25*.
[37] Cameron, *James V*, p.20.
[38] *Ibid*, pp.26-27.

the tresonable art and part of the halding of oure soverane lordis persoune
aganis his will ... and aganis the decrete of the lordis of his parliament[39]

Angus was pursued, but not with the utmost vigour. The Scots were keen to prevent the English intervening on his behalf, given how strongly he identified with their interests. A five-year truce was signed at Berwick on 14 December, the English negotiator writing home that:

it were not good to refuse peax for th'Erle of Angus, conseidering the warre of Scottlande is never to the proufite of Einglande.[40]

Jonnie Armstrong's Jewels

King now in his own right, James rode out of Edinburgh to return law and order to Scotland, hoping to make a better fist of it than Angus had as regent. For several years prior to the king's escape, the Earl of Angus had grappled with the problem of the Borders to no avail. When the men of Liddesdale on the Scottish side and Tynedale on the English side combined to enable each other's forays across the wild Middle March, Angus realised something had to be done. In 1525 he made a lightning attack on Liddesdale, capturing two of the most notorious Armstrongs and lifting their cattle. As pacification it failed: the men of Liddesdale simply undertook further raiding to recoup their losses.[41] Composer Robert Carver wrote a dark 'Fera Pessima' (terrible beasts) mass, and the Bishop of Glasgow issued a *Monition of Cursing* to be read out in every Border pulpit against them:

...I curse thaim gangand, and I curse thaim rydand; I curse thaim standand, and I curse thaim sittand; I curse thaim etand, I curse thaim drinkand; I curse thaim walkand, I curse thaim sleepand; I curse thaim risand, I curse thaim lyand; I curse thaim at hame, I curse thaim fra hame; I curse thaim within the house, I curse thaim without the house; I curse thair wiffis, thair barnis, and thair servandis participand with thaim in their deides...

---

[39] RPS, *1528/9/10.*
[40] Cameron, *James V*, p.58, p.63
[41] Fraser, *The Steel Bonnets*, p.225.

...And all the vengeance that evir was takin sen the warlde began for oppin synnys, and all the plagis and pestilence that ever fell on man or beist, mot fall on thaim for thair oppin reiff, saiklesse slauchter and schedding of innocent blude. I disserver and pairtis thaim fra the kirk of God, and deliveris thaim quyk to the devill of hell...[42]

The situation was not helped by Lord Maxwell, Warden of the Scottish West March, protecting and using the Armstrongs of Liddesdale in a private feud against his rivals, the Johnstones; or by Lord Dacre, Warden on the English West March, stirring the pot with the employment of 400 Scottish reivers to raid their own country.[43] A year later Angus tried again, this time bringing the young king with him. But his expedition had to be abandoned in the face of an attempt by Walter Scott of Buccleuch, in support of the Earl of Lennox, to free James from Angus' clutches.[44] The English accused Angus of giving sanctuary to their own clan of bandits, the Lisles,[45] and another Border expedition planned for June 1528 was postponed by the escape of the king.[46]

Now the king was free, his first and most pressing issue was to bring peace to the Borders. The border had been a war zone since the end of the 13th century, and Border families, or 'graynes', were even more lawless than Highland clans. Cattle reiving was endemic, and by common custom, it was legal to recover your property by deadly force, provided you did so within six days. The practice was known as 'hot trod', and reivers caught 'red-handed' could expect bloody justice – as could their pursuers, if they weren't careful.[47] A unique system of governance had arisen to adapt to these circumstances. The border was split into six administrative districts: a West, Middle, and East March on both Scottish and English sides, with Parliament-appointed March Wardens given limited powers of diplomatic negotiation with their opposite numbers. On pre-arranged truce days, grievances were

---

[42] Fraser, *The Steel Bonnets*, pp.383-384.
[43] *Ibid*, p.224, p.219.
[44] *Ibid*, p.183.
[45] Emond, *The Minority of James V*, p.544.
[46] Cameron, *James V*, p.21.
[47] Fraser, *Steel Bonnets*, pp.115-116.

addressed and wanted men swapped. That was the theory, anyway: in practice the more powerful graynes formed cross-border alliances, colluded in criminality with the March Wardens, and extorted 'blackmail' from their unlucky neighbours.

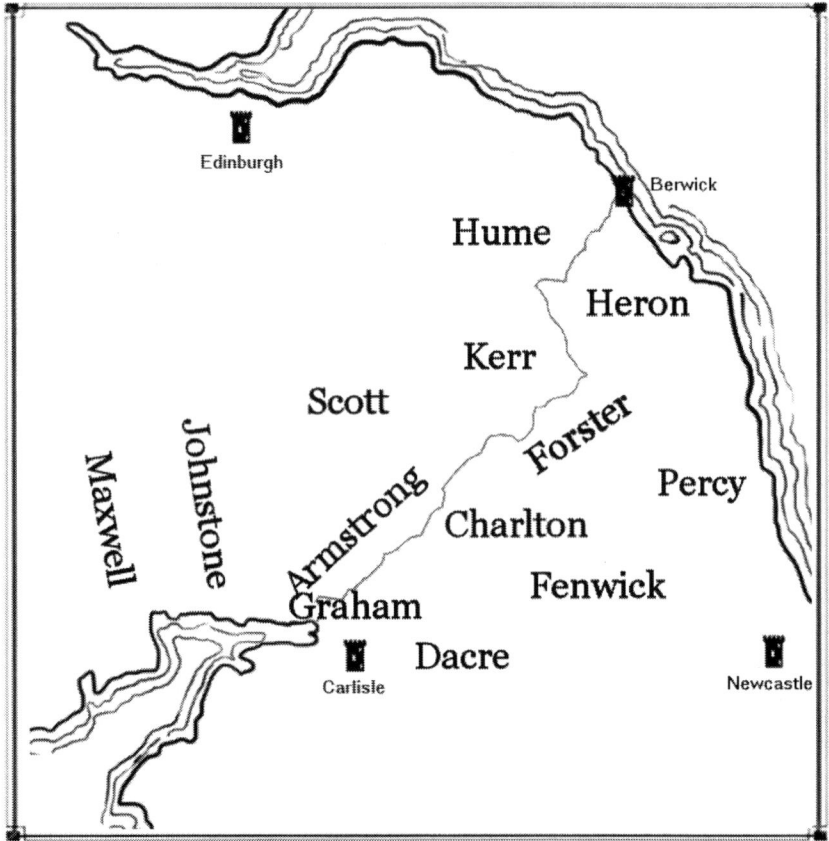

Figure 20: Principal Border graynes

In 1530, having established his rule and dealt with the Douglases, James himself turned his attention towards the Border graynes. Simon Armstrong had met the Earl of Northumberland at Alnwick and boasted that they could lay waste the borders and "not a man in Scotland durst remedy the same."[48] He reckoned without the new king, who summoned the March Wardens and

---

[48] Cameron, *James V*, p.72.

other lords north and briefly incarcerated them in castles across the Central Belt.[49] James then swept through the Middle March of Teviotdale and Liddesdale with an army of 10,000, catching and executing reivers: most famously, Johnnie Armstrong of Gilknockie, of whose splendid dress the king was apparently jealous:

> *Ther hang nine targats at Johnys hat,*
> *And ilk an worth three hundred pound:*
> *What wants that knave that a king suld haif,*
> *But the sword of honour and the crown!'*

Armstrong was a tricky customer. According to popular custom, James offered to meet him under truce, then had him hanged anyway.

> *To seik het water beneth cauld yce,*
> *Surely it is a great folie;*
> *I haif asked grace at a graceless face,*
> *But there is nane for my men and me.*[50]

The Border ballad 'Johnie Armstrong' paints a romantic picture of a man of honour and action. The reality is the deaths of Armstrong, and Scott of the Bog, and other notorious thieves, reivers, extortionists and murderers, would have been a relief to ordinary Borderers, an action that contributed to James' reputation as a 'puir man's king'.[51] A genuine interest in the good application of law led James to found a College of Justice in 1532, with full-time senators funded by the state. According to John Lesley, Bishop of Ross, James' rule brought:

> *gret quietnes, tranquilitie, and pollitie in Scotland as evir wer in ony*
> *Kingis tyme of befoir*[52]

Yet despite James' expeditions and legal reforms, the Borderers remained a law unto themselves, respecting neither king nor nationality, loyal only to the

---

[49] Cameron, *James V*, p.75.
[50] Child, *English and Scottish Popular Ballads,* p.417.
[51] Cameron, *James V*, p.92.
[52] *Ibid*, p.346.

family itself: In 1532 the Scottish Kerrs of Fernihurst & Cesford struck against the English East March. The graynes of Northumberland retaliated by attacking the lands of the Merse and Teviotdale. Kerr in Teviotdale retaliated by burning Coquetdale in Northumberland, fighting off the local hot trod. In 1534 Fenwick led the men of Tynedale against Teviotdale, Scott sought help from Lord Dacre against Kerr, Dacre found himself at odds with Clifford, and in May 1536 Tynedale and Redesdale on the English side and Liddesdale on the Scottish side combined again to harry the rest of the Borders.[53]

The Highlands were another story. The last Lord of the Isles, Domhnall Dubh, was in captivity, but a royal journey to the north was a less familiar undertaking than raising an army to march on the border. James' first attempt to raise an expedition in 1536 had to be abandoned due to difficult weather. The outcome was Alexander Lindsay's 'Rutter (after the French, *Routier*) of the Scottish Seas', the first navigational guide to Scotland's north coast, and the purchase of 'foure horologis (clocks) and ane compas' for the royal flagship *Salamander*.[54] It was 1540 before James followed Lindsay's Rutter anti-clockwise from Leith to Dumbarton in order to dispense justice in Kirkwall and Lewis, making his will beforehand as such a novel trip was an 'uncertane aventuris'.[55]

But if James still had turbulent or hard-to-reach territories to contend with, he at least had one advantage over many of his Stewart predecessors. A lack of money wasn't a problem.

Kist and Kirk

For centuries, religion and royalty had worked together as the twin foundations of feudal society. The church had become incredibly rich as a result. It was the greatest landowner in Scotland, with an income, on the eve of the Reformation, of £300,000 a year. (By comparison, the king's own patrimony brought him only £17,500.)[56] James wanted some of this money. He negotiated a tax of £10,000 per annum, intended as finance for his

---

[53] Sadler, *Border Fury*, p.456.
[54] Cameron, *James V*, p.239.
[55] *Ibid*, pp.239-248.
[56] Mackie, *A History of Scotland*, p.140.

College of Justice. Instead, in 1532 the church paid a one-off levy of £72,000; still plenty money for James to fund his planned scheme.[57]

Meanwhile in England, Henry VIII fell out with the Pope, who refused to grant the divorce Henry wanted from his first wife. Henry's answer was radical. Break with Rome, make himself Pope in England, gain his divorce, and increase his own wealth and influence by distributing church lands to loyal nobles. When David Lyndsay premiered his play *Ane Satire of the Three Estates*, which highlighted ecclesiastical corruption, James mocked the bishops in attendance, threatening to send them to his uncle Henry in England.[58] James' advisors possessed English documentation that could be copied to order a dissolution if desired.[59] The king had no intention of reforming the church, or of following his uncle's example, and was even thanked by the Pope for persecuting heretics.[60] But the very threat of it was enough to concentrate the church's mind, making:

greitar profit to him nor the hole revenew of the crowin.[61]

James' illegitimate sons were placed in lucrative high church office, becoming abbots or priors of Kelso, Holyrood, St Andrews, Melrose and Coldingham at the ages of five, six, seven, and nine respectively.[62] With the church funding his projects, it was time for James to find a wife.

The Gudeman of Ballengeich

In 1530 James' ambassadors wrote to the Pope, guardian of Catherine de Medici, to seek her hand in marriage.[63] Thanks to her family wealth, Catherine was one of the most courted girls in Europe. That she was only eleven years old and may despise her husband-to-be was not a consideration: a marriage contract could be concluded and the successful suitor continue to see his mistresses until the girl was old enough to take up her duties as a

---

[57] Cameron, *James V*, p.260.
[58] *Ibid*, p.264.
[59] *Ibid*, p.291.
[60] *Ibid*, p.288.
[61] Lesley, *The History of Scotland*, p.155.
[62] Cameron, *James V*, p.261.
[63] Hay, *The Letters of James V*, p.172-3.

queen. James was unsuccessful: Catherine would marry the future King of France instead. But Catherine was just one potential match for the Scottish king: no fewer than eighteen women were linked to him as possible brides, from one of James' own mistresses, Margaret Erskine, to Maria, the Queen of Hungary and Bohemia.[64] James himself desired the prize promised in 1517's Treaty of Rouen: a French princess, Madeleine. But Madeleine was unwell, her constitution so weak that her father, concerned for her health, insisted that she live in the mild climate of the Loire rather than in Paris. King François suggested a different bride: Marie de Bourbon, daughter of the Duke of Vendôme, and James travelled to France to see her.

Legend has it the Scottish king appeared secretly at the Duke of Vendôme's court dressed as a servant, but as the lady possessed a portrait of the king and his distinctive appearance, she was not fooled by this 'servant' for a second.[65] James didn't like what he saw, and despite exchanging love tokens with Marie de Bourbon, continued to François' royal court where he met Madeleine in person. Madeleine was smitten with her suitor and persuaded her father to agree to their marriage. They wed in Notre Dame in Paris on 1 January 1537 and, after months of celebrations, left for Scotland in May. But the poor child did not live to see her seventeenth birthday. On 7 July 1537 she died of her illness in her husband's arms in Edinburgh.

Soon after, Marie de Bourbon also died. Robert Lindsay of Pitscottie wrote:

> *the duik of Vandones dochter, quho [who] tuke sick displeasour at the king of Scotlandis marriage that shoe deceast immediately thaireftir: quhairat [whereat] the king of Scotland was highlie displeassed, thinkand that he was the occasioun of that gentlvoman's death.*[66]

It was time for James to try again. One lady in particular had caught his attention: the Duchess of Lorraine, Marie de Guise. She had attended his wedding in Paris as a guest, but her own husband had recently died, leaving her a widow at the age of twenty-one. Unlike Madeleine, she was, in the

---

[64] Cameron, *James V*, pp.132-133.
[65] Lindsay, *The Historie And Cronicles Of Scotland, Vol. I*, p.358.
[66] Lindsay, *The Chronicles of Scotland, Vol 2*, p.374.

opinion of Cardinal Beaton, 'stark, well-complexioned, and fit to travel.'[67] James was not this healthy lady's only suitor. He had a rival: his uncle, Henry VIII. But beyond his relative youth, James had a decisive advantage over Henry, who had recently beheaded his second wife for treason. Henry summoned the French ambassador to insist that Marie was the woman for him as he "had need of a big wife." When Marie heard of Henry's enthusiasm, she responded:

"I may be big in person, but my neck is small."[68]

This was not Henry VIII's only rejection. Princess Christina of Denmark replied to another of his marriage proposals:

"Had I two heads, one would be at his Majesty's disposal."[69]

Marie in fact, had no interest in marrying anybody so soon after her first husband had died. But matters were taken out of her hands when the King of France announced he had found her a new husband in the King of Scots. Generously, he would even provide a dowry. Courted by foreign kings, Marie's marital status had become state business, and in the face of this neither her own opinions nor that of her family mattered.[70] If they did not wish to fall out with the French king, all that could be done was ensure the best deal possible from the terms of her marriage contract. However, it is possible that her sense of mission was fired by a letter supposedly received from James, detailing his political troubles. 'My lords believe,' wrote James, 'that a king who wishes truly to reign over them an insupportable evil.' For a woman as clever and energetic as Marie de Guise, a challenge was more appealing than the promise of wealth and possessions.[71]

Marie travelled to Scotland, marrying James at St Andrews Cathedral on 15 June 1538. The king's mother Margaret Tudor wrote tactlessly to her brother of Marie's excellent qualities:

---

[67] Marshall, *Mary of Guise*, p.45.
[68] *Ibid*, p.47.
[69] Weir, *The Lady in the Tower*, p.358.
[70] Marshall, *Mary of Guise*, pp.41-45.
[71] *Ibid*, pp.51-53.

I trust Sche shal proff a vyss Prynces... I have bene mysch in her company, and Sche berys Her varray honnorabyl to Me, vyth varray good interetyng [entertaining].[72]

James' two marriages proved to be astute business. For dowries, the King of France paid £168,750 – far more than the £72,000 he had already received from the church in Scotland, and more again than James IV's windfall of £35,000 for marrying Margaret Tudor.[73] James' Renaissance court benefitted from the money, which he spent on palaces and clothes:

One day he would wear his new purple satin doublet with the gold buttons. Next morning he would be in crimson silk, another time in white velvet trimmed with gold. His new crimson velvet cassock was lined with red taffeta and sewn with gold and silver, and he had gowns of cloth of gold and crimson velvet.[74]

Renaissance palaces were upgraded at Falkland, Linlithgow, Holyrood, and Stirling, and the court patronised composer Robert Carver and poet and playwright David Lyndsay of the Mount. James' artistic patronage gives the impression that he liked the finer things in life. But he also liked to travel incognito around Scotland in the guise of a farmer, calling himself 'the Gudeman of Ballengeich'. The 'Gudeman' had a genuine interest in law and order and the general condition of his country: these expeditions allowed him to see the land through the eyes of the ordinary people who showed him hospitality. They also allowed him to act the goat, and he delighted in singing a self-penned song called 'The Gaberlunzie Man' about a traveller eloping with his host's daughter.[75] Before his marriages, James had already fathered nine children with his mistresses.[76] Marriage to Marie put an end to this, but their first two children died in infancy.

His marriage also put Scotland firmly on the side of France. Henry VIII's break with the Pope in Rome had made him vulnerable to attack from

---

[72] State Papers Henry VIII, *Vol V Part IV*, p.135.
[73] Cameron, *James V*, p.261.
[74] Marshall, *Mary of Guise*, pp.67-68.
[75] Eyre-Todd, *Scottish Poetry of the Sixteenth Century*, pp.176-179.
[76] Weir, *Britain's Royal Families*, p.244.

Catholic monarchs, and the English king was keen to make peace with his Scottish counterpart.

In this he had an influential ally in Scotland: his sister Margaret.

It Cam Wi a Lass

The central aim of James' mother's life, after resolving her complicated matrimonial situation, was to bring about a better understanding between England and Scotland. Her greatest triumph was to persuade her son in early 1536 to meet Henry, a diplomatic coup she boasted to her brother was 'by advice of us and no other living person.'[77] But it would come to nothing: to Margaret's bitter disappointment, James' advisors would not have it. And with the arrival of Marie as queen, James' connection to France and to Catholicism only grew. The worried English ambassador wrote back to Henry 'the young queen was all papist'.[78] Rumours spread of a pan-European Catholic crusade against Henry VIII. If Scotland joined France, the Holy Roman Empire, and Spain in simultaneously attacking England, there could be only one result. Henry keenly sensed his weakness, and wrote again to James to arrange another meeting at York in September 1541. Henry had cause to hope: he had already thanked James in 1539 for proclaiming no 'slandrouse rymes' defaming the King of England should be circulated in Scotland.[79] Henry sent his tapestries and finery ahead to York, following himself in August 1541.

But without explanation, James failed to show.[80] The rebuke stung Henry who became convinced the King of Scots was now his enemy. In 1542 the threat of a Franco-German crusade against England faded, and Henry made his move. As negotiations continued for another peace meeting at York in September 1542, both sides prepared for the contrary.[81] The Earl of Angus, acting on Henry's behalf, reported from Berwick that the Scots:

---

[77] Everett Wood, *Letters of Royal and Illustrious Ladies*, p.134.
[78] Strickland, *Lives of the Queens of Scotland, Vol I.*, p.263.
[79] Cameron, *James V*, p.288.
[80] *Ibid*, p.290.
[81] *Ibid*, p.296.

Speke miche pece and provides for warre like wyse men.[82]

George Gordon, 4th Earl of Huntly, travelled south from Aberdeenshire to Lauder to organise a defence. When Henry sent 3,000 men unannounced across the border, Huntly was ready. With a force of 2,000 he destroyed the English raid at Hadden Rig on 24 August. James wrote to Henry to order all attacks to cease, so that the pair could still meet at York in September: but the same day, Henry commissioned the Duke of Norfolk to raise a full-scale invasion force.[83] Henry did not necessarily want war: rather, the Privy Council wrote to Norfolk, Henry needed 'som notable exployte' to absolve the embarrassment of the rout at Hadden Rig. On 23 October the duke left Berwick with 10-20,000 men, burned Kelso, and retired.[84] James, meanwhile, prepared to face the English army. But as news came on 31 October that they had already returned to England, the Scottish lords counselled dispersal. The weather was bad, victuals low, and the immediate threat over.[85] James however, was 'very desyrous to be in England',[86] and after taking care of business in Edinburgh and visiting his heavily pregnant wife at Linlithgow, ordered a new muster at Lauder for 21 November. The English had no idea where the Scots would strike, but by 23 November Wharton, Deputy Warden of the English West March, was making preparations with 2-3,000 men. Somewhere between 13-20,000 Scots had arrived at Langholm in Dumfriesshire, but the force that entered England was a fraction of this, closer in size of the parties at Hadden Rig. At dawn on 24 November the Scots crossed the River Esk under the command of Lord Maxwell, Warden of the Scottish West March, but became trapped in treacherous boggy ground between the Esk, Solway Moss, and Wharton's riders, who 'pricked' at them in reiver style with fast mobile horse. Astonishingly, the Scots seem not to have had reliable scouts: they 'knew not the passage quhilk they might have saiflie riden,' and surrendered after a desultory skirmish. Only twenty Scots were killed, and 1,200 taken prisoner.[87] If Hadden Rig had been an embarrassment to Henry, then the abject capitulation at Solway Moss was

---

82 Cameron, *James V*, p.299.
83 *Ibid*, p.297.
84 *Ibid*, pp.299-300.
85 *Ibid*, pp.301-309.
86 *Ibid*, p.303.
87 *Ibid*, 314-320.

doubly so to James. At this point, myth takes over: various conspiracies have been aired to explain the defeat, from secret orders for James' court favourite Oliver Sinclair to take control at a crucial moment, to the Protestant lords willingly defecting to a Protestant king.[88] These are later fabrications: contemporary sources state that the Scots simply got stuck in a bog, 'begylit be thair awne gyding.'[89] By the end of November, James was back in Edinburgh issuing orders for the defence of the border. On 2 December, momentous news: a daughter, Mary, was born to Marie at Linlithgow. By 7 December James had visited her. But he had caught a fever: either 'the pest' that was going round Perth, or the cholera that did for the Earl of Atholl whilst campaigning. James' immune system, weakened from previous fevers in 1533, 1536, and 1540, failed to cope. James V died on 14 December in Falkland Palace.[90]

The final myth from the debacle at Solway Moss, made possible by the unfortunate timing of his death, is that James succumbed to nervous tension following the defeat, dying from a lack of will to live.[91] In these accounts the birth of a daughter rather than a son is the last straw, and he turns his head to the wall, saying "it cam wi a lass," referring to the genesis of the Stewart dynasty with Marjorie Bruce, "and it'll gang wi a lass."[92] This may well be myth-making. What isn't in dispute is that for the second time in a row, the Scots had lost their king after defeat to an army of Henry VIII's. And this time, Henry was determined to bring the Scots under his control.

Only a 'stark and well-complexioned' Frenchwoman could save Scotland now…

⊕ CONTINUED IN BOOK TWO ⊕

---

[88] Cameron, *James V*, pp.321-322.
[89] *Ibid*, p.320.
[90] *Ibid*, pp.324-325.
[91] *Ibid*, p.323.
[92] *Ibid*, p.345.

Sources

Aberth, J., 2005. The Black Death: The Great Mortality Of 1348-1350: A Brief History With Documents. Boston, Mass.: Bedford/St. Martin's.

Adomnán, trans. W. Reeves. 1874. *Life Of St. Columba.* [online] Corpus of Electronic Texts. <https://celt.ucc.ie//published/T201040/> [accessed 18 April 2020].

Anderson, A. and Anderson, M., 1991. *Scottish Annals From English Chroniclers: AD 500 to 1286.* Stamford: Paul Watkins.

Anderson, A. O, 1922. Early Sources Of Scottish History, A.D. 500 To 1286, Volume One. Edinburgh: Oliver & Boyd.

Anderson, A. O., 1922. Early Sources Of Scottish History, A.D. 500 To 1286, Volume Two. Edinburgh: Oliver & Boyd.

Aneirin, trans. S. Echard, n.d. *Y Gododdin.* [online] University of British Columbia. <https://faculty.arts.ubc.ca/sechard/492godo.htm> [accessed 19 April 2020].

Armit, I., 1997. *Celtic Scotland.* London: B.T. Batsford.

Bagad de Lann-Bihoué, 2019. *Marche des soldats de Robert Bruce.* [online] YouTube. <https://www.youtube.com/watch?v=eEsDynBjxII&t=90s> [accessed 12 June 2020].

Bain, J., 1884. *Calendar Of Documents Relating To Scotland Preserved In Her Majesty's Public Record Office, London. Vol II.* Edinburgh: HMSO. [online] Internet Archive. <https://archive.org/details/calendarofdocume02grea>.

Balfour Paul, J., 1900. *Accounts Of The Lord High Treasurer Of Scotland, Vol II: 1500-1504.* Edinburgh: H.M. General Register House. [online] Hathi Trust Digital Library. <https://babel.hathitrust.org/cgi/pt?id=chi.097512179>.

Balfour Paul, J., 1901. *Accounts Of The Lord High Treasurer Of Scotland, Vol III: 1506-1507.* Edinburgh: H.M. General Register House. [online] Internet Archive. <https://archive.org/details/accountsoflordhi03scot>.

Balfour Paul, J., 1902. *Accounts Of The Lord High Treasurer Of Scotland, Vol IV: 1507-1513*. Edinburgh: H.M. General Register House. [online] <https://archive.org/details/accountslordhig01offigoog>.

Balfour Paul, J., 1911. *The Scots Peerage, Vol VIII*. Edinburgh: David Douglas.

Bambury, P. and Beechinor, S., 2020. *The Annals Of Ulster, 431-1201*. [online] The Corpus of Electronic Texts. <https://celt.ucc.ie//published/T100001A/>.

Bambury, P. and Beechinor, S., 2020. *The Annals Of Ulster, 1202-1378*. [online] The Corpus of Electronic Texts. <https://celt.ucc.ie//published/T100001B/> [accessed 22 May 2020].

Barbour, J., trans. A. A. H. Douglas, 1964. *The Bruce*, Glasgow: William McLellan.

Barbour, J. and Duncan, A.A.M., 1999. *The Bruce*. Edinburgh: Canongate Books.

Barrell, A., 2000. *Medieval Scotland*. Cambridge: Cambridge University Press.

Barrow, G., 1992. Scotland And Its Neighbours In The Middle Ages. London: Hambledon Press.

Barrow, G.W.S., 2005. *Robert Bruce And The Community Of The Realm Of Scotland*. Edinburgh: Edinburgh University Press.

Bergenroth, G. A., 1862. 'Spain: July 1498, 21-31', in *Calendar of State Papers, Spain, Volume 1, 1485-1509*. [online] British History Online. <http://www.british-history.ac.uk/cal-state-papers/spain/vol1/pp167-180> [accessed 23 August 2020].

Berresford Ellis, P., 2003. *A Brief History of The Celts*. London: Constable & Robinson.

Boardman, S., 1996. *The Early Stewart Kings*. East Linton: Tuckwell.

Bourchier, J., and MacAulay. G. C., 1904. *The Chronicles of Froissart*. London: MacMillan & Co.. [online] Internet Archive. Available at: <https://archive.org/details/chroniclesoffroi00froiuoft>.

Bricka, C. F., 1887-1905. *Dansk Biografisk Lexikon, tillige omfattende Norge for Tidsrummet 1537-1814. XI. BIND.* [online] Project Runeberg. <http://runeberg.org/dbl/11/0124.html> [accessed 13 August 2020].

Bromwich, R., 2014. *Trioedd Ynys Prydein: The Triads Of The Island Of Britain.* Cardiff: University of Wales Press.

Broun, D., 2013. *Scottish Independence And The Idea Of Britain.* Edinburgh: Edinburgh University Press.

Brown, C., 2002. *The Second Scottish Wars Of Independence, 1332-1363.* Stroud, Gloucestershire: Tempus.

Brown, M., 1998. The Black Douglases: War and Lordship in Late Medieval Scotland, 1300-1455. Edinburgh: John Donald.

Brown, M., 2000. *James I.* East Linton: Tuckwell.

Browne, G.F., 1908. *Alcuin of York.* London: Society for Promoting Christian Knowledge. [online] Internet Archive. <https://archive.org/details/alcuinofyorklect00browuoft>.

Burns, R., 1787. *MS 15952 - Robert Burns - National Library Of Scotland, letter to Dr John Moore.* [online] National Library of Scotland. <https://digital.nls.uk/robert-burns/manuscripts/cowie.html> [accessed 17 April 2020].

Caesar, C. J., trans. W. A. McDevitte, W. S. Bohn, 1869. *Caesar's Commentaries, Book 6, Chapter 13.* New York: Harper & Brothers. [online] McAdams. <http://mcadams.posc.mu.edu/txt/ah/Caesar/CaesarGal06.html> [accessed 17 April 2020].

Caesar, C. J., trans. W. A. McDevitte, W. S. Bohn, 1869. *Gallic War, Book 5, Chapter 14.* New York: Harper & Brothers. [online] Perseus Digital Library. <http://www.perseus.tufts.edu/hopper/text?doc=Perseus%3Atext%3A19 99.02.0001%3Abook%3D5%3Achapter%3D14> [accessed 28 April 2020].

Calendar of State Papers Spain: see Bergenroth.

Cameron, J., 1998. *James V: The Personal Rule, 1528-1542.* East Linton: Tuckwell Press.

Cannon, J. and Hargreaves, A., 2001. *The Kings And Queens Of Britain.* Oxford: Oxford University Press.

Carney, J. and Greene, D., 1969. *Celtic Studies: Essays In Memory Of Angus Matheson, 1912-1962.* Routledge & Kegan Paul.

Chadwick, H., 2013. Early Scotland: The Picts, The Scots And The Welsh Of Southern Scotland. Cambridge: Cambridge University Press.

Child, F. J., 1904. *English and Scottish Popular Ballads.* Boston: The University Press, Cambridge. [Online] https://archive.org/details/englishscottishp1904chil/.

Clarkson, T., 2016. Scotland's Merlin: A Medieval Legend and Its Dark Age Origins. Edinburgh: Birlinn.

Clarkson, T., 2016. *The Picts: A History.* 2nd ed. Edinburgh: Birlinn.

Connolly, S., 2019. *Heroines Of The Medieval World.* Stroud: Amberley Publishing.

Consitt, E., 1904. *Life of St Cuthbert.* London: Burns & Oates, Limited.

Cowan, E., 2003. 'For Freedom Alone': The Declaration Of Arbroath, 1320. East Linton: Tuckwell Press.

Cowan, E. and McDonald, R., 2005. *Alba: Celtic Scotland In The Medieval Era.* Edinburgh: J. Donald.

Cunliffe, B., 2001. *Facing the Ocean.* Oxford: Oxford University Press.

Davidson, J., 2005. *Scots and the Sea: A Nation's Lifeblood.* Edinburgh: Mainstream.

Davies, N., 1999. *The Isles: A History.* London: Papermac.

Davies, S, 2007. *The Mabinogion.* Oxford: Oxford University Press.

Dawson, J. E. A. 2007. *Scotland Re-Formed, 1488-1587.* Edinburgh: Edinburgh University Press.

Dio, C., trans. E. Cary, 1927. Loeb Classical Library. *Cassius Dio — Epitome Of Book 77.* [online] Bill Thayer. <https://penelope.uchicago.edu/Thayer/E/Roman/Texts/Cassius_Dio/77*.html> [accessed 16 April 2020].

Doherty, P. C., 2003, Isabella and the Strange Death of Edward II, London: Constable.

Dunbar, W. and Laing, D., 1834. *The Poems Of William Dunbar Now First Collected. With Notes, And A Memoir Of His Life, By D. Laing. Volume First.* Edinburgh: Laing and Forbes. [online] Google Books. <https://books.google.co.uk/books?id=E1ICAAAAQAAJ>.

Duncan, A. A. M. "Honi Soit Qui Mal y Pense: David II and Edward III, 1346-52." *The Scottish Historical Review*, vol. 67, no. 184, 1988. [online] JSTOR. <www.jstor.org/stable/25530360> [accessed 21 September 2020].

Ellis, H., 1825. *Original Letters, Illustrative Of English History.* London: Harding, Triphook and Lepard. [online] Yumpu. <https://www.yumpu.com/en/document/read/3210142/black-white-university-of-toronto> [accessed 30 September 2020].

Emond, K. W., 1988. *The Minority of King Janes V 1513-1528.* St Andrews: St Andrews University. PhD Thesis, St Andrews University, St Andrews. [Online] https://research-repository.st-andrews.ac.uk/bitstream/handle/10023/2969/WilliamKevinEmondPhDThesis.pdf?sequence=3&isAllowed=y. Accessed 13 May 2021.

Encyclopædia Britannica. [online] https://www.britannica.com.

Everett Wood, M. A., 1846. *Letters of Royal and Illustrious Ladies, From the Twelfth Century to the Close of the Reign of Queen Anne.* London: Henry Colborn. [Online] https://books.google.co.uk/books?id=KnZCAAAAcAAJ. Accessed 15 June 2021.

Ewan, E., Pipes, R., Rendall, J. and Reynolds, S., 2018. *The New Biographical Dictionary of Scottish Women.* Edinburgh: Edinburgh University Press. [online] National Library of Scotland. <https://www.vlereader.com/Reader?ean=9781474436298> [Accessed 5 September 2020].

Eyre-Todd, G., 1892. *Scottish Poetry of the Sixteenth Century.* Glasgow: W. Hodge & Co. [Online] https://archive.org/details/scottishpoetryof00eyre. Accessed 11 June 2021.

Ferguson, R., 2010. *The Knights Templar And Scotland.* Stroud: The History Press.

Foedera: see Hardy.

Forbes-Leith, W., 1884. *Life Of St. Margaret, Queen Of Scotland, by Turgot, Bishop of St Andrews.* Edinburgh: William Paterson. [online] Internet Archive. <https://archive.org/details/lifeofstmargaret00turguoft>.

Forester, T., 1853. *The Ecclesiastical History of England and Normandy by Ordericus Vitalis, Vol. II.* London: Henry G. Bohn. [online] Internet Archive. <https://archive.org/details/ecclesiasticalhi02ordeuoft>.

Forester, T., 1854. *The Chronicle of Florence of Worcester.* London: Henry G. Bohn. [online] Google Books. <https://books.google.co.uk/books?id=gpR0iz5GjYgC>.

Fraser, G. M., 1989. *The Steel Bonnets.* London: Collins Harvill.

Fraser, J., 2012. *From Caledonia To Pictland: Scotland To 795.* Edinburgh: Edinburgh University Press. [online] National Library of Scotland. <https://edinburgh-universitypressscholarship-com.nls.idm.oclc.org/view/10.3366/edinburgh/9780748612314.001.0001/upso-9780748612314> [accessed 5 September 2020].

Freedland, J., 2020. *BBC Radio 4 - The Long View, Sovereign Debt And Default.* [online] BBC. <https://www.bbc.co.uk/programmes/b01b9jnp> [accessed 14 July 2020].

Freedman, P., 1999. *Images Of The Medieval Peasant.* Stanford, Calif.: Stanford University Press.

Gemmill, E. and Mayhew, N., 2006. *Changing Values In Medieval Scotland.* Cambridge: Cambridge University Press.

Gerber, P., 1997. *Stone Of Destiny.* Edinburgh: Canongate.

Gidley, L., 1870. *Bede's Ecclesiastical History of the English Nation*. Oxford: James Parker and Co. [online] Project Gutenberg. <https://www.gutenberg.org/files/38326/38326-h/38326-h.html> [accessed 27 April 2020].

Gildas, trans. H. Williams, 1899. *De Excidio Britanniae*. London: The Honourable Society of Cymmrodorion. [online] Internet Archive. <https://archive.org/details/GildasDeExcidioWilliams1899> [accessed 3 May 2020].

Giles, J., 1849. Roger Of Wendover's Flowers Of History, Comprising The History Of England From The Descent Of The Saxons To A.D. 1235; Formerly Ascribed To Matthew Paris. Volume II. London: Henry G. Bohn. [online] Internet Archive. <https://archive.org/stream/rogerofwendovers02rogeiala>.

Goodwin, G., 2013. Fatal Rivalry: Flodden 1513: Henry VIII, James IV and the Battle for Renaissance Britain. London: Weidenfeld & Nicolson.

Goring, R., 2018. *Scotland: Her Story*. National Library of Scotland e-book: Birlinn.

Gosman, M., MacDonald, A. and Vanderjagt, A., 2003. *Princes And Princely Culture, 1450-1650. Volume One*. Leiden: Brill Academic Publishers.
Gregory, D., 1836. *History of the Western Highlands and Isles of Scotland*. Edinburgh: William Tait. [online] Google Books. <https://play.google.com/books/reader?id=rKFfAAAAcAAJ&hl>.

Guerber, H.A., 1994. *Norsemen*. London: Senate.

Hardy, T., 1869. Syllabus (In English) Of The Documents Relating To England And Other Kingdoms Contained In The Collection Known As "Rymer's Foedera. Vol I.". London: Longmans, Green & Co. [online] Internet Archive. <https://archive.org/details/cu31924007439213>.

Hay, D., 1954. *The Letters of James V, 1513-1542*. Edinburgh: HMSO

Hearne, T., 1770. *Joannis Lelandi Antiquiarii, De Rebus Britannicis Colleactanea. Vol IV*. London: G & J Richardson. [online] Google Books. <https://books.google.co.uk/books?id=Bp8uAAAAMAAJ> [accessed 14 August 2020].

Herbert, J., 2014. *Berwick-Upon-Tweed And The Torching Of The Red Hall |*
Scotland And The Flemish People. [online] University of St Andrews.
<https://flemish.wp.st-andrews.ac.uk/2014/01/25/berwick-upon-tweed-
and-the-torching-of-the-red-hall/> [accessed 2 June 2020].

HES Editors, 2019. *Threave Castle: History.* [online] Historic Environment
Scotland. <https://www.historicenvironment.scot/visit-a-
place/places/threave-castle/history/> [accessed 30 September 2020].

Hunt, Edwin S. "A New Look at the Dealings of the Bardi and Peruzzi
with Edward III." *The Journal of Economic History,* vol. 50, no. 1, 1990.
[online] JSTOR. <www.jstor.org/stable/2123442> [accessed 13 July 2020].

Jamieson, J., 1869. Wallace; Or, The Life And Acts Of Sir William Wallace
Of Ellerslie, by Henry the Minstrel. Glasgow: Ogle.

Jillings, K., 2006. *Scotland's Black Death: The Foul Death of the English.* Stroud:
Tempus.

Johnes, T., 1857. *Sir John Froissart's Chronicles of England, France, Spain, and the*
Adjoining Countries, Vol II. London: Henry G. Bohn. [online] Internet
Archive. <https://archive.org/details/chroniclesengla02curngoog>.

Johnstone, J, 1882. *The Norwegian account of Haco's expedition against Scotland,*
a.d. MCCLXIII. Edinburgh: William Brown. [online] Internet Archive.
<https://archive.org/details/norwegianaccoun00stur>.

Jocelyn of Furness, trans. C.W. Green, n.d. *The Life Of Kentigern.* Chapter
XXXVI. [online] Fordham University Internet History Sourcebooks
Project. <https://sourcebooks.fordham.edu/basis/Jocelyn-
LifeofKentigern.asp> [accessed 20 April 2020].

Knecht, R. J., 2014. *Catherine de' Medici.* Abingdon: Routledge.

Koch, J. T., 2006. *Celtic Culture: A Historical Encyclopedia.* Santa-Barbara:
ABC-CLIO.

Kuhns, O., 1897. *The Divine Comedy of Dante Alighieri, Translated By The Rev.*
Henry F. Cary. New York: Thomas Y. Crowell & Co. [online] Internet
Archive. <https://archive.org/details/divinecome00dant>.

Laing, D., 1872. *The Orygynale Cronykil Of Scotland By Androw Of Wyntoun, Vol II*. Edinburgh: Edmonston and Douglas. [online] Google Books. <https://play.google.com/books/reader?id=GvJJAAAAMAAJ> [accessed 19 April 2020].

Laing, D., 1879. *The Orygynale Cronykil Of Scotland By Androw Of Wyntoun, Vol III*. Edinburgh: William Paterson. [online] Internet Archive. <https://archive.org/details/orygynalecronyki03andruoft> [accessed 21 April 2020].

Lehane, B., 2005. *Early Celtic Christianity*. New York: Continuum International Publishing Group Ltd.

Lesley, J. and Thomson, T., 1830. *The History Of Scotland, From The Death Of King James I In The Year MCCCCXXXVI To The Year MDLXI*. Edinburgh: Bannatyne Club. [online] Google Books. <https://play.google.com/books/reader?id=m1oJAAAAIAAJ> [accessed 30 September 2020].

Lindsay, R., ed. Mackay, Æ., 1899. *The Historie And Cronicles Of Scotland, Vol. I*. Edinburgh: Blackwood and Sons. [online] National Library of Scotland. <https://digital.nls.uk/publications-by-scottish-clubs/archive/106036546> [accessed 19 June 2020].

Lindsay, R., ed. Dalyell, 1814. *The Chronicles of Scotland by Robert Lindsay of Pitscottie, Vol. 2*, Edinburgh: Archibald Constable and Company. [Online] https://books.google.co.uk/books?redir_esc=y&id=nQoHAAAAQAAJ. Accessed 12 June 2021.

Linklater, E., 1934. *Robert The Bruce*. London: T. Nelson.

Lucas, H., 1930. "The Great European Famine of 1315, 1316, and 1317." *Speculum*, 5(4). [online] JSTOR. <http://www.jstor.org/stable/2848143> [accessed 3 July 2020].

Lynch, M., 1992. *Scotland: A New History*. London: Pimlico.

Macdougall, N., 1997. *James IV*. East Linton: Tuckwell.

Macdougall, N., 2009. James III. Edinburgh: John Donald.

Macdougall, 2019. *Clan MacDougall Handout.* [online] Clan MacDougall Society. <https://macdougall.org/wp-content/uploads/2019/05/ClanMacDougall-Handout-REVMay2019.pdf> [accessed 27 May 2020].

Mac Eoin, G.S. "On the Irish Legend of the Origin of the Picts". *Studia Hibernica*, no. 4, 1964. [online] JSTOR. <https://www.jstor.org/stable/20495786> [accessed 2 May 2020].

MacInnes, I.A., 2016. *Scotland's Second War Of Independence, 1332-1357.* Woodbridge: Boydell & Brewer.

MacKay, J., 1995. *William Wallace: Braveheart.* Edinburgh: Mainstream.

Mackie, J.D., 1991. *A History Of Scotland.* Harmondsworth: Penguin.

MacLean, J.P., 1889. *A History of the Clan MacLean From its First Settlement at Duard Castle, in the Isle of Mull, to the Present Period.* Cincinnati: Robert Clarke & Co. [online] National Library of Scotland. <https://digital.nls.uk/histories-of-scottish-families/archive/94801891> [accessed 11 September 2020].

Macleod, R. C., 1927. The Macleods of Dunvegan, From the Time of Leod to the End of the Seventeeth Century. Based on the Bannatyne MS. and on the Papers Preserved in the Dunvegan Charter Chest. Edinburgh: The Clan Macleod Society. [online] Internet Archive. <https://archive.org/details/macleodsofdunveg00macl>.

Macquarrie, A., 2004. *Medieval Scotland: Kingship And Nation.* Stroud: Sutton Publishing.

MacRitchie, D. "FRENCH INFLUENCE IN SCOTTISH SPEECH." *Transactions of the Glasgow Archaeological Society*, vol. 2, no. 4, 1896. [online] JSTOR. <www.jstor.org/stable/24680585> [accessed 10 September 2020].

Magnusson, M. and Pálsson, H., 1966. *The Vinland Sagas.* Harmondsworth: Penguin.

Marshall, R. K., 1977. *Mary of Guise.* London: Collins.

Marshall, R.K., 2003. *Scottish Queens, 1034-1714.* Edinburgh: Tuckwell.

218

Marwick, J. D., 1869. *Extracts from the Records of the Burgh of Edinburgh, 1403-1528*. Edinburgh: Scottish Burgh Records Society. [online] Internet Archive. <https://archive.org/details/extractsfromreco01edin>.

Matusiak, J., 2013. *Henry VIII: The Life and Rule of England's Nero*. Stroud: The History Press.

Maxwell, H., 1902. *A History Of The House Of Douglas From The Earliest Times Down To The Legislative Union Of England And Scotland, Vol. I*. London: Freemantle & Co. [online] Google Books. <https://books.google.co.uk/books?id=Y9ztAgAAQBAJ>.

Maxwell, H., 1907. *Scalacronica : the reigns of Edward I, Edward II and Edward III, as recorded by Sir Thomas Gray*. Glasgow: James Maclehose & Sons. [online] Internet Archive. <https://archive.org/details/scalacronicareig01grayuoft>.

Maxwell, H., 1913. *The Chronicle Of Lanercost, 1272-1346*. Glasgow: James Maclehose and Sons. [online] Internet Archive. <https://archive.org/details/chronicleoflaner00maxwuoft/>.

McDonald, R. A., 2016. Outlaws of Medieval Scotland: Challenges to the Canmore Kings, 1058-1266. Edinburgh: John Donald.

McGladdery, C., 1990. *James II*. Edinburgh: John Donald.

McKirdy, A., 2015. Set in Stone: The Geology and Landscapes of Scotland. Edinburgh: Birlinn.

McNamee, C., 1997. *The Wars of the Bruces*. East Linton: Tuckwell.

McPhee, K., 2013. *Somerled: Hammer Of The Norse*. Glasgow: Neil Wilson Publishing.

M'Lauchlan, T., 1862. The Dean of Lismore's Book. A Selection of Ancient Gaelic Poetry From a Manuscript Collection Made by Sir James M'Gregor, Dean of Lismore, in the Beginning of the Sixteenth Century. Edinburgh: Edmonston and Douglas. [online] Internet Archive. <https://archive.org/details/deanoflismoresbo00macluoft> [accessed 11 September 2020].

Moffat, A., 2002. The Borders: A History Of The Borders From Earliest Times. Selkirk: Deerpark.

Moffat, A., 2005. *Before Scotland*. London: Thames & Hudson.

Moffat, A., 2010. *The Faded Map*. Edinburgh: Birlinn.

Moffat, A., 2011. *The Scots: A Genetic Journey*. Edinburgh: Birlinn.

Monro, D., 1774. Description Of The Western Isles Of Scotland, Called Hybrides; by Mr Donald Monro High Dean of the Isles, Who Travelled Through the Most of Them in the Year 1549. Edinburgh: William Auld. [online] Google Books. <https://books.google.co.uk/books?redir_esc=y&id=bpsHAAAAQAAJ>.

Mooney, L. and Arn, M., 2005. *James I Of Scotland, The Kingis Quair*. [online] Robbins Library Digital Projects. <https://d.lib.rochester.edu/teams/text/mooney-and-arn-kingis-quair-and-other-prison-poems-james-i-scotland-kingis-quair> [accessed 2 August 2020].

Morris, J., 1984. The Age of Arthur: A History of the British Isles From 350 To 650. London: Weidenfeld & Nicolson.

Murison, A.F., 1899. *King Robert The Bruce*. Edinburgh: Oliphant Anderson & Ferrier. [online] Internet Archive. <https://archive.org/details/kingrobertbruc00muri>.

NRS. n.d. *Transcription And Translation Of The Declaration Of Arbroath, 6 April 1320 National Records Of Scotland, SP13/7*. [online] National Records of Scotland. <https://www.nrscotland.gov.uk/files//research/declaration-of-arbroath/declaration-of-arbroath-transcription-and-translation.pdf> [accessed 6 July 2020].

ODNB, Oxford Dictionary of National Biography. [Online] https://www-oxforddnb-com.nls.idm.oclc.org.

O'Grady, O., 2018. "Accumulating Kingship: The Archaeology Of Elite Assembly In Medieval Scotland." *World Archaeology*, 50:1, 137-149. [online] Taylor & Francis.

<https://www.tandfonline.com/doi/full/10.1080/00438243.2018.148973 6> [accessed 13 May 2020].

Oram, R., 2011. *Domination And Lordship: Scotland, 1070-1230*. Edinburgh: Edinburgh University Press.

Oram, R., 2013. *Alexander II: King Of Scots 1214-1249*. Edinburgh: Birlinn.

Oram, R., 2020. *David I, King of Scots 1124-1153*. National Library of Scotland e-book: Birlinn.

Pálsson, H. and Edwards, P., 1978. *Orkneyinga Saga: The History Of The Earls Of Orkney*. London: Hogarth Press.

Penman, M., 2014. *Robert The Bruce: King Of Scots*. New Haven: Yale University Press.

Pitscottie: see Lindsay

Prestwich, M., 1997. *Edward I*. New Haven: Yale University Press.

Pryde, G., 1965. *The Burghs Of Scotland: A Critical List*. Glasgow, Oxford: Published for the University of Glasgow by the Oxford University Press.

Rankin, E. B. "Whitekirk and 'The Burnt Candlemas'." *The Scottish Historical Review*, vol. 13, no. 50, 1916. [online] JSTOR. <www.jstor.org/stable/25518888> [accessed 22 September 2020].

Reid, N. "The Kingless Kingdom: The Scottish Guardianships of 1286-1306." *The Scottish Historical Review*, vol. 61, no. 172, 1982. [online] *JSTOR*, <www.jstor.org/stable/25529476> [accessed 19 June 2020].

Robb, G., 2013. The Ancient Paths: Discovering the Lost Map of Celtic Europe. London: Picador.

Rogers, C. J., 2014. *War Cruel And Sharp, English Strategy Under Edward III 1327-1360*. Woodbridge: Boydell Press.

Rolleston, T., 1994. *Celtic Myths And Legends*. London: Senate.

Ross, S., 1993. *The Stewart Dynasty*. Nairn: Thomas & Lochar.

Routt, D., n.d. *The Economic Impact Of The Black Death.* [online] Eh.net. <https://eh.net/encyclopedia/the-economic-impact-of-the-black-death/> [accessed 8 July 2020].

RPS. The Records of the Parliaments of Scotland to 1707. [online] http://www.rps.ac.uk.

Sadler, J., 2006. *Border Fury.* Abingdon: Routledge.

Sadler, J., 2008. *Bannockburn: Battle For Liberty.* Havertown: Pen and Sword.

Scott, W., 1803. *Minstrelsy Of The Scottish Border, Vol. I.* Edinburgh: James Ballantyne. [online] Internet Archive. <https://archive.org/details/minstrelsyscotti01scotiala>.

Scott, W., 1828. Tales Of A Grandfather; Being Stories Of The History Of Scotland. Vol. I. Edinburgh: Cadell and Company.

Setton, K., 1984. *The Papacy And The Levant (1204-1571), Volume III.* Philadelphia: The American Philosophical Society. [online] Google Books. <https://books.google.co.uk/books?id=EgQNAAAAIAAJ>.

Severin, T., 2018. *The Brendan Voyage.* Amazon e-book: Endeavour Media.

Shirley, J., 1818. *The Dethe Of James Kynge Of Scotis / Translated By John Shirley.* Glasgow: John Wylie & Co. [online] University of Michigan. <https://quod.lib.umich.edu/c/cme/deathjas/> [accessed 17 April 2020].

Skene, W. and Skene, F., 1871. *John of Fordun's Chronicle of the Scottish Nation.* Edinburgh: Edmonston & Douglas.
Skene, F., 1880. *The Book Of Pluscarden, Vol II.* Edinburgh: Paterson. [online] Internet Archive. <https://archive.org/stream/liberpluscarden00unkngoog>.

Smith, D., Schlaepfer, P., Major, K. et al., 2017. "Cooperation and the evolution of hunter-gatherer storytelling." *Nat Commun* 8, 1853 (2017). [online] Nature Research. <https://doi.org/10.1038/s41467-017-02036-8> [accessed 3 August 2020].

Starkweather, K. and Hames, R., 2012. "A Survey of Non-Classical Polyandry." *Human Nature*, 23(2). [online] University of Nebraska-Lincoln.

<https://www.unl.edu/rhames/Starkweather-Hames-Polyandry-published.pdf> [accessed 16 April 2020].

Stevenson, J., 1836. *The Scalacronica of Sir Thomas Gray.* Edinburgh: The Maitland Club. [online] Internet Archive. <https://archive.org/details/scalacronica00unkngoog>.

1836. *State Papers Henry VIII, Vol 5, Part 4.* [Online] https://books.google.co.uk/books?id=pM0_AAAAcAAJ. Accessed 25 April 2021

Stevenson, J., 1854. *The Church Historians Of England, Vol II-Part II. The Chronicles of John Wallingford.* London: Seeleys. [online] Internet Archive. <https://archive.org/stream/thechurchhistor202unknuoft>.

Stevenson, J., 1855. *The Church Historians Of England, Vol III-Part II. The Historical Works Of Simeon Of Durham.* London: Seeleys. [online] Internet Archive. <https://archive.org/details/historicalworks00simegoog>.

Stevenson, J., 1856. *The Church Historians of England, Vol IV-Part I. The Chronicle of Melrose.* London: Seeleys. [online] Internet Archive. <https://archive.org/details/churchhistorians41stev>.

Stevenson, J., 1856. *The Church Historians of England, Vol IV-Part II. The History of William of Newburgh.* London: Seeleys. [online] Internet Archive. <https://archive.org/details/churchhistorpt204unknuoft>.

Stevenson, K., 2014. *Power And Propaganda: Scotland, 1306-1488.* Edinburgh: Edinburgh University Press.

Strickland, A., 1850. *Lives of the Queens of Scotland, Vol I.* Edinburgh: William Blackwood and Sons. [Online] https://books.google.co.uk/books?id=tfwXAAAAYAAJ. Accessed 15 June 2021.

Sturlason, S. n.d. *Heimskringla, By Snorri Sturlason.* [online] Project Gutenberg. <https://www.gutenberg.org/files/598/598-h/598-h.htm> [accessed 11 May 2020].

Summerson, H., et al. *The Magna Carta Project.* [online] <http://magnacarta.cmp.uea.ac.uk/read/magna_carta_1215/Clause_39> [accessed 25 May 2020].

Sumption, J., 1991. *The Hundred Years War, Volume I: Trial by Battle.* Philadelphia: University of Pennsylvania Press.

Sutton, D. F., 2009. *George Buchanan, Rerum Scoticarum Historia (1582).* [online] University of Birmingham. <http://www.philological.bham.ac.uk/scothist/contents.html> [Accessed 23 May 2020].

Sutton, D.F., 2010. *Hector Boethius, Historia Gentis Scotorum (1575 version).* [online] University of Birmingham. <http://www.philological.bham.ac.uk/boece/contents.html> [Accessed 9 June 2020].

Suzman, J., 2020. *How Neolithic Farming Sowed The Seeds Of Modern Inequality 10,000 Years Ago.* [online] The Guardian. <https://www.theguardian.com/inequality/2017/dec/05/how-neolithic-farming-sowed-the-seeds-of-modern-inequality-10000-years-ago> [accessed 13 April 2020].
Swanton, M., 1997. *The Anglo-Saxon Chronicle.* London: Dent.

Tanner, R., 2001. *The Late Medieval Scottish Parliament.* East Linton: Tuckwell Press.

Taylor, R., 2013. *Hornshole.* [online] Hawick Callants Club. <https://www.hawickcallantsclub.co.uk/cr07-hornshole.shtml> [accessed 25 August 2020].

Taylor, S., 2000. Kings, Clerics And Chronicles In Scotland, 500-1297. Dublin: Four Courts Press.

The Scots Guards, 2009. *Flower of the Forest.* [online] YouTube. <https://www.youtube.com/watch?v=rfsasAllCo8> [accessed 12 June 2020].

Thomson, T., 1819. *The Auchinleck Chronicle.* Edinburgh: Printed for private circulation. [online] <https://play.google.com/books/reader?id=jwAHAAAAQAAJ> [accessed 17 April 2020].

Thomson, T., 1834. *Instrumenta Publica Sive Processus Super Fidelitatibus Et Homagiis Scotorum Domino Regi Angliae Factis, A.D. 1291-1296.* [online] Internet Archive.

<https://archive.org/details/instrumentapublica00thomuoft/> [accessed 10 June 2020].

Tichy, O. and Rocek, M., 2019. *Wilisc.* [online] Bosworth-Toller Anglo-Saxon Dictionary. <https://bosworthtoller.com/035767> [accessed 20 September 2020].

Tytler, P. F., 1831. *Lives Of Scottish Worthies, Vol. I.* London: John Murray. [online] Google Books. <https://books.google.co.uk/books?id=09k5AAAAcAAJ>.
Uncredited, 2012. *Special Delivery: The William Wallace Letters - Visit & Learn : Scottish Parliament.* [online] The Scottish Parliament. <https://www.parliament.scot/visitandlearn/45948.aspx> [accessed 12 June 2020].

Uncredited, 2016. *Who Wore Scotland's Oldest Piece Of Tartan?* [online] The Scotsman. <https://www.scotsman.com/whats-on/arts-and-entertainment/who-wore-scotlands-oldest-piece-tartan-1470161> [accessed 20 September 2020].

Wærdahl, R., 2011. The Incorporation And Integration Of The King's Tributary Lands Into The Norwegian Realm C. 1195-1397. Leiden: Brill.

Wales, K., 2006. *Northern English: A Social and Cultural History.* Cambridge: Cambridge University Press.

Watson, W., 1926. The History Of The Celtic Place-Names Of Scotland, Being The Rhind Lectures On Archaeology (Expanded) Delivered In 1916, By William J. Watson [online] Hathi Trust Digital Library. <https://babel.hathitrust.org/cgi/pt?id=mdp.39015010209701&view=1u p&seq=112> [accessed 20 April 2020].

Watt, D. E. R., 1987. Scotichronicon by Walter Bower, in Latin and English, Volume 8. Aberdeen: Aberdeen University Press.

Watt, D.E.R, MacQueen, J, MacQueen, W, 1995. Walter *Bower's Scotichronicon, Volume 3.* Aberdeen: Aberdeen University Press.

Way, G. and Squire, R., 1998. *Collins Scottish Clan & Family Encyclopedia.* Glasgow: HarperCollins.

Weir, A., 2008. Britain's Royal Families: The Complete Genealogy. London: Vintage.

Weir, A., 2008. *Henry VIII: King and Court.* London: Vintage.

Weir, A. 2010. *The Lady in the Tower: The Fall of Anne Boleyn.* London: Vintage.

Winroth, A., 2016. *The Age Of The Vikings.* Princeton: Princeton University Press.

Wood, M., 2017. *Brunanburh: Where Did The Battle That Saved England Take Place?.* [online] HistoryExtra. <https://www.historyextra.com/period/anglo-saxon/where-did-brunanburh-battle-take-place-location-england-michael-wood/> [accessed 15 May 2020].

Woolf, A., 1998. *Pictish Matriliny Reconsidered.* [online] Academia. <https://www.academia.edu/313141/Pictish_matriliny_reconsidered> [accessed 7 May 2020].

Woolf, A., 2014. *From Pictland To Alba, 789-1070.* Edinburgh: Edinburgh University Press. [online] National Library of Scotland. <https://edinburgh-universitypressscholarship-com.nls.idm.oclc.org/view/10.3366/edinburgh/9780748612338.001.0001/upso-9780748612338> [accessed 11 September 2020].

Wright, T., 1888. *The History Of Scotland From The Earliest Period.* London: London Print. and Pub. Co.

Wyckoff, C.T., 1897, *Feudal Relations Between the Kings of England and Scotland Under the Early Plantagenets. Chicago: University of Chicago.* [online] Internet Archive. <https://archive.org/details/feudalrelations00wychgoog> [accessed 4 July 2020].

Yorke, B., 2014. The Conversion Of Britain: Religion, Politics And Society In Britain, 600-800. Abingdon: Routledge.

Acknowledgements

Did you like this book? Confession time. None of it is mine. The real authors are the historians listed in the sources: people like Skene, Sadler, Moffat, Woolf, Watson, Duncan, Mackie, Lynch and Tanner, people whose work I've extensively referenced. Where I've written something demonstrably wrong, as opposed to the kind of clearly labelled tradition, myth, or legend that is sometimes as much a part of Scotland's early story as the known facts, then it's because I haven't paid enough attention to scholars like them.

Speaking of which, if it wasn't for Midlothian Libraries and the National Library of Scotland, this book wouldn't have existed. Thank you for providing free books and, in the strange summer of 2020, for re-opening so that I could check my references. It is amazing what you can find online these days, and the Internet Archive is a treasure-trove of out-of-copyright works. But there is no substitute for experiencing that book in all its dusty glory, (or in the case of the NLS, remarkably undusty), and few recent books are available outside the libraries without spending a small fortune. Thank you again.

Any published author can tell you that *writing* a book is the easy part. I am indebted to everyone who has guided me in the other parts of this process: Robbie Inman whose coaching chats proved invaluable; Jeff Sanders who persuaded me of the benefits of 5am starts in regards to book writing; Moira Cormack, Ceris Jones, and Augusta Paulikaite who cured my aversion to social media; citethisforme.com and Andrew Macdonald Powney whose advice around citations has saved you a lot of eyeache; John Fawkes whose excellent battlefield maps bring military manoeuvres alive; Elizabeth Richardson who allowed me to quote from her husband's song *Scotland Will Flourish*; beta reader Shaun Adams whose advice improved the book; and the AfterWords group of self-publishing authors who said *"just publish it already!"*

And to Katherine, who insisted I check my facts: the book works now, thanks to you.

Usually at this point, authors admit that any errors in the book are theirs alone. I bet you've found some. So please help your fellow readers: e-mail me craig@craigweldon.com with any glaring issues. If your message causes a correction in a subsequent edition, I'll be eternally grateful, add your name to the acknowledgements of that edition if you wish, and will be delighted to send you a copy.

Craig Weldon, Midlothian, 2020.

Tell Others What You Think...

As an indie author, I am highly reliant on reviews to help other readers decide if this book is for them. So, if you enjoyed it, please tell your friends, and leave a review on Amazon.

Read the next instalment in *A History of Scotland* ...

**A HISTORY *of*
SCOTLAND**

Book Two

Covenant

CRAIG WELDON

The Scots must choose their allegiance. Will it be to England, or to France?
As a revolutionary new religion sweeps the country, the decision they make
will change world history.

Preview: craigweldon.com/a-history-of-scotland

Printed in Great Britain
by Amazon